Psychological Portraits of Adolescents

Psychological Portraits of Adolescents

AN INTEGRATED DEVELOPMENTAL APPROACH TO PSYCHOLOGICAL TEST DATA

Carol J. Eagle
Lillian Schwartz

LEXINGTON BOOKS
An Imprint of Macmillan, Inc.
NEW YORK
Maxwell Macmillan Canada
TORONTO
Maxell Macmillan International
NEW YORK   OXFORD   SINGAPORE   SYDNEY

Library of Congress Cataloging-in-Publication Data

Eagle, Carol J.
   Psychological portraits of adolescents: an integrated developmental approach to
psychological test data / Carol J. Eagle, Lillian Schwartz.
      p.   cm.
   Includes bibliographical references and index.
   ISBN 0-669-27800-9
   1. Teenagers—Psychological testing.   2. Adolescent psychology.
I. Schwartz, Lillian.   II. Title.
BF724.25.E34   1994
155.5'028'7—dc20   93-3194
                                                                                      CIP

Lexington Books
An Imprint of Macmillan, Inc.
866 Third Avenue, New York, N.Y. 10022

Maxwell Macmillan Canada, Inc.
1200 Eglinton Avenue East
Suite 200
Don Mills, Ontario M3C 3N1

Macmillan, Inc. is part of the Maxwell Communication
Group of Companies.
Printed in the United States of America

printing number
1   2   3   4   5   6   7   8   9   10

This book is dedicated to our nieces and nephews,
Judy Maguire, Betsy O'Connor, Jason and David Johnson,
and Bruce, Phil, and Ken Schwartz,
and to the memory of our fathers,
Evan S. Johnson and Phillip Schwartz

Contents

Introduction

T he intent of this book is to provide clinical practitioners with demonstrations of the analyses of psychological test materials and their integration according to developmental expectations. In our previous volume, *Psychological Portraits of Children* (Schwartz/Eagle 1986), we traced the psychological development of the child from 3 to 12 years. In this volume we continue the psychological developmental sequence from 12 to 21 years.

To provide the most complete and useful picture of a given adolescent's functioning, the psychologist must understand the clinical interpretations of each psychological test performance in light of appropriate developmental expectations and, finally, arrive at a comprehensive integration of the productions of the adolescent. This way of evaluating the data has evolved through our years of experience in testing thousands of adolescents in school settings, guidance clinics, psychiatric hospitals, private practice, and experimental programs for normal adolescents. These protocols are representative of all ages from 12 to 21 years, all socioeconomic levels from the welfare subsistence level to the wealthy, and most predominant ethnic and religious groups within the United States.

The theoretical principles underlying our understanding of developing coping strategies in relation to developmental needs derive from the ego psychological model of adaptation as conceptualized by S. Freud (1923/1961), Hartmann, Kris, and Loewenstein (1946), and Rapaport (1951). In this view the ego is seen as the organizer of internal and external events in the organism's efforts at adaptation. This theory is represented in the contemporary object-relations schools (Greenberg & Mitchell 1983).

This conceptualization is that human neonates begin their existence with the capacities for the development of primary autonomy utilizing innate faculties of perception, motility, sensation, affect, language, thinking, and memory. These rudimentary ego functions, in interaction with a biological constitution and an "average expected environment" (Hartmann, 1958), lead to the development of the self. The ego represents the organizing process by which experiences are assimilated and through which emerges an individuated sense of self.

By the third year of life the basic structures for the development of the stabilized ego have begun. Therefore, from this time on, specific ego functions can be evaluated. Beres (1956) has provided an outline of ego functions in seven areas: relation to reality, regulation and control of instinctual drives, object relations, thought processes, defense functions, autonomous functions, and synthetic functions of the ego. All of these functions in their evolvement determine the sense of self. Self is the totality of the ego structure (psyche), the body, and self representations, which are "the unconscious, preconscious and conscious endopsychic representations of the bodily and mental self in the system ego" (Jacobson 1964, p. 19), as described by Hartmann (1950).

The developmental conceptualizations of Erikson (1959), A. Freud (1934) and Piaget (1967) have guided our understanding of the maturation of ego function as the individual grows.

We utilize the concepts of ego psychological theory because we find these concepts to be the most elaborated and detailed system in which we can account for normal as well as pathological development. These concepts also provide a psychological portrait of how the adolescent experiences himself or herself in relation to the world. We summarize Beres' seven ego functions into cognition, dynamics, defenses, and affect as the most efficient way of organizing all the data provided by an adolescent's test battery.

A basic grounding in the fundamentals of administration of psychological tests, history taking, and report writing is helpful in understanding the principles underlying the level at which this book begins.

Standard texts on the administration and scoring of the intelligence tests in the battery are the Wechsler Intelligence Scale for Children (Wechsler 1949), Wechsler Intelligence Scale for Children–Revised (Wechsler 1974), Wechsler–Bellevue I and II (Wechsler 1944), Wechsler Adult Intelligence Scale (Wechsler 1955), and Wechsler Adult Intelligence Scale–Revised (Wechsler 1981). Texts on the other tests include the Bender–Gestalt (Bender 1938, 1946); figure drawing (Machover 1949), Rorschach (Ames, Metraux, and Walker 1971; Klopfer, Ainsworth, Klopfer, & Holt 1954; Rorschach 1942/1921), and Thematic Apperception Test (Murray 1943). Compilation of different tests with administration and scoring, examples of adolescent protocols, and descriptions of report writing are provided in books by Goldman, Stein, and Guerry (1983) and Palmer (1970).

Although norms for developmental levels have been provided for the intelligence tests and the Rorschach (Ames, Metraux, & Walker 1971), the meaning of the adolescent's response has not been integrated into the overall understanding of the adolescent's ego functioning. This book begins at the point after the tests have been administered and scored. The psychodynamic interpretation of the adolescent's productions within his or her age group makes obvious the need for appreciating each developmental level in understanding the significance of the adolescent's responses. In integrating these interpretations in light of developmental expectation, diagnostic clarity as to the ego's strengths and weaknesses become evident, as well as an understanding of the adolescent's sense of self and of the world.

Although each test protocol presented is produced by an actual adolescent, all identification data and information suggestive of identification have been altered or removed to protect the adolescent and his or her family. Batteries have been selected from our thirty-five years of testing experience as well as from those administered by other examiners; the batteries selected present examples of normal to pathological adaptation. We chose batteries produced by adolescents who for the most part were highly verbal, so that the nature of their ego functions is more clearly conveyed to the reader. Although adolescent interests and behavioral manifestations can change from time to time according to socioeconomic, ethnic, and cultural values, the essential nature of the development of the adolescent's ego functions progresses on a consistent and predictable path. It is necessary to comprehend the nature of the integration of the ego functions for any given adolescent in order to provide recommendations for the optimal intervention.

It is our hope that this method of interpretation and evaluation of each adolescent's psychological portrait will be helpful to all professionals who work with adolescents.

1
Diagnostic Categories

T he hallmark of adolescent development from the onset of puberty (11–13 years) through middle adolescence (14–16 years) and late adolescence (16–18 years) and into young adulthood (18–21 years), is inconsistency. This inconsistency is produced by the ongoing physical changes inherent in the growing adolescent. As the physiology of the body undergoes its changes, preexisting ego defenses become less reliable and can break down. Adolescence by definition is a period of growth of normal disintegration of defenses with the requirement for ultimate reorganization into a fixed personality pattern.

Adolescent ego development has been described by Erikson (1959) as that of identity versus role confusion on the way to the young adult stage of intimacy versus isolation and by Blos (1974) as a secondary period of separation-individuation.

During the onset of puberty, 11–14 years, the impact of the rapidly changing body with its endocrinological changes leaves the newly arrived adolescent frightened and unclear. He cannot identify with the child he was or the adult he will become.

This creates a need in the middle years for the 14- to 18-year-old to become part of a peer group. The group can provide identification for the individual of values, ideals, and so forth. The group is ordinarily chosen by the individual to meet his own ego needs and to provide strength in numbers.

The adolescent is coping with new conflicts over independence, sexual drives, self-identification, and his changing body. His need for independence stems from both an internal push and societal expectations; his sexual drives are experienced as not within his control and are multifaceted; his self-identification is dependent upon his peer group and is unmoored from his childhood and family; and his changing body is unpredictable and unfamiliar.

The 18- to 21-year-old is now able to begin the process of consolidation and integration that will lead to a more or less fixed personality structure.

1

This period is exemplified by self-searching and a drive to establish an identification usually based on ego ideals.

The loosening and failing defenses in response to the stress of body growth and changes (concurrent with social pressures to mature), as well as the eruption of new strong sexual drives (relating to endocrinological changes), lead to feelings of vulnerability. Those unresolved aspects of earlier stages of development, no longer able to be defensively contained, burgeon forth. It is the degree to which the earlier stages have been worked through during their normal developmental phases that determines the degree of ease the adolescent experiences in coping with adolescence. In *Psychological Portraits of Children* (1986) we offered protocols of children whose rigidity and limitations of defenses led us to recommend treatment so that severe pathology may be averted later. The fewer the available defenses and the degree of rigidity of the defenses up to the onset of adolescence determine the extent of pathology. Those with a wider and more flexible array of defenses can best proceed through the stress of adolescence.

As we noted in our earlier book, there have been no clear or specific nosological designations to clarify the different diagnoses that would be applicable to the developing adolescent. DSM-III-R, the most recent diagnostic manual (American Psychiatric Association, 1987), includes adolescent diagnoses with child and/or adult diagnoses. Although DSM-III-R makes a contribution to nosology by its detailed specification of symptoms, as well as its requirement for multiaxial evaluation, it in no way furthers our understanding of the various neurotic and psychotic disorders of adolescence, because it lacks a developmental conceptualization. Similarly, there have been increasing contributions made by theoreticians and researchers to the developing years of the infant and young child, yet there has been no commensurate investment in charting the course for latency and adolescence.

Diagnostic test batteries of adolescents can reveal responses that might be considered evidence of psychosis for a child or an adult protocol but may be a normal representation for the period of turmoil the adolescent is currently experiencing. As there is no consensus on the nosological labels for adolescent syndromes, and because designations adopted from adult nosology increase the likelihood of confusion in communication from place to place and person to person, we have selected the following broad nosological groupings to describe the emotional status of the adolescent: *psychotic, borderline, neurotic,* and *normal.* In addition, there is general agreement on categories related to conditions considered to be engendered by physical factors: *mental retardation, organicity,* and *learning disabilities.* Consensus in the use of these broad labels enables us to employ them with a fair degree of confidence in communication.

Because adolescence is a unique time of disorganization of ego defenses resulting from new conflicts and fears, certain problems are peculiar to this age. The Conduct Disorder group type (DSM-III-R 312.20), and the Eating Disorders (Anorexia Nervosa, DSM-III-R 307.10, and Bulimia Nervosa, DSM-III-R 307.51) are such syndromes. In addition, personality disorders in adulthood usually show their characteristics in the adolescent period. The nature of the pathology of these syndromes and personality disorders can be subsumed within the broad diagnostic groups of psychotic, borderline, and neurotic.

Psychoses

There is no reference in DSM-III-R to psychoses in adolescence. Our description of psychoses in the adolescent is based upon the deviations we find from normal developmental expectations. When these deviations are so severe or distorted that negotiation through the years of adolescence is severely impaired, it portends a total break with reality. The task of diagnosis is made particularly difficult because of the developmentally normal disintegration of the ego defenses during this period.

The psychotic adolescent may appear to have developed normally until puberty or immediately post puberty. The history, however, will usually include a description of an isolated child who has demonstrated excesses in behavior of one kind or another: over- or underachievement; withdrawal from others; sudden eruptive impulsive actions; disturbances in school attendance, eating, or sleeping; and so forth. This child may not come to the attention of clinicians because he has been able to conform sufficiently so that he does not cause distress to the adults in his environment. But with the breakdown and disorganization of defenses normal to adolescence and the developmental need to reach out to peers, the controls that made it possible to conform are no longer available. At this point the lack of ability to relate to his peers makes his isolation particularly threatening and makes him appear to others as strange. Unable to modulate his affective experience, he can display unusual outbursts of inappropriate emotional response to the stimulus. With the breakdown in his intellectual defenses his academic work begins to suffer; as his earlier conformity was based on these rigid defenses, there is no array of defenses available to weather this period of turmoil. His thinking becomes disorganized, confused, and sometimes bizarre.

The psychotic adolescent with paranoid features differs from this portrayal because his psychic energy becomes exclusively invested in ideation. This means that he can maintain his academic level, but at great cost to his developing the ability to interrelate with others and to meet the task of ego reintegration and restructuring. He is at greak risk for the investment in fantasy overtaking his tenuous hold on reality.

Another form of psychoses in adolescence is the reactive psychosis. The requirements for this diagnosis follow those of DSM-III-R Brief Reactive

Psychosis (298.80). This diagnosis is no different than that which would be applied to either a child or an adult.

Diagnoses of psychoses for adolescence will be described in the portraits with reference to DSM-III-R diagnoses that most closely seem to resemble the portrait.

Borderline

The DSM-III-R description of Borderline Personality Disorder (301.83) is essentially for adults and therefore is not applicable for the adolescent who is in transition. The borderline adolescent for the most part retains his connection to reality. At times under stress, however, reality can be lost. More often than not he is able to correct this failure in reality testing. The childhood history of the borderline adolescent indicates that his defenses have been operative until he meets the stresses of puberty and adolescence. It is at this time that he begins to exhibit borderline features.

The normal disintegration of ego defenses during this developmental period leaves this adolescent particularly vulnerable to excesses. This is expressed in uncontrollable, intense, and labile affective explosions of giggling, crying, shouting, and motoric discharge beyond that normally seen.

Although the borderline has a greater array of defenses than the psychotic, they are brittle and therefore become less and less depenable under the pressures of adolescence. This creates a state of affairs where the borderline adolescent becomes inordinately fearful. With fewer and more brittle defenses than normal, his capacity to relate and become an acceptable group member is severely impaired. This difficulty in interpersonal relatedness leaves him isolated from his peers or, at best, on the fringe of the group. This means that there is no feedback from the group to help him in the identification process, and he feels particularly alone and insecure.

In spite of the changing cultural attitudes towards the sexes, adolescent boys and girls differ in their clinical presentations. Borderline girls are still brought to attention primarily through their expression of depressive affect and self-destructive behaviors. Borderline boys, in contrast, most often present with uncontrollable acting out.

Neurosis

The neurotic adolescent is essentially reality oriented. At times his perception of reality can tend to overexaggeration or distortion, but there is no real break with reality. In childhood this adolescent has been related and conforming and has had an array of flexible defenses available to him. In response to the demands of adolescence, with its breakdown of defenses, unfinished tasks of earlier developmental phases are no longer containable. The neurotic adolescent compared to the normal has more unresolved areas with which to contend, so that these experiences are more disruptive to his functioning. This can result in overanxious, regressive, and avoiding behaviors. Separation anxiety in view of the adolescent demand to mature and become self-reliant is a major problem; independence and dependence conflicts at this age become exaggerated. These are designated in DSM-III-R as Anxiety Disorders of Childhood and Adolescence (309.21, 313.21, and 313.00).

Normal

The normal adolescent has arrived into this phase of development with a full array of flexible defenses. He has mastered each preceding developmental stage adequately, so that he is in good stead to meet the demands of the adolescent period. With plentiful and flexible defenses, he is able to weather the breakdown and reintegration of the defenses into a personality structure. This does not preclude the fact that the adolescent stage is disruptive to his self-esteem, his relationships with others, and his affective stability; yet he is still able to enjoy new experiences and achievements and to establish rewarding friendships. This provides the basis for his developing independence and growing maturity.

DSM-III-R includes conditions "not attributable to a mental disorder" that could bring an adolescent for evaluation under V codes (62.30, 71.02, 15.81, 61.20, 62.81, 61.80, and 62.82).

Summary

The major diagnostic categories described in this section are utilized in the evaluation of the test batteries presented in the text. Any one of these categories can be delineated further into specific descriptive groupings appropriate to the psychological portrait presented by the child.

2
The Classic Battery

The child moving into adolescence is facing new biological changes with concomitant alterations in his cognitive and emotional development. Achievements are reached at different stages, and needs have to be met, expressed, and experienced in order for there to be normal growth. Each test that will be discussed has within it the capacity to elicit the appropriate response for each age level; however, the norm for each age level varies from each other age level.

Peculiar to the adolescent stage of development is the requirement for a disintegration of ego defenses requiring ultimate reorganization into an integrated adult personality pattern. Beginning with the onset of the pubertal years (typically 11–13 years of age for girls and 12–15 years of age for boys), the adolescent begins to feel the unreliability of his defenses and suffers a loss in his confidence. Within the next stage, the middle years (14–16 years of age), there is a period of reintegration of the defenses and a beginning sense of the self. By late adolescence (16–18 years of age) the integration of the defenses moves toward a personality structuring, and there is an increasing sense of self-recognition. Finally, in young adulthood (18–21 years of age) there is a definable personality pattern consisting of these integrated defenses and a need for self-definition through introspection.

The adolescent's test responses offer a remarkably specific reflection of the point in development he or she has reached. If we judge the responses to be normal, it is because we are using established developmental norms based on the testing of many adolescents rather than comparing the productions to standards established for adults. The purpose of testing is to determine where a given adolescent is at a given moment in time with respect to age peers. Not to recognize this purpose will result in skewed or distorted interpretations not applicable to the specific age of the adolescent. Inherent in this as well is determining the presence or absence of pathology in the adolescent.

The classic battery is one that we feel provides us with the broadest base of data concerning the adolescent as a whole. It has been adopted by

6

adolescent psychologists from what has been considered to be the classic adult battery. The battery consists of an intelligence test, the Bender–Gestalt (B–G), figure drawings (FD), the Rorschach and the Thematic Apperception Test (TAT). In addition, when necessary an academic achievement test, a test for language competence, and a test for perceptual ability should be used. Many other tests exist, but they tend to be redundant to this particular battery once competence with this battery has been achieved. If one should prefer or have special competence with a different test, however, there is no reason it cannot be substituted or included, provided it taps the same area of functioning.

Intelligence Tests

The intelligence tests for the battery include the Wechsler tests: the Wechsler Intelligence Scale for Children (WISC), Wechsler Intelligence Scale for Children–Revised (WISC–R), Wechsler-Bellevue Form I (W–B, I), and the Wechsler Adult Intelligence Scale (WAIS). The Wechslers used in the test protocols were current at the time of test administration. The WISC–R is applicable for adolescents until 16 years of age, when the WAIS becomes the appropriate choice.

The instructions for the administration of the Wechsler tests offer cut-off points for each subtest. We have found that going beyond these points can provide information on potential for the particular function being tested. This in no way should alter the scoring, however, which follows the standardized procedure.

It is important to note that often there are instrusions of cultural factors in the test items that may or may not be appropriate for some given group. This in no way allows one to deviate from the standardized procedures of administering and scoring the tests to obtain a valid score. It is necessary to be particularly aware of the possibility that these cultural factors may impinge upon and therefore lower the score of a particular adolescent, however, and they should be taken into consideration in the total evaluation of the adolescent. Equally important, it should be remembered that these tests are standardized in English and therefore may present difficulties to the bilingual adolescent, not only in language production but also in the comprehension of directions.

Bender–Gestalt Test

The B–G is an additional test that generally, but not always, is sensitive to central nervous system disorders of a perceptual-motor nature. The Bender figures should be accurately copied by adolescents.

Projective Tests

The projective tests include the FD, the Rorschach, and the TAT. All of these tests are sensitive to the changing developmental stages.

Figure drawings from adolescents should represent an adequately sized (usually two-thirds of the page) and proportioned complete person. Generally there are details of features, clothes, and the figure can be represented in motion; by middle adolescence, profile drawings put in an appearance. The variability in the drawings diminishes with age, and by 16 to 18 years of age there will be an increasing consistency in the production. This is commensurate with the emerging personality structure.

Our method of administration of the Rorschach is the same as is used with adults (see Klopfer et al. 1954). Scoring of the Rorschach protocol is consistent with adult procedures, that is, number and location of the responses, determinants, and so forth. Our scoring method follows the scoring system of Klopfer et al. (1954). Different scoring systems have been developed over the years, each system having its own strengths and weaknesses (Beck 1949; Exner 1974; Piatrowski 1957; Rapaport, Gill, & Schafer 1968). We limit ourselves to a simpler rendition of the Klopfer method, as his system was the original from which most of the others were developed. The resultant protocol must be interpreted and evaluated in terms of the expected developmental stage at which we find the particular adolescent.

We generally select a few choice TAT cards, limiting the number to ten to twelve cards. The basic set should include at least the following cards: 1, 2, 3 BM, 4, 5, 8 BM, 12 M, 13 MF, 16, and for males 6 BM and 7 BM, and for females 7 GF and 18 GF. In general, it should be remembered that one can add particular cards that may be reflective of the particular problem presented, or cards that one has found through experience to be valuable. Cards do not have to be presented in numerical sequence.

Summary

All portions of the test battery reflect some aspect of the adolescent. It is therefore essential that no single test or response be used as the primary focus for interpretation. All aspects of the test productions must be taken into consideration and integrated in order to provide a coherent picture of the adolescent.

In reading the following diagnostic studies, two points should be kept in mind. The first is that we are not writing a formal psychological report; rather, as stated in the Introduction, we present a working model of the thinking that goes into the organization of the test data. The second point is that we do not presume that our summaries present an exhaustive use of the data. We are confident that our approach takes into account the salient material in the data leading to our conclusions. Ultimately, to the good clinician, the data will reflect the nature of the adolescent.

3
The 12- to 14-Year-Old

Developmental Expectations

For most children, puberty begins around the age of 12. Puberty by definition refers to hormonal changes leading to the development of secondary
sexual characteristics, including body changes in height, weight distribution,
facial structure, and extremities. All of these changes lead to a heightened
concern with the body as well as a preoccupation with the self. Children
who are either delayed or precocious in this physical development can become concerned about these changes as they compare themselves to their
peers. There are wide variations among children as well as between the
sexes in their rates of development. As a matter of fact, it is difficult to gen-
eralize about developmental expectations during this period because of these
wide variations. Never before and never again in the life cycle does the individual have to cope with the impact of so many biological and psychological changes.

Cognitive Functioning. The 12- to 14-year-old is in transition from the concrete operational stage of cognitive development to the ability to think more
logically and abstractly. These adolescents are increasingly interested in
moral and societal issues and are attempting to formulate their own value
system. Their cognitive integrity is highly variable as their interests seesaw
from the more mature to the more childlike.

The budding adolescent begins to take pleasure in using words and
phrases that have been given special meaning by the peer group. There is
pleasure in the obvious fact that adults do not understand the new values attributed to the words. At the same time, their humor is becoming more so-
phisticated and appealing to adults.

Perceptual-motor coordination in these years is extremely variable de-

10

pending on the rate of overall body changes. For example, one child can be extremely awkward at puberty but will later become smoothly coordinated. Another child will grow so gradually he never has to experience this disruption from awkwardness to smooth coordination.

Dynamic Picture. Nothing in the developmental sequence has prepared the child for the intensity of the onslaught of puberty and its effects. Perhaps the most critical area to be assaulted is that of the self-concept. The new adolescent is now plagued with questioning what he really looks like. With each perceived body change, the adolescent has to go through a reintegration of the change into his self-concept. Attempting to provide some stability in his self-concept leads to a seeming fascination with the self (for example, an unusual emphasis on bathing and looking at one's reflection). This experience is felt to be shared only by others in his peer group. The group becomes the means of support, and this is expressed in solidarity of opinions, interest, dress, and language.

The conflict between dependence and independence is extreme. This is expressed in the highly variable behaviors that make adolescents so difficult for adults. All stages of development seem to appear off and on during this time, leading to highly labile and unpredictable behavior.

Sexual and aggressive impulses overtake the adolescent, and he can be overwhelmed by intense feelings of love or hate that disappear as easily as they came. Throughout this time there are mounting sexual feelings leading to fantasies, which in and of themselves can cause anxiety. These fantasies contain homosexual and/or heterosexual contents; in contrast, the actual sexual act is ordinarily masturbation.

Due to the intensity of feelings and the concomitant experience of lack of control, the adolescent needs his parents to be strong and protective. At the same time, however, he demands acknowledgment of his own maturity, wisdom, and superiority.

Defenses. The highly variable nature of the adolescent is seen also in his fluctuating defensive maneuvers. He feels his defenses to have become more unreliable, and he fears for his emotional stability. This is a period in which defenses must be flexible and resilient. A major avenue the new adolescent has for fulfilling defensive needs is the peer group. The group can provide reassurance as to the individual's concerns and through group membership can give a sense of support. The group itself can provide defenses against anxiety by its exclusivity and ability to extrude any threatening member. The group, through its own identity, can perceive itself as different and superior to others, as well as to adults. This sometimes can take the form of cruelty to those on the receiving end. This period is a test of the quality of the defensive structure already laid down from the previous years.

Affective Expression. The variability in this period is seen most obviously in affective displays ranging from elation to depression, from love to hate, and so forth. Feelings are intense one way or another. At times the adolescent acts as if he were stimulus deprived—playing tapes at deafening volumes, roughhousing with both sexes, and talking and laughing at raucous levels, among other actions. At other times there are periods of withdrawal and sadness that are felt as devastating. This is because all affects, positive or negative, are exaggerated during this time of pubertal development.

Normal Expectations on Tests

Intelligence Tests. The affective and dynamic disruptions in the adolescent are not expected to interfere in his cognitive performance. Therefore, the achievement on the Wechsler tests should show across-the-board consistency.

Bender–Gestalt. By now, with completed perceptual-motor coordination, the B–G should conform to adult standards.

Projectives. Figure drawings most typically produced by the new adolescent resemble adolescent figures: they are more realistically proportioned and fully clothed, and sexual differentiation is clear. The body outline can be sketchy, and there is great variability in the use of embellishments.

In the Rorschach, content now reflects many more concerns with body changes. M increases to at least 5. The FM can still be higher than M, and m can be expected because it is responsive to the tension of the ongoing pubertal changes. It is expected that there will be a great variability in percepts from the immature to the mature. FC and CF can be equal, and C is not expected. F+% should be close to 50%. W:D:d should be equivalent to adult norms.

The TAT stories can be melodramatic, with romance or mystery as their themes. The new adolescent can easily comply to the task, but in elaborating his tale he can become convoluted and overly detailed. On the other hand the adolescent can also produce concise and terse stories. In carrying out these tasks, the adolescent often responds to his productions with affective accompaniments. He can laugh or look sad as he describes his percept or story, introduce the ridiculous into his product, and be humorous about his own work.

Representative psychological test interpretations and psychological test batteries for adolescents within this age range now follow. The raw test data from the psychological test battery follow the discussion of each portrait so that easy reference can be made to the examples selected for illustration of the interpretations. We include examples of adolescents diagnosed as having a reactive disorder, being mildly disturbed, moderately disturbed, or severely disturbed in order to demonstrate how a psychological portrait is developed. Each adolescent's tests are analyzed, interpreted, and concluded with an integrated summary.

As stated before, the summary is not a complete report but represents the salient features leading to the diagnostic portrait.

Psychological Test Portrait

A: 12–3 Female

A was referred by her school for evaluation because her teacher was concerned that she was not functioning up to her potential. The teacher felt that she was quite depressed.

A's parents were motivated to have her evaluated because after having achieved in her previous school year, she had now become a mediocre student. They felt that she was unhappy but did not know why.

A lives with her parents and an older brother. She is an attractive girl who seems mature for her years. She was interested in the tests, although quite anxious.

Cognitive Functioning

WISC–R: Although there is a 16-point discrepancy between *A*'s Verbal IQ of 145 and Performance IQ of 129, this does not reflect cognitive deficits in her functioning. Her consistently very superior scores are only lowered by her scores on Picture Arrangement (11) and Object Assembly (13).

All areas of cognition, i.e., abstract reasoning, language usage, memory, attention, numerical conceptualization, and fund of knowledge, are very superior. The lower scores on PA and OA are obviously related to dynamic issues rather than any cognitive dysfunction.

B–G: This test was not administered.

FD: Although the B–G was not given, we can see from the FDs and the Performance items in the WISC–R that *A*'s perceptual-motor system functions extremely well. She is able to portray human figures well enough to be recognizable, i.e., they are well proportioned and appropriately drawn.

Rorschach: Consistent with her very superior WISC–R, *A* finds clear and well-defined percepts in all areas of the blot. She gives popular responses and is sufficiently flexible to turn the cards to find new responses. She primarily relies on form to create her responses, tending to avoid color and texture. The number of responses, i.e., her productivity, is in keeping with her superior abilities, but she does not use the blots as creatively as one might expect.

TAT: In spite of the fact that A is able to develop a story line and to include the figures as portrayed on the card, she often moves far away from the stimulus. She introduces people and settings in an idiosyncratically creative way into her stories. The stories are immature and, therefore, are not commensurate with her superior intellect. She does not utilize a creative approach, which her cognitive level suggests is possible.

Summary Statement of Cognitive Functioning: A is an intellectually gifted girl who should not be experiencing any academic difficulties. Her cognitive abilities are solidly within the very superior range. We would have expected, therefore, a greater degree of creativity in her responses to the projectives than she provided.

Dynamic Picture

WISC–R: A's overall performance on the WISC reveals few dynamic issues. There is an implication of concern over her body integrity (Comprehension, 1 and 11) as well as her psychic integrity (Comprehension, 4 and 11; Vocabulary, 16 and 25).

The PA and the OA, which contributed to a lowered Performance score, suggest A's conflict with aggression. In the PA she fails an item (11) by introducing competition, seemingly to explain the aggression, and she reverses two cards in a mother-daughter sequence (12) that begins with a confrontation. In the OA she achieves maximum points in the Girl and Face but is slowed down in her solutions to the Horse and Car. The latter could reflect her age-appropriate concerns with phallic representations.

B–G: This test was not administered.

FD: A's female drawing is noteworthy for its immature and asexual presentation. Her conflict over aggression is again suggested in the extreme narrowness of the arms, as well as their dangling quality. Her associations also suggest a preadolescent girl's wish for phallic achievement.

A's choice to draw an 89-year-old male figure sitting in a rocker is most unusual for any age. This certainly reflects a conflict she experiences with phallic representations referred to above (*viz.* WISC–R, OA).

Rorschach: A's Rorschach is unusually immature ($M{:}FM$ is 1:5) for someone her age and for someone who is able to produce as many responses as she does. The few dynamic concerns that emerge are focused on orality (III,

1; V, 2; VI, 4) and phallic symbols (III, 4; VI, 2 and 3; IX, 2 and 3). Contained aggression is implied in many of her animal percepts (I, 1; II, 2; IV, 1 and 3; V, 2; VI, 1; VIII, 1). Despite her many percepts, *A*'s overall Rorschach does not reveal her individuality.

TAT: In contrast to the Rorschach responses, *A*'s TAT stories are replete with feelings of hopelessness and inadequacy and expressions of aggression. Her stories concerning females or children stress a recurrent theme of not measuring up and not being adequate to achieve (Cards 1, 2, 8 GF, and 3 BM). Their only salvation, if female, is to have a man marry them or, if children, to grow up bigger than anyone else (13B). In contrast, her stories that relate to men reflect strength (13 MF), aggressive confrontations (8 BM and 4), and the ability to salvage the inadequate women by marrying them (8 GF, 8 BM, and 7 GF).

Summary Statement of Dynamic Picture: A reveals her perception of herself as a needy, vulnerable, inadequate, asexual child. This may be in response to her explicit anxiety regarding phallic aggression. She is able to perform in the intellectual arena without conflictual dynamic intrusions, whereas she portrays interpersonal interactions as fraught with conflicts and difficulties.

Defenses

WISC–R: The WISC did not challenge *A*'s psychic integrity, so there was little need for defensive operations. On a few occasions when the content of the question seems to threaten her, she becomes more overtly obsessive or compulsive (Similarities 17, Vocabulary 21, and Comprehension 1, 2, 4, and 11).

B–G: This test was not administered.

FD: In her female drawing and associations, *A*'s major defensive strategy is regression. She draws a "10-year-old," prepubertal, asexual girl.

Her drawing and associations for the male figure are unusual in the degree of denial and avoidance. The use of these defenses permit her to avoid any reference to phallic sexuality and/or aggression. This may reflect an extreme measure to ward off her awareness of puberty.

Rorschach: In spite of *A*'s intellectual approach to the Rorschach resulting in a high *F*+%, her overall defensive strategy prohibits dynamic concerns being expressed. This produces an unusually immature and noncreative record. A produces only one *M*(I, 1) and one (*M*) (IX, 1), in contrast to an adequate number of *FM* (I, 4; V, 2; VII, 1 and 2; VIII, 1). This implies a preference for regression when confronted with the stimulation of the card. In addition, there is only one color response (IX, 2) and two texture responses (VI, 1 and 2), suggesting an inhibition and constriction in her interpersonal interactions.

A's difficulties with aggressive and sexual impulses are seen in the extreme use of denial (I, 1 and 2; III, 5; IV, 2 and 3; V, 2; VI, 1; and IX, 2) and the amount of regression seen throughout the record. One instance of a breakdown of this defensive pattern is seen notably in Card VI in her first response, where her language becomes confused, i.e., she moves from an animal skin to a skinned animal. This is in contrast to her responses to Card VII, which reflect purely immature responses. Another instance of a breakdown in her defensive approach is in Card III, where she produces a clear F- (III, 5) after the only response suggestive of projection (III, 4). Why projection suddenly appears is unclear. It is clear, however, that this "fingers pointing" percept is followed by a breakdown in her more usual rigorous control.

TAT: As in the Rorschach, avoidance and regression are the preferred defensive strategies A brings to the TAT. Her storytelling throughout reflects attempts to avoid the task as well as avoidance of attributing any value to the stimuli (the pictures). Her only way of complying to E's requests is to develop childlike stories that at times become silly and absurd. Over and above her avoiding style, clear instances of avoidance are seen in Cards 1, 2, 12 M, 8 GF, 9 GF, 4, and 16. Examples of regression are found in Cards 1, 8 GF, 8 BM, 7 GF, 3 BM, and 13. The extent of A's efforts at avoidance and the particular refuge she seeks in regression suggest the need to skip over puberty and adolescence and go from latency to adulthood, as personified in Card 7 GF.

In addition A also uses projection, as seen above in Card III of the Rorschach. She introduces omnipotent attributes as the only defense against aggression (8 BM). This use of projection suggests a paranoid orientation.

Finally, her blatant use of denial is seen throughout in her inappropriate leap to happy conclusions to her depressive and aggressive stories.

Summary Statement of Defenses: A's record is replete with several defensive operations. She has excellent obsessive-compulsive defenses that work well for her in structured intellectual areas. She resorts to more immature defenses of denial, avoidance, and regression, however, in response to ideas of aggression, sex, and affect. Additionally, at times she uses projection.

Affective Expression

WISC–R: *A* works very hard throughout the WISC, only betraying her anxiety through her behavior of cracking her knuckles, biting her nails, and expressing concern over how well she is doing.

B–G: This test was not administered.

FD: *A* complies with the task and even in her association does not reveal the affective status of her people.

Rorschach: Consistent with *A*'s major defense of avoidance in this test, there is no expression of or reference to affect. She utilizes *C* on one occasion (IX, 2) and *c* on two occasions (VI, 1 and 2), which is a remarkably constricted use of these determinants.

TAT: In contrast to all the other tests, *A* emerges with affective reactions to the cards in the TAT. Overall she seems to be disturbed by the "pull" of the pictures, possibly because of the affect they arouse in her. She responds to this discomfort with anger and depression. Her stories mock interactions between people and their feelings, which conveys a sense of her hostility toward the test and *E*.

Summary Statement of Affective Expression: The hallmark of *A*'s affective expression is unhappiness. In intellectual tasks she is anxious, presumably over achievement. In some projective tasks she avoids affective expression while in one, the TAT, she expresses anger and resentment. This at times comes across in her disdainful, mocking elaborations.

Summary

A is an intellectually gifted pubescent girl who conveys a sense of great unhappiness. She is caught in the struggle between wishing to remain a child and the inevitability of her pubertal changes toward adolescence. She obviously is experiencing extreme difficulties in accepting sexual and aggressive impulses. Her energies are expended in maintaining herself as a young child. As a result, she is utilizing her intellectual abilities through a variety of immature defensive operations that curtail her creativity and interfere with actual achievement in school. She is out of step with her peers, leading to difficulties in the interpersonal sphere. All of this results in feelings of inadequacy, incompetence, and loneliness.

Generally *A* makes heroic attempts to control any affective reaction to anything. At times, however, her anxiety breaks through in self-punishing behaviors; at other times this anxiety results in self-demeaning productions. She is very angry but is unable to express it directly. She is only able to convey the degree of her anger by a mocking, derisive style.

A's overall personality organization is rooted in reality. She utilizes many different defensive strategies to cope with her concerns. Often anxiety can break through in spite of her attempts to control any feeling states; unavailable ways of expressing anger leave her feeling hopeless and sad. At times she resorts to a paranoid-like orientation when faced with threatening ideas. All of these defensive measures require so much psychic energy that she is left feeling very inadequate, with little available energy for academic achievement.

Diagnosis

DSM-III-R

Axis I: 308.28 Adjustment Disorder with Mixed Emotional Features
Axis II: V71.09 (No diagnosis)
Axis III: None
Axis IV: 2-Mild
Axis V: 70-Mild

A is an excellent candidate for psychotherapy. She has many strengths and is experiencing enough pain to motivate her to work in therapy. The initial phase may present difficulties because of her suspiciousness and feelings of hopelessness. Once she is able to engage in the therapeutic process, she has an excellent prognosis.

Psychological Test Data

A: 12–3 Female

WISC–R

	Scaled Score
Verbal Tests	
Information	16
Similarities	18
Arithmetic	16
Vocabulary	17
Comprehension	18
(Digit Span)	(16)
Total	85

Performance Tests

Picture Completion	14	
Picture Arrangement	11	
Block Design	16	
Object Assembly	13	
Coding	16	
	——	
Total	70	

	Scaled Score	*IQ*
Verbal Scale	85	145
Performance Scale	70	129
Full Scale	155	141

[Very anxious, cracks knuckles, bites nails. Worried about doing well—a lot of checking.]

Information

		Score
1–6.		6
7.	Seven	1
8.	April	1
9.	Pig	1
10.	12	1
11.	Winter, summer, spring, fall	1
12.	Columbus	1
13.	Digests food	1
14.	West	1
15.	February	1
16.	Edison	1
17.	England	1
18.	Chemical properties—I don't know.	0
19.	Canada and Mexico	1
20.	2,000 pounds	1
21.	South America	1
22.	Antimone. [Q] Air, I don't know. [*Describes how they blow glass.*]	0
23.	Athens	1
24.	5 foot, 8 or 9 inches	1
25.	Measures air pressure	1
26.	Water. [Q] Hydrogen.	0
27.	3,000 miles	1
28.	Egyptian picture writing	1
29.	Scientist, theory of evolution	1
30.	I don't know.	0
		——
	Total	26

Picture Completion

		Score
1–4.		4
5.	Whiskers	1
6.	Doll	1
7.	8	1

8.	Leg	1
9.	Steps	1
10.	Handles	1
11.	Holes	1
12.	Nose	1
13.	Hinge	1
14.	Diamond	1
15.	Sock	1
16.	Button holes	1
17.	Band	1
18.	Screw	1
19.	Ear	1
20.	Handle on top? I don't know.	0
21.	[OT] Hoofs not divided	0 (1)
22.	Number wrong—no, mercury.	1
23.	Shadows	1
24.	Missing something on dial. [Q] No cords.	1
25.	Eyebrow	1
26.	I don't know.	0

	Total	23 (24)

Similarities

		Score
1–4.		4
5.	Both fruits	2
6.	Both alcoholic beverages, illegal for under 18	2
7.	Both animals—both mammals	2
8.	Both parts of body with major joint	2
9.	Both methods of communication	2
10.	Both measurements in the English system	2
11.	Both emotions	2
12.	Both made out of minerals. [Q] Metal—both domestic appliances.	1
13.	Both land forms	2
14.	Both rights with privileges. [Q] Civil rights.	1
15.	Both ways of expressing a sequence, both things in a sequence. [Q] They are the ends.	2
16.	Numbers. [Q] Both prime—no—nothing comes to top of my head.	0
17.	Both composed of molecules. Both used in cooking. Both vital to our survival.	2

	Total	26

Picture Arrangement

	Time	Order	Score
1–2.			2
3.	29"	FIRE	2
4.	9"	WALK	2
5.	24"	THUG	3
6.	7"	RUSH	5
7.	22"	VAMP	3
8.	18"	CASH	3

9.	16"	CHASE	4
10.	39"	WORMS	3
11.	1'21"	BCNEH	0
12.	35"	COLUD	2

Total 31

Arithmetic

		Score
1–7.		7
8.	14	1
9.	7	1
10.	24¢	1
11.	$27	1
12.	11	1
13.	9	1
14.	10¢	1
15.	18	1
16.	$1.20	0
17.	$42	1
18.	$12	1

Total 17

Block Design

	Time	*Score*
1–2.		4
3.	5"	2
4.	8"	7
5.	6"	7
6.	7"	7
7.	8"	7
8.	10"	7
9.	38"	5
10. This is hard.	1'58"	4
11.	1'11"	5

Total 55

Vocabulary

		Score
1–5.		10
6.	A tool used to hold two things together. [Q] Made of metal and you hit it with a hammer. Usually used for wood.	2
7.	The letters that make up a language.	2
8.	Animal sort of like a horse. Used for carrying stuff.	2
9.	Someone who takes things belonging to other people.	2
10.	To bring together.	2
11.	Courageous.	2
12.	A gem. A precious stone.	2
13.	To wager money on the outcome of a certain event. To wager something.	2
14.	Words that don't have a clear or precise meaning, or not sense.	2
15.	To stop or to stop from doing something.	2
16.	Being able to pass a disease onto other people.	2
17.	A bother.	2
18.	A story with a moral. A fictional story with a moral.	2
19.	Harmful or endangering.	2
20.	To move from place to place.	2

21. A group of lines in a poem or something that fits together in one idea and are said in rhyme with one another.   2
22. To be away from other people.   2
23. I don't know.   0
24. A plan between two countries. What happens in spy stories. [Q] Against a different party. I don't know exactly, like to take over.   1
25. An attic. Bats in your belfry.   0
26. Rival, an opponent. Rivalry, they're against somebody. Fighting between two people who are enemies or opponents.   2
27. Different parts in the Constitution. 1st Amendment, 13th Amendment. [Q] Listing in the Constitution.   1
28. To draw somebody towards you. When something makes you do something, a compulsion.   2
29. Like a sickness.   2
30. To cross out. Erase entirely.   2
31. Prominent.   0
32. Something to do with diligent. I don't know..   0

Total   54

Object Assembly

	Time	Score
G	18"	8
H	60"	5
C	39"	6
F	33"	9
	Total	28

[*H—she spends half the time figuring out how a horse goes, before trying to place the pieces together.*]

Comprehension

               Score

1. It depends on how bad a cut. Wash it out. If really bad, sterilize it with alcohol, then put a Band-Aid on it. In a few days, take Band-Aid off. If it's really bad, you should bandage it every few days, frequently.   2
2. You should take it right away to the cash register, because they have an easier way to locate the person in the store. If they are not in the store, you can see if there is an address in it and send it back. If there isn't, you can take it to the police station.   2
3. Call for fire department. You should check it out. Call fire department and then go over and see if you could help.   2
4. To keep traffic under control. To make sure people don't get too crazy at events like ball games. To keep criminals —to find them and bring them to justice and to generally keep things under control.   2
5. Look for it and if you can't find it, buy another one and tell the friend it all.   2
6. Stop fighting. Don't fight back and stop her.   2
7. Brick is better insulated, warmer, and can't be destroyed by fire.   2

8. To keep track of how many cars and for ID of car if someone steals your car.   2
9. So that they can't get out and do anymore harm. *[Q]* As a
punishment.   2
10. It's a tax. *[Q]* It's another way of paying taxes to help pay
the mailman and people who work at the mail.   2
11. So that stuff doesn't get shipped out to public that isn't
worthy of the public—and so that someone homicidal doesn't
putpoison in all the meat and people don't get killed. So
meat is not all rotten.   2
12. Charity is more organized, less likely to spend it on alcohol
and drugs. People will be helped by it. It will make your
money go further.   2
13. That way people can't come up to you and say, "You voted
for my opponents, grrrr!" Who you vote for is your business,
and nobody needs to know.   2
14. Easier to carry around, and they are cheaper.   2
15. If you promise somebody, they put trust in you, and if you
break your promise, it proves you're not worthy of being
trusted. And not to mention that they don't get done what
they wanted you to do.   2
16. It's produced in the USA. Cheaper, soft and sells well.
[Q] 'Cause people buy it.   1
17. If you have two parties, then you have votes for different
choices. And when you have different people working together
you get different ideas, more opinions. [Q] They both have
different duties. Both houses have different duties, so they
need both. *[Duties?]* Congress declares war, executive or
judicial pass bills that other people suggest.   1

Total   32

Digit Span

Score
F 12 + B 8   Total   20

Coding B

Score
Total Score   71

Bender–Gestalt was not administered.

Figure Drawings

[Female]   She's 10 years old. She likes to do models and stuff and long-term ambition is to become an airplane captain. She doesn't like school and her brother, who is 14. You can understand what he does to her.

[Male]   He's 89 years old but very spry. He likes to see his girlfriend, who is 94 and also in good health. They like to play checkers and eat pizza.

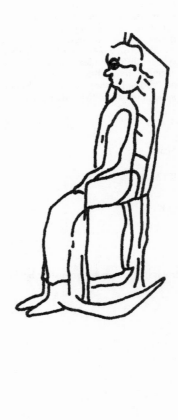

Rorschach

Inquiry

I.

↑↓ 1. This way it looks like an eagle, like in one of those flags.

1. Eagle. Head turned to side. Like the kind on a flag. These are sort of his wings and his body down here.

↑ 2. These look like Pegasus or something.

2. Winged horses. Wings and head. [Q] I am imagining the rest—in my mind.

3. A combination of a dolphin and a fish.

3. [*doesn't remember the dolphin*] Fish—head, eye, body tail.

→ 4. A bird flying.

4. Birds, head and wings. [Q] Also imagining the rest. [*Flying?*] The wings look like they are spread.

II.

↓ 1. A butterfly. [*lower center red*] Two butterflies.

1. The antennas and the way it's shaped. Head and wings.

↓ 2. A sting ray, [S] sort of.

2. Head, wings, stinger part.

→ 3. Rabbit. [*side D*]

3. [*she doesn't remember at first*] Head, nose, tail, ears, feet. There is another one here [*opposite side*].

↑ 4. Two seals. [*upper red*]

4. The positions, just the way they were sitting, sort of the head and sort of the body.

III.

↑ 1. Two people.

1. There are the people and they are doing something. This is like a pot or something

	[*lower center* D] [*Q*] Heads, arms, feet. [*Pot?*] It looks like they were stirring something.
2. Butterfly. [*center red*]	2. [*again did not remember*] The bow-tie part? [*Q*] The wings and the middle part of the butterfly.
3. Some stringed instrument. [*upper side red*]	3. Stringed instrument this looks like keys, neck.
↓ 4. Fingers pointing. [*on usual legs*]	4. Looks like that. [*demonstrates with finger pointing*]
↓ 5. A person with a bow tie.	5. A man with a bow tie, head, tuxedo—oh, why did I say tuxedo? Just looks like a jacket and here are his arms. [*Q*] I am just seeing the top.

IV.

1. Bigfoot. [*W*]	1. Bigfoot. This looks like some kind of monster and these look like his feet.
2. Caterpillar. [*lower center projection*]	2. Antennas, body.
3. Badger. [*Top center D*]	3. Just the badger's head. The stripe of his head.

V.

1. Butterfly. [*W*]	1. Antennas, wings. [*Q*] Standing still.
2. Alligators.	2. Crocodiles, or alligators. Just the mouths. Just the way the mouths are open.

[*At this point, A is noticeably upset.*]

V.

↓ 1. Tiger skin. [*W*]

1. A tiger skin. The head, neck, whiskers, stripes [*indicates shading*], arms, legs. [*Skin?*] It doesn't look like a real tiger. Just looks like a skinned one. I saw a skinned lion at the zoo. [*Q*] Because of the position.

↑ 2. Thermometer.

2. [*does not, at first, remember*] This post down the middle. This looks like the mercury. [*Mercury?*] It's just darker.

3. Totem pole.

3. Just like the thermometer but this part here too [*includes the feathery extension on top*].

→ 4. A fish. [*Dr center*]

4. Here with its mouth open. It doesn't look like a fish at all. [*Q*] Just the shape.

VII.

↓ 1. Dancing elephants. [*D*]

1. Trunks, ear, body. Hands like that [*demonstrates*], like young elephants. they just look like they are dancing.

↑ 2. More dancing elephants. [*D*]

2. These elephants look like they are doing ballet. Head, trunks, feet.

→↑ 3. People. [*center third*]

3. Just the head of people.

→ 4. Sunbathing elephants.

↓ 5. Butterfly.

5. Don't remember where it was anymore.

↓ 6. A hall. [*lower* D, with d *as passage-way*]

6. Steps, passageway, and it's all a hall. Like in the Wizard of Oz when they are coming in.

VIII.

→ 1. Cats.

That's all.

1. Mountain cats—legs, body, head. The way they are proportioned makes them look like a wild cat, and they look like they are climbing.

IX.

1. Wizards. [*top orange* D]

1. Wizards. Hat, hands, and they look like they are battling over something.

2. Another thermometer.

2. The red stuff is the mercury and this is the rest of it. [Q] The red makes it look like mercury.

↓ 3. An icicle. [*center column*]

3. This part looks like an icicle. This [*red*] looks like a roof, and down here the icicle is hanging.

X.

1. Lots of insects. [W]

1. A lot of insects. These look like insects, all the legs and stuff.

↓ 2. Sea horses.

2. Just the shape.

TAT

1. There was a little boy that did not want to practice his violin. He stared at it for hours, hoping it would go away. But his courageous attempts were in vain. His next idea was to throw a temper tantrum. That day he'd have to practice his violin. Instead he went to his room with no supper. The next day he was faced with the same problem, so he finally decided to practice it and get it over with. So he kept with it and even though he never got very good, he had a lot of fun with it. Happy ending. [*laughs, but won't say why*]. [*Feel?*] In the beginning he felt mad at having to do it, and then he got discouraged, because nothing was working. And he still had to do it, and then he felt glad that he had given it . . .

2. [*Smiles a lot to herself—long time in trying to think. Stares off a lot. Grimaces, sighs.*] Can't think of anything for this picture. It doesn't lend itself to stories. [*Spends a long time looking—grimaces, laughs to self, holds her head, gets more and more depressed looking as her head drops down into her body. E suggests going on to another card, and A is clearly relieved.*]

12 M. [*A shakes head jerkily.*] I don't feel creative—it's boring. [*E suggests she take one person on the card and describe him, and then something will come as she talks.*] You mean I don't have to have a whole creative story? [*Of course not!*] This guy in the bed looks

sick, and the other guy is the doctor. The guy who is sick is asleep and he's not thinking anything. The doctor guy is worried, 'cause this guy is really sick and he doesn't think he can save him. And what's his family gonna say and stuff. The guy dies. The family yells at the doctor for a while, and then the doctor goes off and treats somebody else.

8 GF. This girl is like an actress. This is her dreaming between acts. And she doesn't know what to do, 'cause she's really not that good and doesn't think she will have a really big future in this. And she has a boyfriend who wants her to give up the theater and marry him. She's not sure if she wants to or not, because she may be able to salvage her career, which isn't going too well at the moment. And so finally she decides to hell with the theater. She goes off and marries the guy and they have nine kids, whose names are Georgie, Porgy, Raggedy Ann, Raggedy Andy, Mickey, Minnie, Donald, Daisy and Goofy. And they all lived happily ever after.

8 BM. This guy on the bed's asleep. The other guys are murdering him. The other guy fell in with the murderers but he doesn't really believe in it, but he sorta does, 'cause he didn't have anything else to do. The guy is worrying because the guy who is getting murdered wants to do something for him. So he is having qualms over it. So he is not helping, but he is standing there. And then the guy who is getting murdered turns out to be Superman, and nobody can cut through his flesh because it's as tough as steel. So he leaps up, turns the murderers in and they live happily ever after again. And he set this other guy free. [Q] He feels guilty, so he reforms and he becomes a hermit until a beautiful girl comes along and he takes her off and—they live in the big city forever.

13 MF. [*A looks really depressed.*] This is getting me really depressed. Mind if I make them funny? This man is playing hide and seek. He has his hands over his eyes, and he's counting. The lady is a mannequin. He bought her for $3.29 at a store, no, at a garage sale. So everybody gets hiding here. And then he finds the other people hiding. They are his children, his great-great-grandfather, his wife. He finds them all and they all leave this dismal room and go out to Burger King and then go to a movie. And they, too, live happily ever after. I like ending things like that.

9 GF. These people are taking part in a special kind of square dance that has to do with washing clothes. What they do in this dance is they take their clothes, do complicated dance steps, and then dive into the river holding their clothes. And then they take soap out and throw it at—and then they take all the clothes and throw the soap at it so that it gets clean. And they all think it's a very effective way to do their laundering.

7 GF. These people are at a rich fancy party—aristocratic. This little girl was dancing with this guy, and he stepped on her feet the whole time and she didn't want to dance again. It was her birthday party. And so she . . . this lady is bugging her to go dancing again because it will seem like she is spoiling her own party. So finally when she won't go out and dance again the lady has the butler bring out Pin the Tail on the Donkey and Duck, Duck, Pour—and they all played games and lived happily ever after. Incidentally, she married the guy who stepped on her feet, later in life.

3 BM. This person is very sad. Such a sad story. They can't find their Legos. And they look all over the house. They had to have their Legos because it's their favorite thing to do on a rainy day or a sunny day or a snowy day. So when they couldn't find their Legos, they were very distressed. And so finally she or he looked in their underwear drawer and found their Legos, and they all lived happily ever after.

4. This guy—somebody insulted his haircut and he wants to go and fight that guy who called his haircut unsuitable. But his wife doesn't think it's a good idea because the other guy is the mayor, and he's having to get a job so he doesn't want to fight him. So he went home and shaved off his haircut and the mayor was pleased and gave him his job.

16. Once upon a time there was nothing. It was plain white and it lived in a piece of cardboard. Since nothing ever happened to it, it wasn't a very interesting person, but it lived happily ever after in its piece of cardboard. [*Thinks?*] It thought of nothing. It was a nothing and it felt nothing, too.

13 B. This is a little boy. He is sitting on his front step, not feeling particularly happy at this moment. He's thinking that Billy never gave him a turn with the toy truck, and he is very angry with him. Since Billy is eight years older and six feet tall, he can't go and express how angry he feels. And so he went off into the forest and made himself his own truck, a whole lot better than Billy's, and grew to be seven feet tall.

2. The whole scene was going perfectly until the girl forgot her lines and stood staring into space like an idiot. She wasn't feeling bad over it, but she was almost in a state of unconsciousness. She stared off into space thinking sentimental thoughts—well, not exactly. The director stormed on stage shaking his fists, and she fell into a dead faint. The end. [*Feeling?*] Not feeling anything.

Psychological Test Portrait

B: 13–1 Male

B was referred for evaluation by his therapist of two years. The therapist wanted confirmation of the vastly improved clinical picture she now saw: *B* now makes friends and does well in school, with only occasional behavior problems.

   B is a well-developed, attractive youth. He is the eldest of three children who live with their mother. He and his mother have a history of conflict that still persists. He has had no contact with his father, who left the famly when *B* was five.

   B is in a special class for the visually handicapped, indicating that his corrected vision is at most 20/200. In order for him to see adequately, it was necessary for him to be no more than ten to twelve inches away from the testing material. He was cooperative throughout the testing and seemed to enjoy the tasks and the interaction with *E*.

Cognitive Functioning

WISC–R: *B* achieves a low average Full-Scale IQ of 87, with a small discrepancy between his Verbal score (85) and his Performance score (91). His subtest scores range from 6 to 12, indicating an inconsistent pattern. The Coding and Picture Arrangement scores may be lowered by his severe visual problems; the inconsistent pattern, however, is also noted within the Similarities test. The overall contrast of test scores where he does well (Block Design) to those where he does poorly (Information, Comprehension, Digit Span) does not indicate any specific cognitive deficits, thus suggesting motivational problems.

B–G: *B*'s approach to compensate for his severe visual problems is clearly demonstrated in the Bender: he confines his figures to the upper half of the page, separates each figure with a vertical line, and achieves the diamond in 8 in an extraordinary way. The fact that he does not draw horizontal lines leads to a collision of design 6 into 3. B experiences great difficulty when one figure must overlap into the integrity of another figure within the same design (as in 6, 7, and 8). This, in addition to the above, suggests the possibility of a nonspecific organic problem.

FD: *B*'s figure drawings are well executed inasmuch as they occupy two-thirds of the page, tend to be placed in the center of the page, and are complete (including details and movement). In addition, the bodies are well proportioned, although he exaggerates the heads in size and attention to details. Again, minor indications of his possible organic and/or visual problems are seen in the female's misplaced elbow and the transparency of the right thumb on the skirt.

Rorschach: *B* uses a great deal of effort to integrate the structure of the blots into *W*'s. He manages to achieve an adequate form level with the exception of Card VII. When he experiences difficulty in his effort at integration, however, the form level becomes vague (II, VI, IX, and X). He uses very few determinants, which does not seem to reflect a cognitive problem but rather a problem in expressing fantasy.

TAT: Although *B*'s stories to the TAT cards are somewhat limited and immature, he complies with the instructions and tells adequate stories.

Summary Statement of Cognitive Functioning: B presents a picture of a boy with cognitive deficits related to an unspecified organic problem and severe visual limitations. He often manages to compensate adequately for these problems through dint of effort and creative tactics. He shows a good average intellectual ability but is constricted in his use of fantasy.

Dynamic Picture

WISC–R: There is little dynamic material presented by *B* in the WISC. There is the suggestion of insecurity about his ability inasmuch as he does not attempt to answer questions when he is not sure of the answer.

B–G: The Bender does not reveal any dynamic considerations.

FD: The figure drawings suggest *B*'s openness to the world with some degree of confidence. His sexual differentiation is clear-cut, with the male drawing suggesting his wish to be older. His emphasis on detailing the heads (as well as the size of the heads) suggests *B*'s narcissism, typical of the adolescent. The bodies of his figures, however, suggest that he is still rooted in a prepubertal stance. The one suggestion of feelings of insecurity is represented in the tiny feet. The strong emphasis on the eyes (in both drawings) most probably reflects his concern about his visual problems.

Rorschach: Similarly to the figure drawings, *B*'s Rorschach percepts vacillate between an expression of adolescent and prepubertal issues. His initial response to Card I, as well as his emphasis on phallic-shaped percepts (II, 1; VI; VIII, 1; IX, 1; and X, 2), reflect adolescent masculine strivings as well as fears. This is in contrast to the more childlike percepts on II and IV. The record is replete with free-floating anxiety (smoke, fire, and electricity) and explosiveness (II, IX, and X) related to phallic representations, which would explain the extreme inner tension (as in m's in II, VI, IX, and X).

The limited use of M and FC when ordinarily we would expect three to five M's and at least two FC's indicates that B has not yet developed a secure sense of self or the capacity to relate to others on a more mature level. He, however, shows promise for growth in these capacities.

TAT: The content of B's poignant stories reveal a boy who feels very isolated. When there are interactions between people, they are superficial (3 BM and 7 BM) or expressing concern over possible loss of the others (5, 6 BM, and 13B). He conveys an overall sense of vulnerability (3 BM, 8 BM, 13 MF, and 16) that may stem from inner feelings of damage or external threats of danger (8 BM, 13 MF, and 20). Although B's expression of fantasy is limited, it should be noted that Card 1 elicits a reference to the possibility of daydreaming.

Summary Statement of Dynamic Picture: B's test responses convey a sense of a lonely, isolated boy who feels damaged and vulnerable. He has yet to establish a sense of self adequate for his age, which would provide a source of security and safety. He has not developed the ability for interpersonal relationships, which increases his sense of vulnerability and isolation.

Defenses

WISC–R: The hallmark of B's use of defenses in the WISC is his use of avoidance ("I don't know"). He is unwilling to attempt to test his potential intellectual abilities, which are evident throughout.

B–G: The Bender is a testimony to B's intellectual potential, as he has developed many adaptive coping strategies to deal with his visual/organic problem.

FD: The portrayal of human figures with large heads indicates B's reaching for intellectual defenses as a way of coping with his underlying dynamics. He uses denial of sexuality in drawing immature bodies.

Rorschach: Similarly to the figure drawings, B attempts to control his responses to the Rorschach blots through intellectual defenses. He produces a *W* for 8 out of the 10 cards, and he gives 7 *F*'s out of 13 responses. His reliance on constriction is seen in the small number of total responses and in the lack of detail and elaboration of the responses he gives. The fantasy he does express is too frightening (II, 1; III, 2; IV, 1; VI, 1; VIII, a; IX, 1; and X, 2) to be available to him for defensive purposes. There is an attempt on Card VIII to use denial in mastering underlying feelings of sadness.

TAT: Constriction of fantasy is again evident in *B*'s TAT stories. When some fantasy emerges, we again hear dangerous and frightening ideas (3 BM, 6 BM, 8 BM, 13 MF, and 20).

Summary Statement of Defenses: *B* does not have an array of flexible defensive strategies that would be more appropriate for his age. Rather, he relies extensively on avoidance and constriction and seems to be making an effort at developing intellectual defenses.

Affective Expression

WISC–R: Although *B* was compliant throughout the WISC, his feelings of insecurity precluded his experiencing this test as positive.

B–G: The execution of the Bender figures, including the use of the vertical lines to separate each figure, suggests that *B* was experiencing some tension and anxiety in this test.

FD: There does not seem to be the same degree of anxiety in *B*'s drawings as there was in the Bender figures, and the drawings themselves suggest a pleasant feeling of openness to the world.

Rorschach: *B* appears to experience excitement in his explosive percepts of spaceships, which in turn elicit a depressive feeling (see *C'* in V).

TAT: For the most part, *B*'s stories conclude with a positive and hopeful solution. This is true even in stories concerned with danger and loss. The one exception is 13 MF, and notably there is no compassion expressed by the husband/father.

Summary Statement of Affective Expression: *B* communicates the sense of a sad and lonely boy who can also feel pleasantly open to the world and others. His inner tension and anxiety appear at times when he is most stimulated by adolescent sexual impulses.

Summary

B is a boy who is not only handicapped by his visual problems and nonspecific organic problems but also by his sense of insecurity and inadequacy. He demonstrates good cognitive capabilities but is limited in the expanded use of those abilities by his need to constrict and avoid intellectual challenges. He feels sad and lonely, worries about abandonment, and feels his impulses as threatening. The challenge of adolescence, with the implication of independence as well as newly intense sexual drives, is frightening to him. He would prefer to remain in a dependent, childlike stance. There is evidence, however, of the potential for growth in establishing a self-identity and reaching out for good interactions with others.

Diagnosis

DSM-III-R

Axis I:	313.81 Oppositional Defiant Disorder–Improved
Axis II:	315.90 Developmental Disorder NOS
Axis III:	Visual handicap—"legally blind"
Axis IV:	4-Severe
Axis V:	65-Mild–Moderate

B shows remarkable improvement in response to his two years of therapy in spite of his home circumstances having stayed the same. He is presently moving toward a more secure sense of self and a greater ability to make trusting relationships. It is necessary for therapy to continue in order to improve on and solidify the gains he has made. He has shown his capability to make a trusting therapeutic relationship, which is reflected in his TAT statement, "and the doctor made him well" (Card 3 BM).

Psychological Test Data

B: 13–1 Male

WISC–R

	Scaled Score
Verbal Tests	
Information	6
Similarities	8
Arithmetic	9
Vocabulary	9
Comprehension	6
(Digit Span)	(6)
Total	38

Performance Tests

Picture Completion	9	
Picture Arrangement	7	
Block Design	12	
Object Assembly	10	
Coding	6	
Total	44	

	Scaled Score	IQ
Verbal Scale	38	85
Performance Scale	44	91
Full Scale	82	87

Information

		Score
1–4.		4
5.	Five	1
6.	Calf	1
7.	7	1
8.	April	1
9.	Pig	1
10.	12	1
11.	Spring, summer, fall, winter	1
12.	C. Columbus	1
13.	I don't know.	0
14.	I don't know.	0
15.	I don't know.	0
16.	T. Edison	1
17.	I don't know.	0
18.	I don't know.	0
19.	I don't know.	0
20.	I don't know.	0
21.	Alaska	0
	Total	13

Picture Completion

		Score
1.	[*points*] These are missing.	1
2.	Mouth	1
3.	Ear	1
4.	Fingernail	1
5.	Whiskers	1
6.	Doll missing in mirror	1
7.	Number 8 is missing	1
8.	One leg	1
9.	One of the steps	1
10.	Everything is here	0
11.	Holes	1
12.	Other half of nose	1
13.	Other screw. [*points*] I don't know what you call it.	1
14.	Diamond [*points*]	1
15.	Sock	1
16.	The holes where you put buttons	1
17.	Wristband from the watch he has on	1

18.	The screw from middle	1
19.	The ears	1
20.	The thing on top where you put screwdriver in [*demonstrates*].	1
21.	I think everything is there	0
22.	The liquid here [*points*].	0
23.	Everything here	0
24.	Letters part—to be here to the right	0
25.	Nothing missing	0
26.	I don't think anything's missing.	0
	Total	20

Similarities

		Score
1.	They are round.	1
2.	They give light.	1
3.	You can wear a shirt and a hat.	1
4.	Musical instruments.	1
5.	Fruits	2
6.	Something to drink	1
7.	They are animals	2
8.	Parts of the body	1
9.	Because you listen to them.	1
10.	What kind of pound? I don't know.	0
11.	Some kind of feelings.	2
12.	I don't know.	0
13.	They are places. [Q] Both places that you can get to.	1
14.	I don't know.	0
15.	I don't know.	0
16.	I don't know.	0
17.	I don't know.	0
	Total	14

Picture Arrangement

	Time	Order	Score
1.			2
2.			2
3.	42"	FIRE	2
4.	20"	WALK	2
5.	16"	THUG	3
6.	33"	RUSH	3
7.	20"	VAMP	3
8.	29"	CASH	3
9.	68"	ECHAS	0
10.	4'	—	0
11.	35"	BCHNE	0
		Total	20

Arithmetic

		Score
1–4.		4
5.	2	1
6.	4	1

7.	6	1
8.	14	1
9.	7	1
10.	24¢	1
11.	27	1
12.	26	1
13.	I don't know.	0
14.	10¢	1
15.	I don't know.	0
16.	$1.20	0
17.	I don't know.	0
18.	I don't know.	0

Total 13

Block Design

	Time	*Score*
1–2.		4
3.	10"	2
4.	11"	6
5.	27"	4
6.	23"	4
7.	20"	5
8.	16"	6
9.	49"	5
10.	84"	4
11.	88"	4

Total 44

Vocabulary

		Score
1–5.		10
6.	Like, um, some kind of tack that if you want to nail something to the wall, you hit at it with a hammer.	2
7.	A group of letters. Twenty-six letters, you know.	2
8.	Is like a baby horse . . . no, no, wait. Is it like a baby horse? Small horse.	2
9.	A man or woman that likes to break into houses or rob stores. [Q] They are lazy, they don't want to earn their own money.	2
10.	Like unite.	2
11.	Fearless.	2
12.	Like a kind of rock or crystal that sparks. [Q] Like it glitters.	2
13.	Like you gamble for money. [Q] I don't know.	1
14.	Like silly.	2
15	Avoid. [Q] Like trying to stop something from happening.	2
16.	You can catch something. Like a disease you can catch.	2
17.	Like a bother.	2
18.	Some kind of story.	2
19.	Like bad for you. [Q] Like smoking is hazardous to your health.	1
20.	I don't know.	0
21.	I don't know.	0
22.	I don't know.	0
23.	I don't know.	0

24. I don't know.   0
25. I don't know.   0
                                                    ──
                                        Total   36

Object Assembly

	Time	Score
G	35"	6
H	23"	6
C	53"	5
F	79"	6

                                        Total   23

Comprehension

                                                    Score
1. Wash it and put Band-Aid on it.   2
2. Take it to the police station.   2
3. Call fire department. [Q] Run to the house. Run to the
   neighbor's house. Go over there to see if anyone's there.   2
4. Protection. So to see that everybody obeys laws. 2
5. I'd try to look for it. If I can't find it, replace it.   2
6. Tell him to stop. If he doesn't stop, get my little brother and
   he'll fix him, 'cause I'm not going to beat up a little kid.   2
7. They used to be built of wood. Wood burns. [Q] Bricks
   can't burn.   1
8. If driver does something bad, police will write down license,
   write down number on the plate. Then they go look for
   driver and the car.   1
9. For doing things bad, because they did stuff against the law.
   [Q] I don't know.   1
10. I don't know.   0
11. I don't know.   0
12. I don't know. Charity goes to kids that need food.   0
13. I don't know.   0
                                                    ──
                                        Total   15

Digit Span
F 4 + B 5   Total Score   9

Coding   Total Score   35

Bender–Gestalt

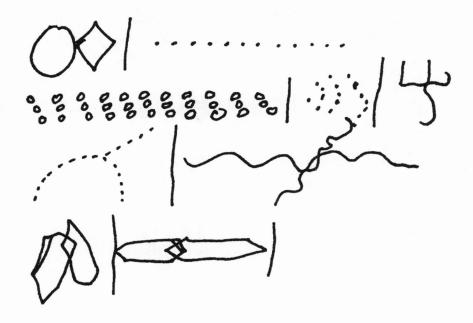

Figure Drawings

Rorschach

Inquiry

I.   27"

1. This looks like a body right here. This middle part looks like a body. Looks like a lady with a dress on, no head.

1. Shaped like a woman, looks like it has a dress on, looks like a collar. [Q] Here, the shape of the body, too, like this is part of the dress, looks like a collar. Just standing there with no head.

II.	16"		1. To me this looks like some kind of spaceship. this looks like fire coming out from the back. The red fire, and this thing is standing this way—red. [*laughs*] That's it. Black smoke.	1. The shape of it made it look like fire. [Q] Black smoke on the sides of it. I saw it before, but did I say the shape of it made it look like smoke? [Q] The sticking out. Didn't look like it is moving— just standing—fire out and from below.
III.	4"	↓	1. This looks like a butterfly	1. Shape.
			2. Arms right here some kind of monster. Look like the eyes, this is the face right here. That's it.	2. Saw arms, then eyes, then face, and then put it together to make a monster. Looks like a monster wearing a bow tie. [Q] Bug or something.
IV.			I gotta do all?	
	10"	↓	1. This looks like some kind of giant, the feet. This is some kind of head, two arms here and another head on top.	1. This looks like feet, little arms. This is head on bottom, and this is head looking at it. From here [*demonstrates*], from top perspective.
V.			1. This looks like a bat—the wings, the antennas—a bat. That's it.	1. [Q] This looks like wings and, you know, the antennas and face. Shape makes it look like a bat. And the color, too—I—oh— black.
VI.		↓↑	I don't know—this looks like—I don't know—[*shakes head*] I don't get nothing out of this.	

	80"	↓ 1.	Could be like some kind of spaceship, and this is an antenna sticking out. And this looks like some electricity going out. That is what is on my mind. That's it.	1. [Q] Shape—antenna sticking out. This is like sparking electricity, 'cause of the sparks. Just thought it up. Shape of it—I thought of it because of the shape of it.
VII.	50"	↓ 1.	Looks like crooked legs, crooked, that's all.	1. [Q] Just by shape. Looks crooked, because I saw this movie, *The Black Hole.* There was this robot. Robot had crooked legs like this. Crooked legs, that's what I thought of. Looks like his crooked legs.
VIII.			This is nice.	
	18"	↓ 1.	This looks like some kind of face, some kind of clown face—different colors.	1. Eyes, some kind of makeup. Shooting stuff, shooting through the nose. This is like the mouth. [Q] By the color and shape of things.
		← 2.	And right over here looks like some kind of animal. Like a lion or something. And on this side, too, looks like the same thing.	2. This looks like lion or tiger. Face, legs, shape of it.
IX.	25"	1.	This looks like some kind of rocket, and this is like the smoke right here. And this is the smoke coming up here. That's it.	1. [Q] Because of shape of it. Smoke doesn't have shape, but I just thought it up like that. I don't know what makes it look like smoke, just looks like it. a. Now that I think of it, the green part looks like the side of a face. [*profile*] The eyes, nose, mouth.

X.   These are nice colors, let's see—um—I seen this one
                                before.

12"   ↓ 1. This looks like a   1. [Q] Like eyes, nose.
                      horse face. This is   [Q] Shape of white
                      the eyes right here,   right here, looks like a
                      the nose, and the   horse-face shape.
                      mouth. And upside
                      down—

                 2. It looks like a   2. Shape of it looks like
                    rocket shooting up.   rocket shape. [*Smoke?*]
                    That's it.   Shape just came to my
                                                    mind. [*Shooting up?*]
                                                    Looks like it is going
                                                    up, the smoke.

TAT

1. This looks like a boy with a violin. He's thinking or daydreaming. [Q] Thinking about how it would be to play a violin. When he grows up, he's the greatest violin player that ever lived.

3 BM. What is that man? I think it is somebody that just got beat up or else maybe he has a stomachache. Somebody took him to the hospital because he was really sick—had a bad pain in his stomach. And the doctor made him well.

5. This is a mother. She's looking for her children. She's mad—and, um—then she finds the children hiding under the bed. She tells them that they are punished 'cause they did something bad in school. That's it. [Q] Started getting fresh with the teacher. And mother told them that they are punished. That's it.

6 BM. These two people look sad because their son just got hit by a car. [Q] No, no, not their son—uh. They are sad and worried altogether. No, 'cause this is the mother and this is the father. Wait—see this lady. She's the mother of his wife. And then his wife and son went out and didn't come for a long time. And then the father and, you know, his mother-in-law, they were worried. Then the mother comes back at ten o'clock in the nighttime. That's all. [*Before you said—*] Yeah, but I changed my mind.

7 BM. This man is—see him—his father. They are having a talk. About how—first the father starts with, "How is school?" Then they, you know, they talk and talk. That's it.

8 BM. I think that this boy right here, that's his father. His father is getting operated. He got shot and they are taking the bullet out of his stomach. The boy feels sad. A few hours later the father recovers from the bullet.

13 MF. I think in the picture, this is his wife. He just got home from work and finds his wife, you know, laying in bed. Somebody broke into the house and, you know, raped her. You know some kind of madman broke into the house, you know, raped her. The father found her lying in bed. He calls the hospital and the police. The ambulance takes her to the hospital and she dies a few hours later because she got stabbed.

13 B. I think in this picture there is a boy in a cabin sitting on the stoop. He is looking for his mother. He gets worried about her because he can't find her. And—[*shakes his head*] I can't. [Q] I don't know. Then he finds his mother. [Q] Shopping.

20. I think that this is an undercover agent and he has a gun. Shooting at robbers. Instead of shooting at the policeman, they, robbers, shoot the streetlight and it blows up—right. Then more policemen came and caught the robbers. They got arrested.

16. The man was driving and his shocks broke down. He sent it to a garage. They put new shocks in. After that they told him how much it would cost. He told them he couldn't pay for it. That's all I can think of. [Q] I think he made like a down payment on it, they took away his car. He had to pay, like, the rest of the money.

Psychological Test Portrait

C: 12–2 Male

C was brought in for evaluation by his parents at the request of his teacher. His teacher was concerned because he was being teased and seemed not to have any friends. C is the middle child, with a teenage sister and a brother in first grade. His parents did not see him as having problems but as just a "normal" boy.

C was very cooperative throughout the testing and seemed to enjoy the tasks. He communicated a sense of needing to please the authority. He was guarded, however, in response to any questions as to his personal life and feelings. He is slim, small, and looks like a prepubertal boy.

Cognitive Functioning

WISC: C scores a high average Full-Scale 117. There is little discrepancy between his Verbal (114) and Performance (117) scores. He shows excellent intellectual capabilities except for lowered Arithmetic and Picture Completion test scores, which do not reflect cognitive deficits (see below).

His frequent inconsistencies in the subtests suggest that he cannot sustain his attention and concentration throughout each subtest. This is undoubtedly the result of dynamic factors that will be discussed later. Inconsistencies seen in C's abilities to do better on harder items than easier items, plus the quality of some of his responses to Vocabulary (7, 12, 21, and 22) and Similarities (13) suggest a much higher intellectual potential than he currently achieves.

B–G: Although C's Bender drawings are adequate, there are many inconsistencies in each figure. There is a variation in pencil pressure, a larger gap in Figure 1, shading lines (Figures 7 and 8), double loops (Figure 2) and a loss of directionality (Figure 5). This, in addition to the disorganized sequencing in the placement of the figures, raises the possibility that C experiences *absences*. This may relate to the inconsistencies mentioned above in the WISC.

FD: C's drawings are recognizably male and female. He experiences great difficulty in attaching the arms, as well as in drawing them proportionally. The quality of his sketchy line (which at times evolves into scribbles), the seeming inability to end the lines at the waist, the empty eye sockets, the cup suspended in space, and unfinished hand in the male drawing all again raise the possibility of *absences*.

Rorschach: *C* demonstrates a powerful drive to organize nine out of the ten blots into *W*'s. He utilizes most of the determinants as well as incorporating small details. Frequently the form level suffers as he attempts to bring all aspects of the blot together. He conveys a sense of unusual perceptions in the way he describes the perspectives on certain blots (Cards II, III, and IV). In spite of this he has five *P*'s, demonstrating his ability to see the world as others see it.

TAT: *C*'s TAT stories demonstrate accurate perceptions of the pictures, as well as sequential plotting. Unfortunately his language usage and thought processes become confused and, at times, idiosyncratic.

Summary Statement of Cognitive Functioning: *C* is a bright young man who demonstrates in many instances a far higher intellectual potential. Unfortunately, he is unable to realize his potential because of idiosyncratic language and conceptualizations, along with the possibility of experiencing *absence* states.

Dynamic Picture

WISC: Generally *C* does not express dynamic concerns throughout the WISC. The one preoccupation he seems to express is the perception of danger to the self (Information, 27; Comprehension, 1; Similarities, 11; and Vocabulary, 13, 27, and 28), which may reflect a feeling of inadequacy and/or vulnerability. This perception of potential danger in the external world may contribute to his lowered scores in Arithmetic and Picture Completion. There is also the suggestion of a problem in *C*'s maintaining the integrity of the self, seen in a fluctuation in boundaries between animate and inanimate (Similarities, 11 and 14; Vocabulary, 13).

B–G: The Bender does not reveal any of *C*'s dynamic issues.

FD: Although *C* draws the male figure first, he minimizes its overall size in contrast to the female. This again suggests his perception of himself as inadequate and inferior, particularly in relation to women. It is possible that the drawing of the male in profile with a fedora (unusual for this age) may represent his concern in facing the world; the blank eyes in both drawings and the lack of ears on the male drawing also emphasize this point.

C seemingly cannot handle aggressive content, which is exemplified in the amorphous manner in which the arms are drawn on both figures. The hands are notably missing or truncated, as is the case with the arms.

The stories accompanying the drawings attribute nothing of dynamic significance except that both speak to oral concerns (nurturance).

Rorschach: As seen in the FD, C suggests difficulty or fearfulness in facing the world through his unusual perceptions of figures from the back and on their knees (II, 1; IV, 1; and IX, 1, Inquiry). His fears of facing the world seem related to a concern with the threat of aggression (I, 1; II, 1; and X, 3), as well as a conflict in his sexual identification (II, 1; VII, 2; and IX, 1) beyond that usually associated with pubertal children. Some of this stems from feelings of inadequacy, vulnerability, and damage (I, 1; II, 1; III, 1, Inquiry; and VI, 1).

An unusual emphasis for his age on self-scrutiny (seen in the reflections on Cards VIII and IX) suggest C's inordinate concern over his own identification, sexual and otherwise.

TAT: C's TAT stories portray, again, his sense of inadequacy (Cards 1 and 2) and a sense of being different (Cards 2 and 7 BM). This may be a reflection of the difficulties he perceives in communication between people (Cards 5, 7 BM, and 6 GF) and a lack of awareness of the feelings of others (Cards 5, 7 BM, and 6 GF).

His expressed sexual confusion (Cards 3 BM and 15) leads him to describe a stereotypic picture of the aggressive male and the victimized female (Cards 6 GF, 4, and 15). Aggressive impulses inevitably lead to murder (6 GF, 4, and 15).

Children of either sex also fare badly (Cards 1 and 2) or die (Cards 3 BM and 8 BM).

Summary Statement of Dynamic Picture: C suffers from intense feelings of inadequacy and vulnerability and a sense of a damaged self. His feelings of worthlessness and insubstantiality relate to confusion in his sexual identification. There is no relief in communication with others, because his people lack awareness and compassion for the feelings and motivations of others.

Defenses

WISC: Throughout the intelligence test there seems to be little need for C to mobilize defenses. The lowered scores in Arithmetic and Picture Completion (10, 11, 12, and 15) may result in his suspiciousness, which is projected on the tests.

B–G: The compulsive defenses utilized by C in the Bender are interfered with by his experience of *absence* (Figures 1, 5, and 7).

FD: The blank eyes in both figures, the lack of ears on the man and the man in profile, at this age, all suggest a paranoid orientation by C (the use of projection).

Rorschach: Throughout the Rorschach, projection is seen as C's major defense. Nine out of ten cards are a W, suggesting an extreme need for control of every aspect of the environment. This is underlined by his inclusion of tiny details and the specificity of his descriptions. This need to control leads to a constriction in his freedom to fantasize. This effort at defense, however, does not prevent bizarre and idiosyncratic percepts from emerging.

TAT: C's initial approach to the new task of the TAT is to become very concrete by naming his characters, which gives him the sense of control over his emerging story. As fearful ideas are projected he must call upon magical thinking as a primitive defense (Cards 5, 8 BM, and 15). These defenses, however, do not work, as peculiar phrasing and idiosyncratic ideas emerge in practically every story.

Summary Statement of Defenses: Unfortunately, C's defenses do not protect him from paranoid ideation and fearful aggressive fantasies elicited in the projectives. He is able to perform his best in the more structured intelligence and Bender tests.

Affective Expression

WISC: C seemed to accept this task without any obvious signs of affective disturbance.

B–G: The Bender figures do not suggest any particular affective response on C's part.

FD: In spite of the anxiety expressed in the sketchy and scribbly lines in his drawings, C did not seem to react with any negative feelings.

Rorschach: C's limited and inappropriate use of color in his percepts speak to his experience of constricted affects. If these affects are felt, they are experienced as confusing.

TAT: The TAT evokes disheartening feelings from C: either his characters are mad, or they die or are murdered. We would have to assume that for so much emphasis on death, C must have an unexpressed reservoir of anger and rage.

Summary Statement of Affective Expression: C's overt affective expression is extremely constricted and limited. Although he was pleasant throughout the testing, there were no indications of any real enjoyment.

Summary

C is a very intelligent boy who has a pleasant and unflappable demeanor. His test protocol, however, indicates a boy who is in serious trouble within himself. He feels inadequate, vulnerable, and damaged. He presents confused and distorted ideation, as well as strange perceptions of the interactions with others. There is a paranoid flavor conveyed in his frightening projections. There is an extreme constriction in his own affect, as well as a confusion in his perception of the feelings of others. His language often is peculiar and idiosyncratic.

C's portrayal of himself as vulnerable, damaged, and sexually confused seems to be in response to sexual abuse clearly evident in his Rorschach percepts (II, 1; IV, 1; VI, 1; and IX, 1) as well as in his unique response to some WISC items (Similarities 5, and Picture Completion 10). The experience of sexual abuse may have caused his precocious emphasis on introspection in the effort to understand who he is, male or female. He seems to be in a quandary as to why he is being so used and sometimes resorts to fantasied magical solutions, including animating the inanimate. The suggestion of states of *absence,* as well as his severely constricted affect, may indicate a way of coping with the traumatic impact of this experience. We can conjecture that this is his way of dissociating himself from the actual event.

Diagnosis

DSM-III-R

Axis I:	309.89 Post-Traumatic Stress Disorder
Axis II:	301.22 Schizotypal Personality Disorder
Axis III:	R/O *Absence*
Axis IV:	5-Extreme
Axis V:	50-Serious

A careful and sensitive investigation of C's probable sexual abuse is immediately necessary. The facts will determine the course of intervention to be taken, such as separation from the abuser. In addition, a neurological examination (specifically, an EEG) should be carried out to rule out the possibility of *absence* states. In any case, C's lack of affect, damaged self-image, isolation from others, and bizarre ideas and perceptions warrant immediate treatment. He should be in ongoing therapy, and if placement is necessary, he should be sent to a residential treatment facility.

Psychological Test Data

C: 12–2 Male

WISC

Verbal Tests		Scaled Score
Information		13
Comprehension		16
Arithmetic		9
Similarities		11
Vocabulary		12
(Digit Span)		(12)
	Total	61

Performance Tests		
Picture Completion		8 (9)
Picture Arrangement		15
Block Design		12
Object Assembly		14
Coding		13
	Total	62

	Scaled Score	IQ
Verbal Scale	61	114
Performance Scale	62	117
Full Scale	123	117

Information

		Score
1–3.		3
4.	Cow and goat.	1
5.		1
6.		1
7.		1
8.		1
9.	Leif Erickson and Christopher Columbus	1
10.		1
11.		1
12.		1
13.		1
14.	Digests	1
15.	Special chemicals. [Q] Oil's lighter.	1
16.		1
17.		1
18.		1

19.	6'	0
20.	Europe	0
21.		1
22.		1
23.	Paint—I don't know.	0
24.	I don't know. 2,000?	0
25.	November	0
26.	I don't know.	0
27.	Tells us when earthquakes are coming.	0
	Total	20

Comprehension

		Score
1.	Wash it with soap and water, sterilize it, and bandage it.	2
2.	If you can't find it, pay for it.	2
3.	Go to a different store.	2
4.	Either walk away or give one good wallop—he'd stop. [Q] Give him one good wallop. If he didn't stop, I'd just ignore him.	0
5.	Wave something—I don't know what it could be—something red. Signal him.	2
6.	Brick more sturdy, wood burns.	2
7.	If let them go, they might do something again. If not locked up, would be more crime in city because they think they could get away with crime.	1
8.	Children have longer life ahead, and men are stronger than women. Can take more punishment than lady can.	2
9.	Easier to carry.	1
10.	Many people in need of money, and charity could give it to them. Person could disguise self as a beggar with money.	1
11.	See if they were good enough for the job and not do poor work.	1
12.	Make it stronger. [Q] Softer.	2
13.	Should be people representing cities, towns, so few big shots shouldn't run everything.	1
14.	Show that you're trustworthy, that you're a good person.	2
	Total	21

Arithmetic

		Score
1–3.		3
4.		1
5.		1
6.		1
7.		1
8.		1
9.		1
10.	OT	0
11.	6	0
12.		1
13.	49	0
14.	OT	0
15.	OT	0
	Total	10

Similarities

		Score
1–4.		4
5.	Has same crease. [Q] They start with "P," taste pretty much the same. [*explanation*] But peach has furry skin.	0
6.	Have two tails, whiskers, nose, mouth. [Q] Both animals.	2
7.	Both have alcohol in them.	2
8.	Both instruments.	1
9.	Both can burn.	1
10.	Both measurements.	2
11.	Both do something. [Q] Pan could cook and scissors could cut.	0
12.	Both have rocks in them.	0
13.	Both compounds that could be separated. [Q] If mix them could be separated.	2
14.	both want peace. [Q] Both mean to be fair, so both want peace.	0
15.	Same category. [Q] One, two, last.	0
16.	Both can be divided by 7—no, both can be divided by 8.	0
	Total	14

Vocabulary

		Score
1–5.		10
6.	Soft pillow.	2
7.	What kind? [*Up to you.*] Piece of iron or metal with head and point.	2
8.	Mule.	2
9.	Skin of some mammal.	2
10.	Valuable stone.	2
11.	Link, put together.	2
12.	Playing card or shovel.	2
13.	Long knife that could cut you.	2
14.	Bother to you, hangs on to you, and asks questions you don't like.	2
15.	Courageous.	2
16.	Foolishness, bother to you.	2
17.	Brave.	1
18.	Play games for money.	2
19.	Fluid, highly explosive.	2
20.	Instrument that magnifies things.	2
21.	European coin. [Q] Ireland—they have one—worth 24¢.	2
22.	Untrue story that teaches a lesson. Animals often talk.	2
23.	Don't know.	0
24.	One country works against another, like France works against America.	1
25.	Don't know.	0
26.	To include—don't know.	0
27.	Don't know. [*Thought E said strangle.*]	0
28.	Chinese—I think somebody commits suicide.	1
29.	To cut off—not to go any farther—don't know.	0
30.	To put out. [Q] I guess.	0
31.	Don't know—never heard of it—rhymes with chalice.	0
32.	Not cocoon—catacomb—beginning of—I don't know.	0
33.	Do wrong—I don't know—never heard of it.	0
	Total	45

Digit Span

F6 + B5   Total Score   11

Picture Completion

		Score
1–6.		6
7.	Lady's pinky nail.	1
8.		1
9.		1
10.	Lapel slit.	0
11.	Side fin.	0
12.	Head too big.	0
13.		1
14.		1
15.	Other eye.	0
16.		0
17.	Buttonhole.	0
18.	What you push up to open it.	0
19.		(1)
20.	Part of tree.	0
	Total	11 (12)

Picture Arrangement

	Time	Order	Score
A–D.			8
1.	20"	FIRE Looks like the mother died. [*points to lady in building.*]	4
2.	11"	THUG	5
3.	5"	QRST	7
4.	6"	EFGH	6
5.	10"	PERCY	7
6.	40"	FSIHER	4
7.	20"	MSTEAR	2
		Total	43

Block Design

	Time	Score
A–C.		6
1.	9"	7
2.	15"	6
3.	14"	7
4.	9"	7
5.	62"	5
6.	OT	0
7.	OT	0
	Total	38

Object Assembly

	Time		*Score*
M	5"		7
H	35"		6
F	37"		8
A	33"		7
		Total	28

Coding B   Total Score   53

Bender–Gestalt

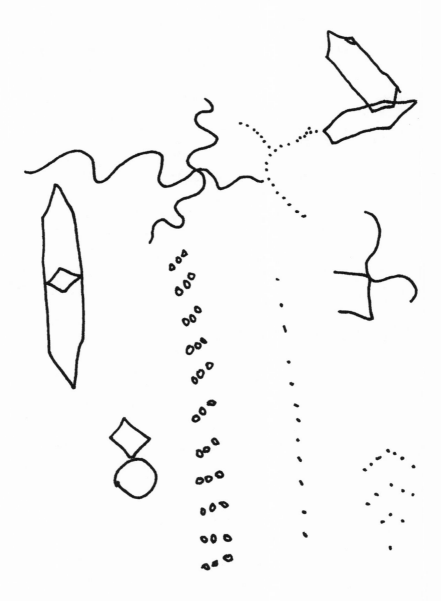

Figure Drawings

[Male:] About 30. Holding a cup and other person—have to imagine, is pouring tea. [*Do?*] Guess he likes tea. He's a regular, ordinary person.

[Female:] Mother about 30 years, like the other one. Mean mother—no, nice one. Making dough balls. Likes to sleep late, but more industrious than lazy. Cooking for her family.

Rorschach

<table>
<tr><td></td><td></td><td>Inquiry</td></tr>
<tr><td>I.</td><td>4"</td><td>1. That looks like a bug, sort of corroded butterfly. That's all. Few blots of his blood.</td><td>1. See if it is the butterfly. He's dead. Except little spots, that's his blood. Eyes and antenna, tail—I don't think butterfly has a tail. I'll say he does.</td></tr>
</table>

II.	20"	↑↓ 1.	Looks like little legs with socks on it. [*top red*] Whatever it is it looks down on its knees. Looks like a ripped cape. Looks like a lady with her hair up. Like scared out of her wits—like Phyllis Diller.	1. Looks like lady with two socks on her feet, down on her knees with a ripped cape. Back to me, arms holding cape up. [*Hole in cape?*] Yeah. [*laughs*] Also hole right through her body.
III.	20"	↑↓ ↑ 1.	I know what it looks like. Looks like man with hands over his head, wearing a white shirt with a red bow tie. That's the scenery. [*side red Ds*]	1. [*Scenery?*] Like champagne popping out of bottle since he's formally dressed. Two black eyes, fat, bald, some hair coming down on sides. Arms up. Ends before his waistline. Nose. [*Mouth?*] I never thought of that. Doesn't show it. Nose covers it, like a bull goes out head first.

[*From this point on E did not administer a separate inquiry*]

IV. 25" ↑↓↑→ Oh wow!

    ↑ 1. Looks like a dog from the top. Nose, ears, tail, hind paws. Doesn't look like a dog much, but that's the best I could do. And he's furry—lots and lots of fur. [*Else?*] No.

V. 5" ↑↓ 1. I can tell you right now. This looks like a butterfly. Two antenna. Looks like two-headed butterfly. [*Two heads?*] Well, now that I look at it, it looks like a bat, wouldn't you say? [*Up to you.*] Well, yeah.

    ↓ 2. Bat hanging upside down. Wings, feet, ears and head. [*Butterfly with two heads?*] Two heads [*points to wings.*] [*Where see them?*] Don't see them. Maybe in museum. [*Q*] Have to get two caterpillars in same cocoon.

VI. 20" ↑↓ 1. Looks like a thermometer that's just been broken [*center*]. This is where mercury was kept [*bottom*]. Was a very hot day and mercury went to top and it burst—voom—went all over. Or somebody knocked it off a wall and it broke. [*Q*] Knocked it off a wall. [*Q*] If mercury burst on a hot day, it would probably just run down inside and not make a big mess. If knocked off wall it could actually look like that.

VII. 5" 1. Looks like a U.

    2. This is a really interesting one. What it really looks like is two dancing girls. Have real long hair but it's up, like in a bun. Have feathers in hair. Head twisted around. Hands, both clutched together, like Hawaiian dancers. Dress [*bottom D*].

VIII. This is a colorful one. I like this one.

    15" ↑← 1. Looks like a cougar. He's in a forest. This is the scenery and it is reflected in the water. [*Scenery?*] Grass, leaves falling off trees. Very clear lake and shows all reflections. [*Cougar?*] Just walking along. [*points to all the parts*]

IX. 20" ↑← 1. Pretty much looks like same thing as that one [*VIII*]. Reflection in water but with different scenery. Looks like little girl in pink looking at a big bushy bush. [*green*] The line separates land from water. That's just another bush. [*orange*] See, looks like a windy day. [*Q*] Reflection is spread out, like ripples caused by wind. [*Girl?*] Small little girl wearing a dress, covering her legs, down on knees more logically. [*Girl?*] Hair comes down to neck, and there is a flip in back.

X. ◎ Oh wow! This is an interesting one. Looks like everything put together.

◎ Looks like a whole bunch of bugs.

25" ← 1. Two spiders [*blue*]
2. Two caterpillars, pink caterpillars
3. Two black widow spiders [*top*]
4. Moth [*green*]
5. Two fish [*yellow*]
6. Two reindeers jumping [*brown*]
7. Looks like bug nobody's ever seen before [*center*] with two beams coming out with eyes on it.
8. Rest looks like mud [*green, brown*]

TAT

1. "The Violin." Boy's name is Ted. Ted wants to play the violin. Father knows how to play it, and he wants to know, too. But his father keeps on saying, "Don't touch the violin, you might break it." But he really wants to play it. One day he saw the violin case with the violin in it. He took it out and started to play it and broke two strings. Then his father punished him. Ever since then he never played the violin again. [*Feel?*] Mad that he broke the violin. Felt he could do it, but he couldn't. [*End?*] He still wants to play the violin.

2. This girl's name is Terry, and she lived on a farm with her mother and father. Her father always liked to farm—that's why they lived on a farm. Every day she goes out to school and then—all her friends would tease her because their parents worked on regular jobs in the city. She told her mother and father what her friends were saying. Nobody liked the whole family. [*Q*] They say that they're slobs or something. So they all moved away to where the entire state was farmers, and they lived happily ever after. [*Feel?*] Like no one liked them. [*Feel?*] Hurt. Probably disappointed and that's about it.

5. This doesn't tell much. Her name is Mrs. Smith. This is her house. She always liked to peek through the door, because she was scared somebody might be there. She lived all alone. She was a widow. One day she was peeking through the door and heard someone. She was always mean and grouchy. She didn't like anybody. People who tried to be friendly—she didn't like them. This was her birthday, and she peeked through and heard a noise. She walked in, and it was a surprise birthday party. I said she was a mean old grouch—so she kicked everybody out. [*Feel?*] She felt everybody was trying to rob her and believed in the spirit world. [*Q*] Like her husband was dead and she could contact him.

7 BM. A man and his boss. The boss is Mr. Jones, and the one with the black hair, call Mr. Andrews. The boss called him into his office, and the boss had to fire him. Since he was a good worker he had to do it in a nice way. He tried all different approaches to say, "You're fired," but none worked because Mr. Andrews, the employee, was always a crazy mixed-up guy and kept thinking he was going to skip him up to a higher

rank. Finally, the boss said, "OK, Mr. Andrews, you're fired." That's all. [*Feel?*] He was real mad and just walked out. Found a new job.

6 GF. These people lived in old times. Say she's 29 and he's 31. He kept on trying to get her to marry him but never succeeded. One day he came in with a gun and said, "You marry me or I'll kill you—I'll shoot you." But, fortunately, she got away. Ever since then he was trying to catch her. One day he cornered her on a dead-end street. There was no escape. He said, "If I can't have you—no one else will." He shot her and she died. He was taken away by police. [Q] Heard shot and caught him. Ever since then his head was chopped off. [Q] In old times they did that. [Q] England.

3 BM. Is this a boy or girl? More like boy. Boy wouldn't wear dress. I'll say it's a girl. She was going to school one day, and there was pushers all around trying to sell her marijuana, LSD, cocaine, pot. She tried it once and she kept coming back for more, and more, etc. One day she was in her room and took an overdose. Fell to the floor and found dead like this. That's all.

4. Oh wow! This man was a sailor. Owned his own boat and was a fisherman. He was married and never let his wife go along with him. One day she stopped him and said, "If you go I'll never see you again." He said, "Get away," and pushed her. Banged her head against the wall and she died. He thought she was only knocked out. He left and was lost at sea and never heard from again. He didn't really love her—just said he did.

8 BM. This is a boy who kept on dreaming he was being operated on and kept dying in the operation. He kept on saying, "I'm never going to take an operation, I'm never going to take an operation." He was going to the doctor for a checkup and he needed an operation. He didn't want it and kept running away from it, but he needed surgery. The doctor grabbed him and said, "You go to the hospital." He pushed the doctor away and wouldn't go. His mother, his father, his brother, his sister kept telling him he needed it, and he kept refusing. He finally decided he'd take it. The night before he went to the hospital he had the dream again, but it was different. He dreamt he was taking the operation and pulled through and was still alive. This gave him confidence. He was in the hospital and being operated on, and all of a sudden his heart gave way and he was dead. The doctors tried to make his heart beat again, but nothing would work. His mother, his father, his sister and brother found out that all his dreams came true, but they didn't want them to come true. That's all. [*Kind operation?*] Lungs. [Q] He sniffed ammonia too much, and one lung got corroded and had to be removed. [Q] His friend said he could sniff ammonia longer than him—but nothing happened to his friend.

15. Oh wow! This is a big cemetery. Hundreds and hundreds of bodies. He was a ghost. Call him The Ghost of the Cemetery. Every night he'd come out and kill somebody— first male, then a female, male, female, and kept on going like that. He'd wear a black suit, and he had gray hair and was bald on top. He was white. One night he was going to kill a man and the man shined the light on him and chased him, trying to get the light on him because it would kill him. He escaped back to the cemetery to his tomb. The next night he tried a female. He went to this lady's house, but she also knew he was afraid of light. She shined her flashlight on him. A hole went right through his body, but that didn't kill him. He escaped. Every night when he went to kill somebody he had a hole in his body. They thought if they could get large searchlight and shine it on the cemetery, he could die. So one night they shined them on the cemetery when he was getting out of his tomb. All of a sudden—all the lights went on and they killed him. He died and never bothered anybody anymore. [Q] All those people tried to kill him before he died [*implying revenge*].

Psychological Test Portrait

D: 13–5 Male

D's mother wanted him evaluated for school placement after he had spent 14 months out of school. She works full-time and apparently had permitted

D to stay out of school because he did not want to go. Now that he expressed an interest in returning, she was concerned as to whether he was at grade level or should be in a special class.

D's parents have been separated since his first year of life, and he has had limited contact with his father. His older siblings live outside the home, and *D* has been alone at home during the day since his great aunt died earlier in the year. *D* would not reveal his reasons for staying out of school, just stating "for personal reasons." His dropping out was the more remarkable because he had completed sixth grade scoring in the ninety-ninth percentile in citywide reading and math tests and had received a school award in mathematics.

D is extremely tall for his age and, in spite of being overweight, appeared well-groomed and attractive. He was very anxious about his performance throughout the testing. He made self-deprecating comments and thought he did poorly even when it was clear he had the answer. *E* needed to provide a good deal of reassurance and structure. At times she permitted a break from the tasks, which seemed to allow him a second wind to complete all the required tests.

Cognitive Functioning

WISC–R: The total IQ score of 132 places D in the very superior range. There is little discrepancy between the Verbal (124) and the Performance (132) scores. Except for his Coding score (11), his scores are all within the superior range. There is little intertest or intratest variability.

Cognitive functions of memory, attention, abstraction, conceptualization, and perceptual-motor coordination are all excellent. Although his verbalizations and language usage can be at a high level (Vocabulary, 11, 14, 15, and 31; Comprehension, 5), frequently his language is strange, bizarre, and/or tangential (Picture Completion, 21; Vocabulary, 12, 15, 16, and 19; Comprehension, 2, 3, 4, 9, 10, 11, and 16).

B–G: Although the Bender figures, on the whole, are accurately reproduced and sequentially organized, the overall impression is of a more immature production. This may be related to a clumsiness in fine motor coordination but is certainly related to extreme tension in *D*'s hand and constricted use of his pencil. This is also seen in the use of limited space, clinging to the edge of the paper, and a reduction in the size of most figures.

FD: *D* minimally complies to the request for drawings after dashing off a stick figure. These drawings are devoid of any identification other than the breast line on the female. Other than this one line (and a recognizable arm and hand), these drawings are extremely simple and primitive. Using the edge of the paper as the base for their stance is similar to the use of the edge of the paper in the Bender.

It is impossible to talk about his cognition with these peculiar drawings because of the lack of any facial, sexual, age, dress, or dimensional features.

Rorschach: Cognitively, there is no resemblance between *D*'s performance on the Rorschach and his performance on the WISC–R. For the most part his responses to the cards are concrete (I, II), vague (I, II, IV), undifferentiated (I, II, IV, and IX), fragmented (III and X), and frequently are *F*–'s (I, II, III, IV, X). He seems to attempt a humorous response on Cards I and VIII, but these attempts are irrelevant to the test and fall short of humor. His whole Rorschach production is strange, and the fact that he only manages 2 *P*'s suggests his idiosyncratic and unusual perception of the world.

TAT: *D* clearly demonstrates accurate perception of the pictures in the TAT. In the stories he produces, however, he offers an oddly worded phrase (Card I, "So to abide of his mother's wishes . . .") and peculiar ideas (2, 14, 7 BM, 18 GF, and 3BM). Similarly to the Rorschach responses, *D*'s TAT stories portray an idiosyncratic relationship to the real world.

Summary Statement of Cognitive Functioning: *D* achieves a very superior IQ and is able to produce at a high level within non-affect-laden test areas. When dynamic areas are tapped, however, his production can become concrete, strange, tangential, idiosyncratic, and peculiar.

Dynamic Picture

WISC–R: *D*'s productions on the WISC–R subtests (Information, Block Design, Digit Span, Object Assembly) are fine when the material does not elicit peculiar thoughts and associations. He shows concerns with body vulnerability (Picture Completion, 21; Similarities, 3 and 17; Comprehension, 1, 3, and 11; Vocabulary, 19 and 29) and guilt about getting away with something (Comprehension, 9; Vocabulary, 9).

B–G: Again in the Bender, *D* demonstrates a sense of insecurity (clinging to the edge of the paper) and a feeling of inferiority (small size of designs), which may all be related to his concern over body vulnerability.

FD: The striking breast line on the female drawing is the only clue to a sexual differentiation in *D*'s figure drawings. The other differentiation between the figures is in the size discrepancy, with the female being almost three times the size of the male drawing. This suggests that D feels females to be far more powerful than himself, and a possible source of their power is from his feeling of oral dependency. His oral impulses are further expressed in his sardonic associations to the female drawing. These dependency feelings in light of the superior power of the female may be the cause of the extreme sense of inadequacy and isolation conveyed by his drawings and through his associations.

Rorschach: D's difficulties in self-representation are expressed throughout his Rorschach percepts. He is unable to produce a good human percept, with the exception of Card VII; all other human representations are either supernatural (III, IV) or fragmented and distorted (III, X). In addition, he is unable to specify the sex of the figures even when he sees "two people dancing" on Card VII.

With the exception of the "mouth eating" on Card III, oral needs are only offered in associations ("garbage can" on Card IV; "Sam Carvel" on Card VIII). There is a reference to symbiotic feeling in Card VII and aggressive impulses on Card VI. Card IX, with its color and lack of structure, is responded to as a "volcano erupting," suggesting fear of his lack of impulse control. This could explain why there is so little evidence of dynamic material in the Rorschach.

D's percepts convey an enormous problem in interpersonal relationships. He is unable to perceive the usual two animals on II and two people on III, and when he does give two people on Card VII, it is not the usual right-side-up percept. His lack of *FC* and *CF* demonstrates an inability to relate to others or, of more concern, the lack of a wish to relate to others.

TAT: There is some limited attempt in D's TAT stories to conform to usual motivations in the real world (Cards 1, 2, 5, and 4). His preoccupations with primitive aggressive impulses, however, dominate his overall TAT productions. His characters either are killed, kill others, or kill themselves. There is no reference to any other type of interaction than that based upon hostility.

Summary Statement of Dynamic Picture: The pervasive theme of hostility expressed in D's TAT stories raises grave concern for the degree to which he experiences murderous/suicidal impulses that are threatening to erupt. This is of particular concern inasmuch as there is seemingly almost no relatedness to others, as well as a profound sense of inadequacy, inferiority, and vulnerability.

Defenses

WISC–R: Generally the structure of the WISC provides *D* with a neutral enough task so that he does not have to become excessively defensive. He is also aided in this by his high intellectual functioning, which precludes his being overly challenged by the nature of the task. For unclear reasons, however, certain items trigger off a defensive flurry seen in verbose responses (Similarities, 14; Comprehension, 1 and 4; Vocabulary, 6), bizarre humor (Comprehension, 3, 9, and 17; Vocabulary, 9), and a single instance of projection (Picture Completion, 26).

B–G: The fact that *D*'s figures cling to the edge of the paper, are reduced in size, and use up less than half of the sheet of paper demonstrates constriction. This implies that he looks to the outside world to provide control and structure for him. There is an indication of regression in the overall immature quality of his Bender productions.

F–D: The constriction referred to in the Bender is amplified here. Again the edge of the paper serves as an external limit for him. There is denial of any individuality, of most sexual distinctions, of all facial sensory organs, and of any movement in his drawings. This denial is seen again in his associations, where he equates the two in their age, location, and occupation. In addition, he distances the figures by age and location.

Rorschach: *D*'s handling of the Rorschach is the epitome of defensiveness. Similarly to the FD's, he distances his percepts by referring them to television (Card I) or a movie (Cards III; IV), or he makes them supernatural or unusual creatures (Cards III; IV; V; X). He denies the impact of the blot on him by associative responses (Cards I and VIII) or concretely avoids a response (Cards I and II). The bizarre quality of his humor (Cards I, IV, V, and VIII) suggests the desperateness of his defensive attempts. This desperate effort is strikingly seen in his first response to each of Cards I and II "I chose the closest thing to reality."

TAT: *D*'s stories are rife with primitive aggressive impulses against which he seems to have no defenses. This is in spite of the fact of occasional glimmers of denial (Card I) and projection (Cards 14, 18 GF, and 12 M).

Summary Statement of Defenses: *D*'s defensive operations, when they are mobilized, primarily rely on denial, avoidance, repression, and inhibition. His ineffective humorous remarks are attempts at denial and distancing from the testing situation.

Affective Expression

WISC–R: *D* expresses little affect throughout the WISC. His performance is marked by high anxiety and tension over his need to achieve.

B–G: The Bender is devoid of any affect other than *D*'s anxiety to a point of breaking the pencil.

FD: In *D*'s associations to his figure drawings, we hear his anger and un-happiness. His sense of hopelessness and worthlessness is conveyed in the phrase, " 'cause he's a waste of space."

Rorschach: Neither the content nor the determinants of *D*'s percepts reflect any affective response. Only Card IX reveals the possibility of *D*'s experience of explosive inner tension. His responses to Cards I, II, and VIII suggest anger at the test, *E*, and the world.

TAT: *D*'s TAT stories are fraught with hostility, anger, and rage to destructive proportions. This rage is expressed toward both others and the self.

Summary Statement of Affective Expression: *D* presents an unusual affective picture because of the total lack of any positive feelings. He functions in intellectual tasks in a highly anxious way but is unable to defend against the degree of his rage elicited by the projectives. He is at grave risk because of the lack of any positive aspects to his experiences with others, as well as the extent of his rage.

Summary

D presents the picture of a boy in danger. Although he is able to achieve on a superior intellectual level, he is unable to relate to others or to the world in a positive manner. He portrays a sense of a very inadequate and inferior self. He feels himself to be vulnerable and worthless, "a waste of space." His intellect in no way helps him to develop adequate defenses or even to provide him with reassuring fantasy. When dynamic concerns are tapped, *D*'s language becomes concrete, strange, tangential, idiosyncratic, and peculiar, revelatory of his thought disorder. The existence of his thought disorder combined with his primitive and unmodulated rage, poses an extreme threat to others and to himself.

Diagnosis

DSM-III-R

Axis I: 295.12 Schizophrenia, Disorganized Type
Axis II: 301.20 Schizoid Personality Disorder
Axis III: Healthy
Axis IV: 3-Moderate
Axis V: 30-Impaired

D is in need of immediate treatment. In light of the extent of D's disturbance and his mother's seeming lack of connection to him and/or awareness of his disturbance, recommendation is made for residential treatment. The prognosis is dim, as there is little evidence for D's experiencing psychic pain or having any ability to form positive attachments.

Psychogical Test Data

D: 13–5 Male

WISC–R

	Scaled Score
Verbal Tests	
Information	15
Similarities	13
Arithmetic	14
Vocabulary	16
Comprehension	12
(Digit Span)	(19)
Total	70

Performance Tests	
Picture Completion	15
Picture Arrangement	14
Block Design	18
Object Assembly	15
Coding	11
Total	73

	Scaled Score	IQ
Verbal Scale	70	124
Performance Scale	73	132
Full Scale	143	132

Information

		Score
1–6.		6
7.	7	1
8.	April	1
9.	Pig	1
10.	12	1
11.	Spring, Summer, Fall, Winter	1
12.	A dispute—Christopher Columbus or America Vespuccio	1
13.	Digests food and then goes "urp!"	1
14.	East, west or east. Say west. I don't know.	1
15.	February. Isn't it minus a day?	1
16.	Thomas Edison	1
17.	England	1
18.	It's lighter.	1
19.	Canada and Mexico.	1
20.	2,000, I think.	1
21.	South America, I believe.	1
22.	Fiber. [Q] Sand.	1
23.	Italy, I don't know.	0
24.	Take a potshot and say 5'9".	1
25.	Indicates what the weather will be like. Say, snowing, raining.	1
26.	Water—air. [Q] Don't know—eats down the chemicals.	0
27.	I think 3,100, something like that.	1
28.	Ancient form of language—sign language on rock—designs mean words.	1
29.	Explorer—the voyage—of a ship—the Beagle.	0
30.	What is it? Sort of a cleanser.	0
	Total	26

Picture Completion

		Score
1.	Bristle	1
2.	Mouth	1
3.	Ear	1
4.	Fingernail	1
5.	Whiskers	1
6.	Doll image	1
7.	Number 8	1
8.	Leg	1
9.	Step	1
10.	Handle on drawer	1
11.	Holes	1
12.	Part of nose	1
13.	Hinge	1
14.	Diamond	1
15.	Sock	1
16.	Things you put button in	1
17.	Watchband	1
18.	Screw	1
19.	Ear	1
20.	Groove	1
21.	Feet problem—hooves missing	0
22.	No red stuff	1
23.	Shadow	1
24.	Cord	1

25.	Eyebrow	1
26.	Person holding umbrella	0
	Total	24

Similarities

		Score
1.	Round	1
2.	Both give off light	1
3.	Both cover part of body	1
4.	Make music	1
5.	Both fruit, both tasty	2
6.	Drink both—make you throw up—alcoholic beverage	2
7.	Animals	2
8.	Joints—not the kind you smoke	2
9.	Hear a person speak—use electricity in one form or another	1
10.	Measurements	2
11.	Emotions, reactions	2
12.	Metal	2
13.	Made up of elements	1
14.	Both in anti-Communist speech—pro-American speech—Statue of Liberty—can't think of much—just more or less a phrase	0
15.	Both point out—both ends of a line	1
16.	Numbers—both be used in measurements	0
17.	Can be consumed together—they make you sick	1
	Total	22

Picture Arrangement

	Time	Order	Score
1–2.			4
3.	3"	FIRE	2
4.	12"	WALK	2
5.	10"	THUG	5
6.	10"	RUSH	5
7.	11"	VAMP	4
8.	7"	CASH, then	
	11"	CSAH	0 (4)
9.	14"	CHASE	4
10.	28"	WORMS	3
11.	40"	BECHN	2
12.	22"	CLOUD	4
		Total	35 (39)

Block Design

	Time	Score
1–2.		4
3.	3"	2
4.	8"	7
5.	5"	7

6.	8"	7
7.	9"	7
8.	12"	7
9.	26"	6
10.	43"	6
11.	40"	7
	Total	60

Vocabulary

		Score
1–5.		10
6.	Piece of metal you use with a hammer—you keep wood together by the tool.	2
7.	System used in different languages to write down the words of language; American, English alphabet has 26 letters.	2
8.	Animal which is used on farms and other places as a work animal	2
9.	A man who could get off on a technicality. [*Right answer?*] A person who steals.	2
10.	Couple together	2
11.	Not cowardly, opposite of—without fear	2
12.	It's an element—not an element. Made by natural causes—valued highly just for looks, used in industry.	2
13.	To make a bet	2
14.	Not make sense, no sense to it, thus, nonsense, illogical.	2
15.	To stop beforehand, or aforehand	2
16.	It's something that can be given away, such as a disease in any form, for example, flu, TB	2
17.	Bothersome.	2
18.	A story, not true	2
19.	Dangerous, Pepsi-Cola—to your health.	2
20.	Move to one place or another. Often birds will migrate. Water animals and certain land animals because of the weather.	2
21.	I believe it's related to musical lines, I don't know—but then again . . .	0
22.	To seclude something—something out of the way—it's more or less secluded.	1
23.	As in the animal—preying mantis—an insect, it preys on other insects	2
24.	Espionage is a type of sabotage.	0
25.	I believe it's a type of tower—if it does relate to bells, I don't know.	1
26.	To compete.	2
27.	Sort of like the First Amendment—can guarantee you certain rights, privileges, but not just you.	1
28.	To make you want to do something.	2
29.	Possess a wound, a physical handicap.	2
30.	I think it's eliminate.	2
31.	About to happen.	2
32.	I don't know.	0
	Total	55

Object Assembly

	Time	Score
G	20"	8
H	16"	7
C	26"	7
F	35"—Is this one person?	9
	Total	31

Digit Span

		Score
F 13 + B 12	Total	25

Comprehension

		Score
1.	Bleed. [Q] Clean off finger—put Band-Aid on it. Depends on size of cut. Use Bactine.	2
2.	Either supposed to look for ID—ask if someone lost wallet—if nothing works, give to police or your mother or guardian.	2
3.	Fire Department. [Q] Go to neighbor's house and turn the steaks. [Q] Go over there—try to get them out or warn them.	2
4.	When police patrol might prevent crime—or arrest perpetrator. [Q] Strike—go on strike—help—save person from fire or try to get a raise.	2
5.	Apologize and replace ball.	2
6.	Don't beat him up—somehow stop the fight. Prevent it—pick him up and put him away.	2
7.	Wood would probably burn easier, wouldn't last as long—needs repair work.	1
8.	Probably mainly—if your car gets stolen—people could know what to look for—I don't really know—registration. I don't know why.	1
9.	To punish them—to tell them what would probably happen if they commit more crimes—that—if they don't get off on a technicality.	2
10.	Post office will know if letter has been duly paid for, so you can continue . . . no freeloaders.	2
11.	To make sure nothing wrong with meat, so meat won't be sold when it's bad—sealed so not contaminated with a kind of germ.	2
12.	Charity—way to put it to essential things. Street beggar might be the same—might be the same thing for him. You don't know which you're getting. Charity you know money goes for good cause.	1
13.	That your friends couldn't get into arguments.	1
14.	Paperback is something which wouldn't take up more space, like you could put it in your pocket, whereas a hardcover wouldn't bend.	1
15.	Because you give your word on something—you want your word to be worth something.	2
16.	I suppose it's as good as any fabric—might be because of price of it—and another question, you don't generally think of.	1

17. Just to have something to complain about—or if you have a
suggestion you might write a letter. They represent your side—
get money for certain projects, etc.   1

               Total   27

Arithmetic

		Score
1–7.		7
8.	14	1
9.	7	1
10.	24¢	1
11.	$27	1
12.	11	1
13.	9	1
14.	10¢	1
15.	I don't know—19	0
16.	40¢	1
17.	$42	1
18.	$12	1
	Total	17

Bender-Gestalt

I'm not good at doing designs. [*Murmurs to self.*]

A.   I broke the pencil.
1.
2.   I lost the slant.
3–8. [*No more comments as he works concentratedly.*]

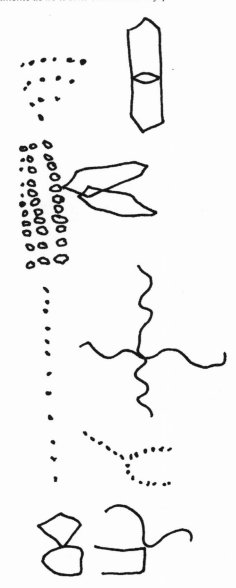

Figure Drawing

[*Person*]: [*While drawing male says:*] No face? Make him from a Stephen King movie. [*Old?*] 150. [*Where live?*] Montana. [*Do?*] A religious leader. [*Q*] Atheistism. [*Best thing?*] He doesn't live in New York. [*Worst thing?*] He doesn't live in China. [*Closest to?*] His pet cockroach Sonny. [*Worst thing happened?*] He was born. [*Worst?*] 'Cause he's a waste of space. [*Happen in future?*] He'll run for President. [*Win?*] No.

[*Female*]: [*Old?*] 149. [*Where live?*] Montana. [*Do?*] Another religious leader. [*Likes to do best?*] Eat coconut ice cream. [*Not like to do?*] Not eat coconut ice cream. [*Closest to?*] Herself. [*Worst thing happened?*] She met the other guy. [*Q*] They didn't exactly get along well. [*Will happen?*] Die of old age. [Q] 151.

Rorschach

Inquiry

I.   ↑→↓◎↑   Any particular way it's supposed to go? [*Up to you.*]

42"   ↑ 1. Inkblot. [*Q*]

57"   2. Richard Simmons doing exercises to a nearsighted man, who, by the way, is colorblind.

II.   2"   ↑↓→ 1. Multicolor inkblots.—Half an inkblot reflected. Nothing else.

    1. [*Q*] You wanted me to see something. I chose the closest thing to reality—not too close to reality, though. [*Q*] General form maybe.

III.   5"   1. A B-movie space creature.

    1. What makes it look like that? Here's the idea of a space creature. Eyes, mouth, arms, body—mouth would be the way, must be eating something. [*Arms?*] Here—body is the rest of it.

IV.   7"   ◎   [*Drops card—picks up, tosses on table.*]
13"   1. A misshapen R2D2.

    1. If you see R2D2 it has three legs and the rest looks like a garbage can—and this looks like a misshapen R2D2—blurry—a blurry R2D2. [*Q*] It's here as seen in *Star Wars*.

V.   7"   ↓↑ 1. An unusual bird.

    1. [*Q*] These may be thought of as wings— the middle could be the body, there's not much of it there. [*Unusual?*] Because it's unusual. It's an inkblot. It's not a lot like the general shape of a telephone, is it?

| VI. | 20" | | 1. Cat. | 1. What makes it look like a cat? Because the top part of it resembles slightly a cat's head, and the large part of it may be a cat's body, and the two things to strike out might be paws. |

| VII. | 42" | ◎ ↓ 1. [*Throws card on table*] Two people dancing. | 1. Because the top part of it resembled two heads touching, and the rest of it might be human bodies. |

| VIII. | 17" | ↓ 1. Sam Carvel's nightmare. | |
| | | 2. Looks like the general form of an animal. This part—these two [*points to D's*] | 2. Because they had heads, resembled the heads of an otter or something—four legs, and a body. No tail. |

| IX. | 12" | 1. Volcano erupting—here [*points around whole blot*]. | 1. [*Q*] Because it might look like—the lava shoots up, and that's what it might look like. Might, might not. |

| X. | 52" | 1. [*throws card on table*] Man with a mustache and an unusual hairdo. | 1. [*Q*] The part in the middle looks like eyes, and the green part a moustache. [*Hairdo?*] I don't know—I suppose you could say there's the hairdo all around the head [*points to red*]. |

TAT

1. The child has a mother who wants the child to play the violin. The child does not like the violin. So to abide of his mother's wishes, he plays the violin for a while. And he grows up hating her, and that's the end. [*Thinking in picture?*] I wonder what she'd do if I broke it in half? [*Feeling?*] He doesn't care what she feels if he broke it in half.
2. The school has opened up in the farm they live on. The girl wants an education. She gets one, she becomes a college grad, she grows up and moves to New York and finds out her parents have died in a fire. [*In picture?*] She's leaving for school. Her father and, or brother, or whatever, is working the farm. [*Thinking?*] About school. [*Feel?*] Puzzled—she's thinking about a problem.

5. The woman has rented an apartment. She lives by herself. She's afraid of burglars. She heard a noise, and she went out to investigate. She doesn't find anyone there. [*Thinking?*] She's afraid that there really is someone there. [*Feel?*] Relieved.

6 BM. They wonder what happened to their grandchild. Or her grandchild, his son. Because he hasn't been seen for two years. And then they find his body and he's been shot, knifed first. And in the picture they're feeling anxious. [*Picture?*] They just found the body, and they're anxious to find out if it's their child. They're waiting in the living room for a phone call to tell them yes or no. [*Phone call?*] There's a skeleton, and they're checking dental records. [*Happened to child?*] Was mugged. [Q] Maybe he was 17. [*Reason?*] He had a Walkman.

4. Looks like the man is going to enlist in the Army to fight Hitler, and he doesn't want him to go. He goes off, he gets wounded. He gets shipped home, and he finds she's been killed in an air raid. [*Who are they?*] Brother and sister. He's a stupid fool. [*Where live?*] New York City. [*He feel?*] Devastated. [Q] Because she's dead.

13 MF. [*pushes card away on table*] He's annoyed at himself because he strangled her. They had an argument. He killed. He got sent to prison, he committed suicide. [*Argue about?*] His gambling habits. [*Killed her?*] He was drunk. [*Related?*] Husband and wife. [*Suicide?*] He felt like it. Because he feels something, he shouldn't have killed her.

14. He was born, he lived, posed for a picture and died. He is feeling that as soon as he gets this done he will have some extra money. Like posing for a picture, or it may be about a man who commits suicide, and the events preceding the suicide. [*His suicide?*] No. [*He die?*] Of a heart of attack [*sic*].

7 BM. A man is receiving fatherly advice from his uncle. [*looks around room*] He hates his father, so he consults his uncle, and on his uncle's advice he shoots the father. [*How come?*] 'Cause he hates him. [*Why now?*] His uncle tells him to. [*Happens?*] He moves to Puerto Rico. [*Caught?*] No.

18 GF. She's psychotic, she's killing a stranger. She goes crazy, she gets put into an institution, she escapes, and she kills strangers. [*Who?*] X-Blot's sister. [*Who?*] Guy in *Psycho*. [*Why?*] No reason. She doesn't like their hairdo. [*End?*] She gets shot in a swamp. The dogs were after her so she ran into a swamp, or maybe they live in the sewer system.

3 BM. What's this? [*points to object*] He's been shot in the face—by the other woman—for no reason. [*He?*] An artist. [*Story?*] He made a painting, but the other guy didn't like it so he shot him. [*End?*] He's dead, and the other guy commits suicide.

12 M. We'll say this guy is supposed to be a faith healer, and this guy wants to be cured from being a cripple, and he winds up not being cured. [Q] He's a cripple who wants to be cured. He can't move his legs. [*Man thinking?*] That he intends to cure the guy. [*End?*] Annoyed because he's been arrested for fraud. Cripple feels annoyed because he's still a cripple. [Q] He was in a car accident.

4
The 14- to 16-Year-Old

Developmental Expectations

Some children, more commonly boys, will be in the midst of pubertal changes at this time and therefore will be more similar to the expectations described in the 12- to 14-year-old chapter. Variations in physiological maturation can be influenced by genetic, nutritional, and geographic factors. What most teenagers share, however, is an increasing interest and involvement in group social activities. In this format the sexes begin to explore their mounting interest in the opposite sex. At this age the teenager has yet to develop ways of handling these new sexual feelings; their behavior is often boisterous because of the need to touch one another that leads to wrestling, shoving, pushing, and the like. They are often totally unaware of their impact on others.

Cognitive Functioning. The hallmark of the cognitive process during these years is in their "testing." They test their ideas, values, interests, and goals against adult standards. With their peers they test whether their likes and dislikes are within the group's standards.

Their cognitive integrity is increasingly more stable as formal logical operations and secondary processes become more solidly available. Pleasure in coining new meanings to ordinary words is part of the group's communication process, providing them with a sense of uniqueness.

Although some teenagers, particularly males, will still be struggling with smoothing out their perceptual-motor coordination during this time, most 14- to 16-year-olds will have achieved a more coordinated perceptual-motor system.

Dynamic Picture. As the physiological changes come increasingly to a resolution, the adolescent can now begin to develop a greater sense of his own self-concept. The heretofore narcissistic investment in the self is replaced by an incorporation of the group's identity into the self representation. This means that it is now possible, but still with the consensus of the group—to experiment in different looks (hairstyles, makeup, clothing, and the like). This is also part of the ongoing testing against adult standards.

The conflict between dependence and independence still plays a major role during these years. Often when an individual has been hurt by his group, he can withdraw from the group and become overtly dependent on his parents in a way unacceptable to him two years earlier. Also, he is now able with his peers to exercise more independent actions, as his judgment of social interactions and his sense of spatial and temporal reality are more reliable. This is commensurate with the parents permitting a greater freedom of action to the adolescent. Although parents are gradually relinquishing some controls and authority over these years, it is still important for the adolescent to know his parents are involved in his emerging independent behavior.

Sexual expression is still experimental, but most physical contact is imbued with sexual meaning. There is a sense of heightened sexuality to the individual during this time. The preferred mode for sexual gratification is still masturbation, although occasionally sexual experimental activity will take place with others. Sexual fantasies preoccupy the adolescent at this time and are frequently focused on movie, television, and musical idols.

Defenses. Multiple and varied defenses should continue to be available. The need for flexible and resilient defenses is paramount during these years. Membership in the peer group still fulfills defensive needs and provides a source of support. Defenses are still being reorganized and reintegrated toward the formation of the mature personality structure.

Affective Expression. All the variability and intensity of feelings in the 12- to 14-year-old remain during this time. There is, however, a gradually increasing sense of control over the intensity of the feeling.

Normal Expectation on Tests

Intelligence Tests. Affective and dynamic intrusions into cognitive functioning are not expected at this age. The adolescent at this age is at the top of the standardized scale of the WISC–R, and because of the resultant downward skewing may achieve a speciously lowered IQ score.

Bender–Gestalt. At this age, production on the B–G should conform to adult standards.

Projectives. Figure drawings by this time should be produced according to adult standards. In comparison to adult standards, however, these drawings may have more elaborations of dress, makeup, hair, and so forth, reflecting the narcissistic concerns of this age.

Rorschach determinants should now be more similar to adult standards: number of responses (15 or more); D predominant in relation to W and d; M should be at least 5, with FM higher but, more likely, equal; and m is acceptable. FK may now put in an appearance as well as c; FC should be higher or equal to CF, with C not expected; and the F+ percentage should be 50 percent or higher. The content in the Rorschach now reflects more concerns with the body. At this time body parts may appear, specifically internal organs, which in an adult's record would signify a more pathological response.

TAT stories can still retain the melodramatic cast of the previous period, but they can also be concise and terse. Generally, they begin now to approach adult expectations in content and organization.

Representative psychological test interpretations and psychological test batteries for children within this age range now follow. The raw test data from the psychological test battery follow the discussion of each child so that easy reference can be made to the examples selected for illustration of the interpretations. We include examples of children diagnosed as having a reactive disorder, being mildly disturbed, moderate disturbed, or severely disturbed in order to demonstrate how a psychological portrait is developed. Each child's tests are analyzed, interpreted, and concluded with an integrated summary.

As stated before, the summary is not a complete report, but represents the salient features leading to the diagnostic portrait.

Psychological Test Portrait

F: 15–8 Male

F was brought by his parents because of their concerns over having learned that he masturbated in front of a young girl. In addition they were worried about his lack of achievement in high school. F, for his part, complained that his parents treated him like an infant.

F lives with his parents and older sister and had received two years of psychotherapy six years earlier, which ended when he improved. A tall, well-developed, attractive young man, F was friendly and eager to please. He worked diligently throughout the tests, and his only complaints concerned his resentment at his parents' treating him like a baby.

Cognitive Functioning

W–B, Form I: *F* achieves a Superior Full-Scale IQ of 117, with little discrepancy between his Verbal score (117) and his Performance score (113). He is obviously a very intelligent young man who loses credit when he impulsively offers associations rather than thinking through the questions (Information, 4, 8, and 12; and Comprehension, 1). His lowest score (9) on Arithmetic demonstrates this tendency, as his reasoning is good but he is under internal pressure to answer quickly. He demonstrates this tendency to impulsive associative responses in Information 19, but in this instance, *E*'s question provokes him to think and provide an erudite answer. His achievement on the W–B is seen to reflect excellent cognitive capabilities of attention and memory, with his score lowered by his tendency to make quick associations in the Verbal area.

B–G: *F*'s overall Bender performance is very good. In the execution of the designs, however, it is clear (see notes on Bender–Gestalt performance) that he breaks up the visual field in an unusual way to carry out the drawing in an idiosyncratic fashion. This approach is usually reflective of a visual-motor coordination problem, but in *F*'s case he shows an excellent compensation for the deficit.

FD: The two figure drawings of *F* are well executed, with good attention to details on the upper torsos and heads. The visual-motor problem referred to above is again noted in the way he holds his pencil (see notes on Bender–Gestalt performance).

Rorschach: *F*'s overall performance in this test is very good. He achieves many *P*'s and one *O* (X, 4). He is able to delineate and describe his percepts well and clearly. The one difficulty he experiences is seen in his reaction to Card I suggesting a disturbance in his cognitive integrity when faced with a new situation. He would seem to be using a similar impulsive style seen in the Wechsler when he does not take time to think through his response.

TAT: *F* performs this task adequately. For some reason he does not amplify his stories, preferring to keep the content regarding people, their motivations, and their feelings ambiguous and/or vague.

Summary Statement of Cognitive Functioning: Although *F* shows superior intellectual ability, his overall test performance does not live up to his potential. He is unable to invest himself in intellectual and creative endeavors; instead, he rigidly conforms to the demands of the task. There is the suggestion of a compensation for visual-motor coordination problems, which may contribute to impulsivity and/or rigidity seen in his performance.

Dynamic Picture

W–B, Form I: There is little dynamic material appearing in the Wechsler. The one exception is the suggestion of the concern over bodily damage (Information, 23; Vocabulary, 11) and perhaps a concern with secrets (Vocabulary, 31).

B–G: The only aspect of dynamics seen in the Bender is *F*'s tendency toward expansiveness (seen in the size of the figures and use of two sheets).

FD: *F*'s drawings are well differentiated sexually and are acceptable portrayals of people. He uses a sketching line typical of adolescents' expression of concern about their developing bodies. As in the Bender, we see the tendency toward expansiveness, with the female figure especially dominant. On the male drawing, the missing fingers suggest difficulties with aggressive impulses. This may relate specifically to problems with sexual expression seen in the strange handling of the waist-to-crotch area (notice that there is no waistline, and there are odd lines around the crotch). There are no details on the shoes, suggesting insecurity in his own feelings of stability. The hooded eyes seem to convey an expression of covert looking.

On the female figure, the missing fingers also suggest concerns with aggression, specifically from females. Problems in the dress (no details on the dress, and odd lines on the skirt) again suggest concern over sexuality. Despite the excessively large figure, with a masculine face and broad shoulders, the insecurity reported above is repeated more graphically (no feet).

Rorschach: As in the figure drawings, *F*'s percepts in the Rorschach reflect anxiety about the body's vulnerability (VI and VIII, 1). There is little evidence of *F*'s concern with sexual and aggressive feelings, because he produces percepts with no sexual differentiation (II, 1; III, 1; VII, 1 and 2) and little aggressive content. (Aggression is implied only in II, 2; IV, 2; IX, 1; and X, 3 and 4).

There is an emphasis on looking (I, 1; IV, 2; VII, 1; IX, 1; X, 2 and 3) in his record. The use of the mirror (I, 1) and reflections (IX, 4) are expected adolescent responses referring to a self-critical examination and possibly some ability for introspection. In addition he suggests a feeling of being small and vulnerable, as expressed in his view of "looking up at someone" in response to 2 on Card IV.

F shows his potential for interrelationships (II, 1; III, 1; IV, 1, Inquiry; IX, 4; X, 6; and minimal use of color), although he may wish to engage in them on a preadolescent level (VII, 1).

TAT: *F*'s problems with the adolescent struggle between independence and dependence are reflected in many of his stories (Cards 1, 13 B, 7 BM, and 6 BM). He also expresses sexual aggression (Cards 3 BM and 13 MF), but the predominant theme throughout is aggression (Cards 8 BM, 13 MF, 7 BM, 6 BM, and 18 BM). It is as if he is a very angry boy and when he is not preoccupied with these feelings, he feels himself lonely and isolated (Cards 3 BM, 13 B, 16). The last card, 12 M, would seem to speak to a fantasied resolution to these disturbing feelings and impulses.

Summary Statement of Dynamic Picture: There is an over-determined concern with the sense of body damage and vulnerability in *F*'s record. This in part is related to his developing body and sexual and aggressive feelings. He remains, however, insecure and fearful about his body, and his impulses, beyond the normal expectations for an adolescent. It is suggested that this may be due to unresolved conflicts with his anger, specifically around the issue of independence-dependence from his parents. His need to regress and remain dependent leaves him fearful and isolated from his peers.

Defenses

W–B, Form I: *F*'s stylistic approach to the verbal items on the Wechsler is one of impulsive and quick responses. In spite of losing him credits, it seems to have been a necessary defense strategy for him to adopt in interaction with an authority (*E*) asking him a series of questions. When the tests permit (Performance items), his compulsive attention to details takes over.

In contrast to his own defensive stance against authority, his responses on two Comprehension items (8 and 9) suggest he feels only authority can control the impulses of others.

B–G: *F* uses good compulsive defenses in the execution of the Bender figures.

FD: *F* shows good compulsive detailing in the upper halves of his drawings. This is in contrast to avoidance of the meaning the lower halves of the torso may have for him (most likely, sexual and aggressive impulses).

Rorschach: Good intellectual defenses with obsessive and compulsive attention to details typify *F*'s responses throughout the Rorschach. He avoids identifying the sex of the people he sees (I, 1 and 2; II, 1; III, 1; IV, 2; VII, 1 and 2; and X, 2) referring to them only as "people" or "children."

The one confused and ambivalent response is in his first percept to the first card, suggesting his manipulative style referred to in the Wechsler.

Here, however, it seems to be in reaction to a new situation, and once he recovers he maintains an excellent performance.

TAT: The predominant use of obsessiveness throughout *F*'s TAT leaves his stories vague and ill defined.

Summary Statement of Defenses: F's overall record demonstrates an adolescent with well-established intellectual, obsessive, and compulsive defenses. He only regressed to more immature defenses of avoidance and impulsivity when faced with a feeling of being controlled or faced with an unfamiliar situation. These, however, are momentary regressions from which he quickly recovers.

Affective Expression

W–B, Form I: *F* worked throughout the W–B diligently, with good attention to the task. His affect was matter-of-fact without any expression. Notably, he did show pleasure when he did achieve a difficult item.

B–G: The Bender was accomplished easily without any expression of upset or of pleasure.

FD: Similar to *F*'s behaviors in the W–B and the Bender, there was no affective expression as he carried out this task. His lack of pleasure in his figures was particularly noteworthy, as he had told *E* of his interest in art and drawing.

Rorschach: *F* has no spontaneous affective responses either to the cards or to the percepts he produces. It is remarkable that the only suggestion of affect is in the inquiry to his first response to VII, where he implies a teasing interaction. His minimal use of color also portrays a young man still unable to integrate his feelings in his interaction with others.

TAT: Surprisingly, the TAT cards elicited stories from *F* with intense affective expression. He was consistent in that he told the stories in a matter-of-fact manner, as he had done on the other tasks. We speculate that the realistic pictures of people's interactions pulled these descriptions of affective reactions from him.

    F sees people more often than not engaged in contention (1, 13 B, 6 BM, 7 BM, and 18 BM), even to the point of murderous rage (13 MF). Otherwise the affect expressed is of sadness (3 BM and 6 BM) and loneliness (13 B).

Summary Statement of Affective Expression: F is able to present himself as a calm person wanting to please E and to do well on the tests. For some reason the TAT elicits responses with intense affect; it is through these stories that we gain a picture of a lonely, isolated person who is very angry at others.

Summary

F is a young man struggling with the typical adolescent conflict between achieving independence and longing for dependence. His struggle is exacerbated by his reluctance to grow up and his projection of his problems onto his parents.

In spite of having superior intellectual abilities and a potential for good social skills, he is not achieving academically and is somewhat isolated from others. He is preoccupied with feelings of sadness, loneliness, and anger that can sometimes reach intense proportions. He has been unable to resolve these disturbing feelings because he feels himself defective and therefore vulnerable. He sees himself as having done something wrong, but he cannot identify what it is. Instead he reacts to parental pressures, as if they know what it is and will not tell him.

At times this unhappiness mounts to a rageful wish for retaliation, and he can impulsively act out. He seems appropriately ashamed of his behavior, but he is unable to understand it himself.

Diagnosis

DSM-III-R

Axis I: 309.40 Adjustment Disorder with Mixed Disturbance of Emotions and Conduct.

Axis II: 315.90 Developmental Disorder Not Otherwise Specified (compensated).

Axis III: None

Axis IV: 1-None

Axis V: 70-Mild symptoms

There is no evidence of any severe disturbance in F's protocol. He maintains a reality orientation and is motivated for help. We recommend individual and group psychotherapy—individual therapy to aid him in accepting his feelings and maturing age, and group therapy for help in resolving his problems with peers. His motivation and unhappiness suggest a good prognosis.

Psychological Test Data

F: 15–8 Male

W–B, *Form I*

	Scaled Score
Verbal Test	
Information	10
Comprehension	12
Digit Span	14
Arithmetic	9
Similarities	13
(Vocabulary)	(11)
Total	58

	Scaled Score
Performance Tests	
Picture Arrangement	11
Picture Completion	12
Block Design	11
Object Assembly	12
Digit Symbol	12
Total	58

	Scaled Score	IQ
Verbal Scale	58	117
Performance Scale	58	113
Full Scale	116	117

Information

		Score
Kennedy		
1.	Eisenhower	1
2.	Measures temperature	1
3.	Tree and plant	1
4.	Europe—in England	1
5.	4	0
6.	52	1
7.	France—Rome, Rome	1
8.	Hong Kong	0
9.	5'5"	1
10.	Wright brothers	1
11.	South America	1
12.	No idea—1,000 miles?	0
13.	Pumps blood through body	1
14.	Shakespeare	1
15.	Twenty million	0
16.	January or February	0
17.	Byrd	0

18.	Asia	0
19.	Tom Sawyer. [*Rep. Q*] Oh, he took name from call from boat—call out—oh, Mark Twain	1
20.	City in Rome where Pope is	1
21.	I don't know	0
22.	Gount, Robert Gount	0
23.	A dead body—no—corpus delecti, I don't know	0
24.	I don't know	0
25.	I don't know	0

Total 13

Comprehension

Score

1. If it wasn't addressed to me—right? [Rep. Q] I'd open it. — 0
2. A big one or just starting? I wouldn't yell fire, because it would start a panic. I would try to notify one of the ushers. — 2
3. Because a bad influence . . . could rub off on you. — 2
4. To help the government run the country. — 2
5. Don't wear so much, are more durable, don't shrink or expand in weather. — 1
6. Because more land in country. In city not so easy to get, because more people in competition for it. — 2
7. Where I was standing, I would mark it and leave marks and walk in one direction. If it didn't work, I'd go back and start a new direction and keep doing this until I got out. I'd leave a note that I'd be back to that place. — 1
8. To keep people from going bad. Show them difference between right and wrong and keep a reasonable amount of order. — 1
9. First of all, it goes on record, and to find out if fit to be married—blood tests, Wasserman. So just don't go out and marry whoever you want. — 1
10. Have no way of hearing language or knowing what language is. Sometimes connection from ear to mouth could be damaged. — 2

Total 14

Digit Span

Score

F 9 + B 6   Total 15

Arithmetic

Score

1.	9	1
2.	14	1
3.	17	1
4.	9	1
5.	72	0
6.	6¢	1
7.	28	1
8.	600	1
9.	10—oh, wait—	0
10.	24	0

Total 7

[*Basic reasoning good but impulsive in verbal area. Jumps at response without thinking through what is really asked of him.*]

Similarities

		Score
1.	Both fruit	2
2.	Clothes	2
3.	Animals	2
4.	Both roll on wheels and are used for transportation	2
5.	Both used for gaining information	2
6.	Without them you couldn't live	2
7.	Is alcohol from trees? No, I don't know. Alcohol is using for polishing wood.	0
8.	Both senses	2
9.	Both foods	0
10.	Sometimes a poem is written about a statue, and a statue could be commemorated to a poem	0
11.	Both ways of expressing feeling to someone else, happy with them or not	1
12.	Both depend on air to live	1
	Total	16

Vocabulary

		Score
1.	Fruit	1
2.	Animal	1
3.	To mix with something. Going to and staying with. Become part of it.	1
4.	A jewel, a rare stone.	1
5.	Somebody who doesn't know how to behave, who is bothering you.	1
6.	From an animal, skin of an animal.	1
7.	Something that makes something softer.	1
8.	Type of currency—English.	1
9.	To take a chance.	1
10.	A meat from a pig.	1
11.	Piece of pointed steel to hold things together. Or on a finger, dead substance on body.	1
12.	Don't know.	0
13.	To add color to something.	1
14.	Where you keep guns and ammunition.	1
15.	An old story, not true.	1
16.	End of something—on a hat, juts out at end.	1
17.	Weapon of execution. Chops off your head—used in France.	1
18.	More than one.	1
19.	To put by itself.	1
20.	A substance that can blow up.	1
21.	Part of a song.	1
22	Something to see things you can't see with naked eye.	1
23.	I don't know.	0
24.	Is it a bat or something?	0
25.	To plant again. [*E spells it*] Where you break away from something, then you go back with it.	1/2

26.	Something that's bothering you, that goes against normal function, a disease.	1
27.	I don't know.	0
28.	A bomb or something, a ballistic missile.	0
29.	Where they bury people, underground.	1
30.	I don't know.	0
31.	Spying, learning secrets from somebody else.	1
32.	I don't know.	0
33.	Bug.	1/2
34.	Japanese suicide, stab selves with knife.	1
35.	No.	0
36.	No.	0
37.	No.	0
38.	No.	0
39.	No.	0
40.	Something where prone to getting a disease, or anything.	0
41.	No.	0
42.	No.	0
	Total	26

Picture Completion

		Score
1.	Tip of nose	1
2.	Other side of mustache	1
3.	Ear	1
4.	One in middle, a diamond	1
5.	One leg	1
6.	Tail	1
7.	I don't see where there should be sails on top of boat like this.	0
8.	Handle	1
9.	Hand on second timer	1
10.	Water coming out of pitcher	1
11.	Hand in mirror	1
12.	Tie	1
13.	Socket	0
14.	Ear—no, her eyebrow	1
15.	Don't see anything missing	0
	Total	12

Picture Arrangement

	Time	Order	Score
1.	4"	PAT	2
2.	8"	ABCD	2
3.	12"	LMNO	2
4.	21"	AJNET	2
5.	41"	SALEUM	1
6.	57"	EFGHIJ	3
		Total	12

[*Examines them first, then quickly shifts to correct position. Much time used examining them with care.*]

Block Design

	Time	Score
1.	12"	4
2.	13"	4
3.	9"	5
4.	21"	4
5.	37"	4
6.	100"	3
7.	250" (OT)	0
	Total	24

Object Assembly

	Time	Score
M	19"	6
P	43"	8
H	73"	6
	Total	20

Digit Symbol   Total Score   52

Bender–Gestalt

Want all on one page or onto another page? [*Suit yourself.*] Okay. I'll put all on one page.

A. [*Works carefully.*]
1. [*Does it quickly and easily. Counts once and produces it.*]
2. [*Has to repeat his counting after first few groups. He varies it by doing a few in a single top row then filling in the other two loops, then returning to the normal grouping of three at a time.*]
3. [*Well and easily done.*]
4. [*Asks permission to recopy it. The curve is done in two opposite directions from the point of contact.*]
5. [*Counts dots carefully. Begins the dots on upper slanting rows as he reaches the top of the curve, then returns to finish the circular figure.*]
6. [*Here the downward organized sequence is broken as he chooses to fill in upper space beside A.*]
7. [*Turns sheet over. As on 4, asks to recopy it.*]
8. [*Does the long figure in one continuous line.*]

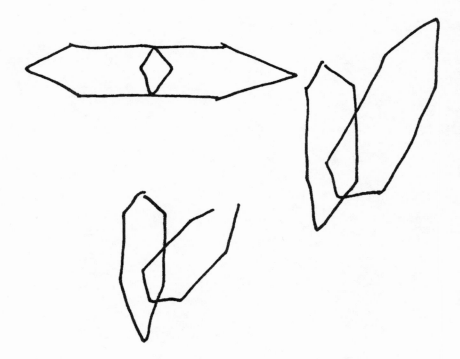

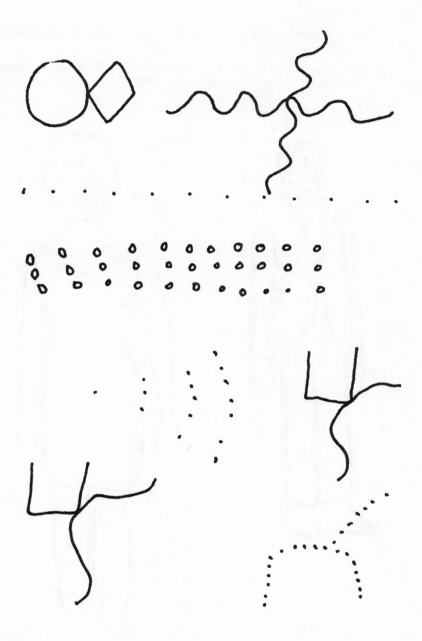

Figure Drawing

[Male]: [*Draws head first, putting in all the details. He then does tie and collar area before the shoulders and body.*]

[Female]: [*Again begins by completing the head and face. He holds the pencil through rather than in his fingers and pushes the point with his thumb.*]

Rorschach

I. 14"

1. I see a face with a hat on. Like a mirror separating it. I see a double image of the face. One eye if look this way (→), two eyes when look this way (←). Nose down here.

1. Looking (→) this way, has one eye, but if (←) this way has two eyes. Nose with one eye. No nose with two eyes.

2. Profile of person [*edge detail side*] on both sides.

2. Only edge detail.

II. 6"

1. Two people running, holding hands.

2. A plane [S] going through the night.

2. A rocket or plane going through the sky, not night. Leaving a stream behind, coming out of back—fire—usually comes out, and it's red.

III. 4"

1. Two people holding something. Something in the middle they're grabbing.

1. [*regular M*] Head, arms, feet and thing in middle.

2. A butterfly. [*center D*]

2. [*Q*] Wings, shape looks like form of a butterfly. Just looks like a figure of it.

IV. 3"

1. Looks like a bearskin rug.

1. The way it's laid out, small here, and comes like this [*outlines it*]. [*A bear skin?*] Texture? No, just the outline looks like it. This looks a little bit like fur.

2. Like you're looking up at someone. Someone towering over people. Looking up at someone.

2. His feet and going up—head. With arms out. Looks like towering over you. [*Frightening?*] In a way, yes.

V.   16"

1. A bird or a bat.

1. Has two things up here like bat wings spread out, and two small feet at bottom like a bat does. Looks like it's flying. The shape of it primarily.

2. Or a butterfly again.

VI.   37"

1. An X ray of a person—their chest— windpipe, spine. Looks like it's cut off. Goes on further to end, and this is center of it.

1. Looks like backbone runs down center, so this would be chest. Like it's dark in middle and lighter, and that's what X rays look like.

VII.   3"

1. Two children looking at each other.

1. Two little elfs, kids looking at each other— sneering, sticking tongue out.

↓ 2. Two people dancing with hands out and feet.

VIII.   8"

1. That looks like a skeleton of a person. Ribs, backbone [*center line from top*], lungs [*blue area*]. This could be intestines and everything, stomach [*lower center* D *red to orange*].

1. Just the shape. Looks like ribs coming around [*between blue* D *areas*], these look like lungs, two of them on both sides of line here, shape of it looks like skeleton.

[*Can you see something else?*]

2. Bears or something, climbing.

IX.   14"

1. An animal, two animals separated by a fence—looking at each other. Like two dogs or two

1. Looks like sheep, too. Have puggy look. Just looking at each other— eyes, nose, like a head—only part of it.

wolves or some-
thing. [*top two-
thirds*]

The rest would be fur-
ther along here [*indi-
cates side space area*].

2. Cow's head, nos-
trils, face looking
down. [*center light
area*]

2. Cow's head, general
outline of cow's head.
The way it comes in
and goes out at nose.
Top of head looking
down.

3. Two moose—look-
ing at each other.
Face and antlers.

3. That oval for face [*top
orange* D] shape and
antlers up here make it
look like it.

← 4. Trees and forest
[*upper half*], and
that's reflection in
water [*lower half*].

4. Tree here in green, and
other foliage or some-
thing. And reflected.

X.   21"

1. House or building
with road leading
up to it and things
or something danc-
ing around. [*top
center grey*]

1. House is at end of
road.

2. Could be a person
looking down the
road far away.
[*tiny detail in
"road"*]

3. Two things looking
at each other, two
lions, I guess.

3. Just the head, mane,
and two feet here.
Don't see the rest of
him. [*top center side
figures*]

4. Roman soldier
with a helmet over
his head. Just face,
yellow thing is hel-
met.

5. Face of a rabbit.
[*top of lower cen-
ter* D]

5. Two ears on top.

6. Sea horses. [*rest of lower center D*]

6. Well, the way curved tails go down. Just the shape. Color reminded me of it a little bit, because they're like green.

7. Spider or crab. [*upper side blue area*]

7. Protrusions coming out.

TAT

1. Now it looks like he's fed up with it. Before he probably made a mistake or ruined the whole piece. Later he'll probably take it up and work on it again. [*Play well?*] Just a kid probably wouldn't play that well. [*Is it he who wants to play, or his parents who want him to play?*] Parents probably want him to. [*How does he feel?*] I don't think he likes it very much. [*But he does it*] Yes.

3BM. Probably she's feeling sorry about something—crying—something happened that disappointed her before. Her or him, probably her. Probably later she'll try to forget about it, whatever happened. [*What happened?*] Something pretty bad, depressing, she's brokenhearted. [*About?*] I don't know, boyfriend or girlfriend, whatever it is.

13B. He's worrying about something that probably happened, or something he did. He's wondering what's gonna happen later as a result of it. He's probably very lonely. [*What did he do?*] Something bad, mischievous. I don't know, something he wasn't supposed to do. [*What happens?*] He will get punished for it. [*Why is he lonely?*] Because he's by himself in the doorway, and he doesn't know if anybody is there. Whole picture looks like he's lonely. [*He makes no move to hold the cards, looking down where they are on the table.*]

8 BM. Maybe someone he knew is hurt. Maybe he's hurt, maybe that's him. Is that a gun? He was probably wounded or shot. Those people are trying to save him. [*Will they?*] I don't know, maybe, maybe not. [*What did you mean, "That was him"?*] Could be him or someone close to him. Maybe this is him now, and that's what happened before and he's thinking about it. And he's out of it and he's still alive.

16. Nothing here, just a blank piece of paper with nothing. [*Can you make up something?*] Emptiness, nothingness.

13 MF. Maybe he just killed her [*laughs*] and wondering why he did it. Maybe he's thinking about what's gonna happen now. Or maybe somebody killed her, and he just came home and found her or something [*laughs*]. And he's crying. [*Why kill her?*] If he killed her, probably hated her and didn't like her. [*Is that a reason to kill?*] Don't kill somebody if you love them! [*Why kill?*] Maybe he had a fight with her. It doesn't look like he planned it. Looks like he's sorry, it was a momentary thing. [*What happens?*] I don't know, that's what he's thinking about. He'll probably get caught, and he'll be killed, too [*grins*].

7 BM. Looks like somebody is very angry and mad about something—and somebody older is trying to console him and make him feel different. Maybe older person said something he's getting mad at. [*Why?*] I don't know, probably said something about him that he didn't like. [*Happens?*] It doesn't look like he's making him happy or anything. [*What happens?*] It all depends on what did happen. If it's just a small thing, might get mad and walk away; if a big thing, might hit the guy, whatever it is. [*If hits him, then what?*] He'll probably just walk away. Maybe he just called him a name, a little thing. I don't know, big thing. Maybe he's not giving him something, or he's taking something away.

6 BM. He probably got some bad news. Somebody left or somebody died. They both look very sad. He looks like he doesn't understand, why did this happen. He probably came a long way, heard something, and then came and found out. [*What happened?*] Something sad, something he can't understand. Somebody left or somebody is leav-

ing—or police, an outsider are coming—or somebody died. Mother or whoever that is looks sad, too. [*Who is this happening to?*] I don't know, one of family, his father, sister, or uncle, aunt, or something. [*Feel about each other?*] Feeling they probably never see each other. He's probably married or something, you know, and came over. [*Feel toward her?*] I don't know, he doesn't understand, he could be angry at her. [*Is it her fault?*] Maybe she had something to do with it, or because of her it happened. [*What happens later?*] She looks like she can't believe it happened, she'll probably feel very sorry, and he'll probably just go away and . . .

18 BM. Looks like something pulling him. He's probably drunk or . . . sleepy—or maybe he's asleep. Somebody pushing him forward. [*Do they mean well?*] I don't know, probably not. He doesn't look like he wants to go or—turning his face from something. He could be just letting himself go, he doesn't care. [*Happens?*] It's probably something bad, or wouldn't have that look on his face. Hands look like they're grabbing him, so couldn't . . . be anything very happy. [*Happens in end?*] I don't know—I don't know.

12 M. Could be somebody is blessing him, a priest giving him extreme unction. Last prayers. Or could be he's asleep, and somebody coming to see if he's just asleep—or somebody trying to wake him up. Somebody casting a spell over him? [*laughs*] I don't know. [*What happens?*] Maybe he'll wake up or—if he's asleep, the other person will probably leave, he could be dreaming about it, I don't know.

Psychological Test Portrait

G: 14–9 Female

G was referred because of truancy from school and rebelliousness at home. The referring intake worker was concerned as to whether she had any motivation for help and any ego strengths.

G presents a facade of bravado, lack of concern, and boredom. She, however, cannot sustain this facade, having a strong need to achieve. She demands reassurance by requiring structure from E. As her anxiety mounts so does her negativism, until on the Rorschach it was not possible to elicit a full inquiry on all the cards. She is a thin, heavily made-up girl with her hair in studied disarray. G lives at home with her parents and brother and is in the eighth grade.

Cognitive Functioning

WISC: G obtains an average Full-Scale IQ (93) and shows little discrepancy between her Verbal score (91) and her Performance socre (97). There is, however, intertest and intratest scatter. The intertest scores range from 6 to 11, and the lowest—Information (7) and Arithmetic (6)—are those tests most closely related to school functioning. Although compliant in responding to all questions and instructions, G conveys someone who is variable in the use of her intellectual energy as it taps into dynamic concerns. This is reflected in the intratest scatter, where memory, concentration, and language usage are all variable.

B–G: G puts forth a great deal of effort in the copying task of the Bender, seemingly because she does not perceive it as a challenge to her intellect. The figures are adequately drawn, and the layout is well organized.

FD: G chooses to draw both of her figures on one page. Although her renditions are clearly differentiated sexually, she draws extremely miniature figures with underdeveloped bodies and legs extending from the waist. In terms of perceptual-motor development and perception of the body, this suggests a girl on a very immature level.

Rorschach: In spite of G's refusal to respond in the Inquiry, her percepts include the important determinants: good form and an adequate number of responses. She develops good percepts in utilizing W's and D's, indicating that her perception of reality is commensurate with others.

TAT: G tells stories to the TAT cards that reflect her accurate perception of the stimuli. In spite of her negativism she manages to give sequentially organized (albeit terse) stories.

Summary Statement of Cognitive Functioning: G's cognitive performance is marked throughout by variability. Although she scores in the average range, there are times when her language and conceptualizations suggest a higher capability. It is difficult to get a true picture of her cognitive abilities because of her relentless negativism.

Dynamic Picture

WISC: G provides some clues into her dynamics on the WISC. She feels herself to be a vulnerable child (Comprehension, 1, 7; Vocabulary, 13, 28, 36) in a dangerous world (Comprehension, 5, 7, 9; Similarities, 14; Vocabulary, 2, 36). Her immaturity intrudes at times into the way she handles intellectual material (Information, 13, 15, and 19; Similarities, 9 and 16). Other than these examples, there is no other evidence of dynamic intrusions.

B–G: The way in which G initially asks E for directions on how to perform the Bender demonstrates a strong dependency need on the authority. When this structure is not forthcoming, G goes on to demonstrate her own inner demands for precision and perfection.

FD: G's vulnerability suggested in the WISC is clearly demonstrated in her figure drawings. Both male and female figures lack any pelvic area, are heavily shaded in the body, and have truncated arms and feet, all of which suggest a feeling of helplessness in dealing with the world. The arms, adhering almost into the body, particularly reflect a fearfulness regarding aggression. The female figure suggests a wish for dominance in the large size of the head in contrast to the male's. In addition the female head has definable features, whereas the male looks more like a mannequin's head that is precariously perched on the shoulders.

Rorschach: Although G presents a healthy Rorschach psychogram, her reduced use of C suggests a preference for and reliance on a fantasy life rather than a willingness to interact with others. She masks her human percepts in clown or animal costumes (I, 1; II, 1) as a way of hiding her true feelings. Her one percept of unmasked human figures fighting (IX, 2) suggests her perception of people's interactions as hostile. Further evidence of her experience of hostility is seen in dead rabbits (III, 3) and a dog about to be killed (IV).

In any human percept she does not identify any gender differentiation, again suggesting a more unformed sexual identity. A poignant longing to remain little and dependent is seen in her unusual number of baby responses (VII, 1, 2, 3; IX, 1). This conflicts with the more usual adolescent responses of concern with the body (VIII, 1) and the need to separate (V, 1).

TAT: The hostility suggested in the Rorschach comes to full fruition in G's TAT stories. Females are described in derogatory terms (5, 12 F, 7 G, and 8 GF), and men meet violent deaths (12 F, 18 GF, 3 GF). There appear to be no positive objects with which to identify, nor any positive interaction possible between people.

Summary Statement of Dynamic Picture: G is a very unhappy adolescent with strong longings to return to a dependent childlike stance. She feels her environment offers no possible positive objects to rely on or to provide an identity. Interpersonal interactions are fraught with hostility and danger. Despite her bravado, she wishes to comply to authority and demonstrate her competence.

Defenses

WISC: On the WISC there is evidence of G's use of obsessiveness (Information, 27; Comprehension, 1; Picture Completion, 11, 15, 17) and language regression (Comprehension, 14; Picture Completion, 19). The use of the obsessive defense at times results in pretentiousness and failure (Information, 27; Comprehension, 11; Similarities, 10).

B–G: G's good use of compulsivity in this task allows her to produce adequate designs.

FD: These immature figure drawings bespeak G's regressive tendencies.

Rorschach: G's good compulsive defenses make it possible for her to achieve good form, utilizing all aspects of the blot. There is a curious rigidity in her approach, however, as she conforms to the way the blot is presented, never turning it. This is curious inasmuch as she presents as an angry, defiant, and rebellious adolescent. Her overt expression of defiance and anger precludes the presence of explosive or pure C responses.

While the drive for growth is seen in the number of W's and M's, it is unclear what positive models G strives for as she avoids identifying her human percepts in any detail, including their sex. The predominance of the ideational aspects of the psychogram (M's, FM's, and m's) speaks to a strong investment in the use of fantasy as a defense against the unpleasantness she perceives as imbued in human interactions. The wish to regress implied in her many baby responses seems to be the only evidence of a comforting fantasy for her.

TAT: The TAT stories are replete with G's use of anger as a defense against depression.

Summary Statement of Defenses: The one positive working defense G has at her disposal is compulsivity. Otherwise avoidance, denial, use of fantasy, a wish to regress, and overt expressions of anger mark her productions.

Affective Expression

WISC: Anxiety seems to pervade G's reaction to the WISC. She was concerned about getting the right answer, which led in one instance to her remarkable recovery of the correct answer forty-five minutes later in the testing (answer to Information, 16, provided in Picture Arrangement, 5), and on another occasion to her concern to whether she was doing it correctly (Picture Arrangement, 3).

B–G: At the outset, G's anxiety leads her to ask E for more directions, but once she begins the task her anxiety is bound by her compulsivity.

FD: Again G's anxiety leads to a request for more directions at the outset, but then she proceeds to complete the task, only betraying anxiety in the heavy shading on both drawings.

Rorschach: There is very little evidence of G's anxiety manifested in the Rorschach protocol itself. Her resistance to the Inquiry, however, reveals anxiety about the acceptability of her responses. For the first time her anger is overtly expressed toward *E*, in withholding on the Inquiry or demeaning *E*'s questions (VIII, 1; X, 3).

TAT: The content of *G*'s TAT stories are replete with anger and rage, primarily directed toward the mother. She does not express this toward *E* on the test, however, with the exception of her sarcastic remark to the blank card (16).

Summary Statement of Affective Expression: Anxiety is expressed by *G* throughout the more structured tasks. Her anger manifests itself once she is confronted with the projectives and whatever she perceives as *E*'s demand on her.

Summary

G presents as an anxious, immature adolescent whose defenses do not serve her sufficiently to handle the tasks inherent in her age. She reacts to issues of independence versus dependence, self-identity versus identity diffusion, sexuality versus asexuality, etc. in a regressive angry and negativistic stance. It is as if she hopes to ward off the maturational process and remain a dependent child. So much energy is expended on maintaining her rebellious, noncompliant position that all cognitive pursuits are diminished.

In seeming contradiction she is compliant, is anxious to achieve, and wants the approval of the authority. This breaks down only when she feels an unspecified criticism of her performance.

Diagnosis

DSM-III-R

> Axis I: 313.81 Oppositional Defiant Disorder–Severe
>
> Axis II: 301.90 Personality Disorder NOS–Immature Personality Disorder
>
> Axis III: Healthy
>
> Axis IV: 1-None
>
> Axis V: 60-Moderate

G's response to the testing situation, including her response to *E*, strongly suggests her ability to respond and relate to therapy. She will need a therapist who is able to be sensitive to the anxious immature child in her as well as to handle the potential anger. She should be seen at least twice a week and in family treatment once a week. If the family is cooperative, the prognosis is good.

Psychological Test Data

G: 14–9 Female

WISC

Verbal Tests		Scaled Score
Information		7
Comprehension		11
Arithmetic		6
Similarities		11
Vocabulary		9
(Digit Span)		(8)
	Total	44

Performance Tests

Picture Completion		10
Picture Arrangement		11
Block Design		8
Object Assembly		9
Coding		10
	Total	48

	Scaled Score	IQ
Verbal Scale	44	92
Peformance Scale	48	97
Full Scale	92	94

Information

		Score
1.	2	1
2.	Thumb	1
3.	4	1
4.	Cow	1
5.	Heat it	1
6.	Supermarket or grocery	1
7.	5	1
8.	7	1
9.	Christopher Columbus	1
10.	12	1
11.	Fall, winter, summer, spring	1
12.	Red	1
13.	Like a mountain	0
14.	[Q] Something inside, the digestive system in there digests your food	1
15.	Because it's heavier—oil is heavier	0
16.	I think I heard it in school. He also wrote Julius Caesar.	0
17.	Our independence	1
18.	From post office—postage—special parcel delivery	0
19.	Now—about 6'	0
20.	South America	1
21.	16	0
22.	I don't know.	0

23.	I don't know.	0
24.	900 miles	0
25.	August 25th	0
26.	I don't know.	0
27.	Tells the weather forecast. [Q] Round circle split into 16, and each has different word for level and has a number on it, and it goes to what it's going to be.	0
28.	No	0
29.	Sounds familiar	0
30.	Type of house natives would use	0

Total 15

Comprehension

Score

1.	Where are you? In school, or home? All depends how bad cut is. Wash with soap and put Band-Aid on. If in school, tell them before doing anything.	2
2.	You could either tell her and you'll have to replace it.	2
3.	Try a different store.	2
4.	Walk away from her.	2
5.	What you do? If train stops near station, tell man in charge. Otherwise start running, because when that train hits it'll really crack up, and no telling what'll happen.	0
6.	In the first place, brick is harder to break and in fire won't burn as fast as wood, and safer.	2
7.	If criminals not locked up, never learn they were doing wrong. If keep doing it, younger generation get bad impression and can do harm to people.	2
8.	Because women and children cannot take as much as men, and men are stronger and able to do more than women.	1
9.	If you're going personally, could be robbed, and could also be taken out of letter—postman sees it and could take it out, but can't steal check unless it's endorsed.	1
10.	Because organization charity know people and what to do with money, but to beggar can never tell if he's lying or what.	1
11.	Well, if just pick somebody from nowhere, he has to have sense of politics and what is going on in the world. Can't just pick somebody off the street and give test—have to have college and be very interested in it.	0
12.	Because they are thin—easy to weave.	1
13.	Because part of government and cabinet, just part of government and men that serve in our government.	0
14.	If keep promise sometimes and don't keep it, after while people aren't going to believe you no more.	2

Total 18

Arithmetic

Score

1–3.		3
4.	2	1
5.	6	1
6.	14	1
7.	7	1
8.	14	1
9.	18	1
10.	OT [Confused]	0

11.		0
12.	I don't know—10—don't know	0
13.	[*Counts on fingers*]	0
14.	[*Confused*]	0
15.	42	0
16.		0
	Total	9

Similarities

		Score
1–4.		4
5.	Two fruits	2
6.	Two animals	2
7.	Could be called liquids or drinks—beer and liquor	1
8.	Both musical instruments	2
9.	Well, paper is made out of coal	0
10.	Equal to same thing. [Q] A pound equals a yard 32 oz., and in the yard—36 inches.	0
11.	Both made of metal	2
12.	Both natural resources	1
13.	Both also natural resources. Salt comes from salt water.	0
14.	Both mean same thing—have freedom and right to speak— not trapped	1
15.	If first at beginning and last at end—in same category—like 1–10, 1 at beginning and 10 at end.	0
16.	[*begins adding and counting, then subtracts and loudly says*] They're both numbers	0
	Total	15

[*Very anxious to do well. Works very intently and hard—anxiety sometimes interferes.*]

Digit Span

F 5 + B 4   Total Score   9

Vocabulary

		Score
1.	You ride on it—a means of transportation in town.	2
2.	What type of knife? [Up to you.] Knife used for cutting, or some crackpots would use it for killing.	2
3.	Wear it on your head—a woman wears it for decoration.	2
4.	They writing it to you, or you writing it to them? Letter is to write news or tell somebody something, or just for pleasure.	2
5.	To protect self from getting wet from rain.	2
6.	Used to make things softer to sit on or to lean against.	1
7.	To hold something in place or hang something on wall.	1
8.	Animal that walks very slow.	2
9.	Comes from animal and make coats out of it—skin.	2
10.	Come from a rock and made with chemicals into diamond. Get one when you're married.	0
11.	[*yawning*] Things that go together.	1
12.	On a card—comes to a point on top, curves on side.	2

13. Weapon to protect yourself.   2
14. Person that bothers you.   2
15. Person that is not afraid of anything or anybody.   2
16. Person or something that does something that's ridiculous.   2
17. Somebody that does something outstandingly brave.   2
18. Person that bets money and loses it most of the time.   2
19. An acid—that's used—I don't know what used for.   0
20. Makes small things larger. Used by doctor to see blood type
    or disease in blood.   2
21. English money.   2
22. Fairy tale.   2
23. I don't know what it is.   0
24. A spy of some kind.   1
25. Phrase written and tells something.   0
26. Place that is blocked off which can't get out of.   2
27. On dress? Moves around. Streamer that flaps.   0
28. Person—Harry Caray—or disease.   0
29. Growing—something to do with body.   0
30. When you—not infection—no—somebody got bad
    influence on you.   0
31. I don't know.   0
32. Something like a hideout for animal.   0
33. Is that impudent? I don't know.   0
34. Animal? A bug—a praying mantis.   2
35. Is it a vest?   0
36. Can catch it or has a disease you can catch.   0
37. To talk a lot.   0
38. A bathroom with a different name—is it? I don't know.   0
39. Float—a fish.   0
40. Not to reduce.   0
                                                                          ―――
                                                        Total   40 (42)

Picture Completion
 1. Teeth   1
 2. Fourth leg   1
 3. Ear on fox   1
 4. Mouth on woman   1
 5. Other side of whiskers   1
 6. Hinge   1
 7. Other nail on finger   1
 8. Spade   1
 9. Nail to hold together   1
10. Buttonholes   1
11. Other side of gill, fin   0
12. Slit   1
13. Antennas   1
14. That horn on leg   1
15. Eye on other side   0
16. Barometer? The 5 on the column   0
17. Other ear   0
18. All wires on top side   0
19. Other milker in middle   0
20. Is there a door? Can't see anything. Oh, some more grass   0
                                                                          ―――
                                                        Total   13

Picture Arrangement

	Time	Order	Score
A–D.			8
1.	9"	FIRE	6
2.	13"	THUG	5
3.	8"	QRST Right? Get them all right so far?	6
4.	9"	EFGH	6
5.	35"	EPRCY	0

[Suddenly G gives answer to Information 16] Shakespeare.

	Time	Order	Score
6.	27"	FISHER	5
7.	65"	MSATER	0
		Total	36

Block Design

	Time	Score
A–C.		6
1.	16"	5
2.	17"	5
3.	OT	0
4.	7"	7
5.	OT	0
6.	OT	0
7.	OT	0
	Total	23

Object Assembly

	Time	Score
M	9"	7
H	57"	5
F	140"	6

This is ridiculous—a dumb thing. [*Talks to herself.*]
His eyebrow is corroded.

	Time	Score
A	104"	6
	Total	24

Coding   Total Score   52

Bender Gestalt

[Asks specific directions, but able to make decisions.]

1. *[Counts]*
2. *[Starts to say, "3–6–9," then counts each group as "1–2–3." Counts aloud as she draws; recounts both model and her reproduction. Last "0" on card not properly printed; she leaves it that way and points out what she did to E.]*
3. *[Brings card close to eyes to see and count. Redoes line because line curves instead of angles. Erases it and corrects last line. Works diligently right through.]*
4. Have to have precise amount of dots? *[E repeats instructions.]* If you want the precise amount of dots, I'll do it. Do you? *[E tells her to do the best she can. She is annoyed; then counts.]*
5. *[Counts curves.]*
6. *[Insists on turning card over herself.]*
7. *[Does diamond over.]*

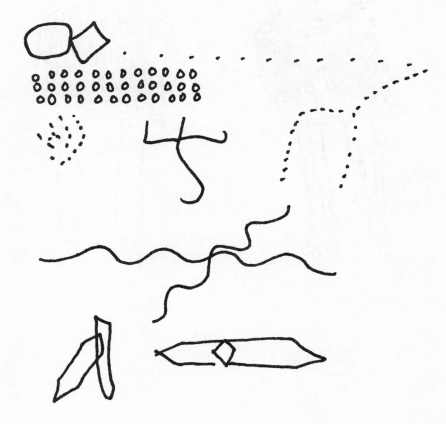

Figure Drawings

Female: [*Female first. Much ado about the hair, then does body.*] Do you want the whole body? [*By now G is smiling a bit.*]

Male: [*Does head, small features, then shoulders and arms, then fills in the center, darkening it.*]

Rorschach

I.   5"

1. Two clowns stand-
ing on another
body of a clown
with no head. [*W*]
Phony body with
zipper down cen-
ter. A stuffed
body—not the
sides, they're real.

II.   3"

1. Two people danc-
ing. Two chubby
people dancing—
an animal or a
clown—something
funny.

1. [*People or animals?*]
Could be people
dressed up as animals.
The back [*looks at
back of card*] don't say
what they are.

III. 4"

1. Two natives play-
ing a war drum.

1. [*Natives?*] Drum—
natives.

2. And a bow tie
[*laughs*] in the mid-
dle.

2. Not part of the natives.
The shape only.

3. And two things
hanging down.
Like rabbits—
they're going to eat
or something.

3. Dead rabbits.

IV.   3".

1. A big gorilla and
two big feet trying
to step on some-
thing. No, walking
toward a dog and
can only see half
the dog's body,
and his big feet are
going to kill it.

1. Big legs and arms.
Hairy. Dog at a dis-
tance.

V.   2"

1. A butterfly, and it's
flying away some-
place.

VI.   4"

1. A turtle upside
down and it's
walking. He's
walking so he's up-
side down. Shell is
on top—so walk-
ing right.

1. [*Shell of turtle?*] [*becomes very resistive;
Won't give description
of shell*] Head out—
looks like moving
slowly.

VII. 3"

1. Two little elves sit-
ting on rocks talk-
ing to each other.

1. [*Very resistive to inquiry.*]

2. Or could be two little bunny rabbits also on rocks.

3. Or bottom could be two little baby bears cuddled up.

VIII.   8"

1. I know what it looks like. The insides. Your chest and ribs. This is the most colorful one of all. Ribs forming a blanket over ribs.

1. [*Insides?*] I don't know—just looks like it a little bit. [*Because of color?*] Could be—no! What has color got to do with it? That's not red, it's paint.

IX.

Looks like a mess. Doesn't look like anything—mess—[*arms in air*] I don't know—has no meaning.

35"   ¨ 1. A little bear. [*lower D*]

1. Baby bear with tongue sticking out—whole red is one baby bear—maybe I like babies. No. They're a bother. I don't know.

2. Two people fighting. [*top*]

← 3. Two hippopotamuses or two Scotty dogs.

3. Hippos. [*but refuses to show E; goes to the bathroom*]

X.   7"

1. Two spiders.

1. All those things coming out—legs—just a mess.

2. Hornets.

2. Cause they do. No movement.

3. Pink clouds—whole rest looks like bugs.

3. I'm sick of seeing blue clouds. That's why. [*very negativistic*]

4. Grasshopper.

TAT

1. A boy who doesn't want to play his violin because he doesn't like violin—thinks it's a bore. [*Do?*] Nothin', doesn't do it. [*Happens?*] Nothing.

5. That's a cuckoo mother walking into neighbor's house to see if neighbor's home. She is and tells her to come right on in, and she does. [*evasive*] And she's going . . . [*stops, refuses to complete*].

13 MF. It's a, mmmm—a man. I guess it's his wife—her tough look—getting up out of bed to go to work—was drunk last night and has to get dressed. [*Why drunk?*] Nobody sleeps with their clothes on.

12 F. It's a woman and mother back of her—mother looks like witch—daughter looks evil. She's got cat eyes. She bothers me. [*Doing?*] She's telling her—old lady telling her daughter to kill her husband. [*Do it?*] Mm-hmm—because she has nothing better to do. [*Happens to her?*] Goes to jail.

16. Now this tells a good story. Artist got bored, so just made a painting of white piece of paper. Man who made that seems to be real crackpot.

7 G. A little girl, little fagged-up girl, and her mother, the glower puss, is reading to her daughter—and girl looks bored, exceptionally bored. [*Mother feel?*] I don't know. [*Girl feel?*] Lousy. That girl must be pretty hard up to have a cracked-up mother like that—fagged-up girl.

8 GF. Here's that cracked-up girl again, posing for her husband so he'll take her picture—painting her picture—feels all right. [*talks of cigarettes*] I smoke Marlboro. It's banded from some states because they do something to you when pregnant. I can smoke because I'm not pregnant.

18 GF. I don't know what it is—is that a man or a woman? A woman trying to choke a man or a woman? [*Why?*] I don't know. [*Does she?*] Uhmmm. [*Happens?*] Goes to jail. I love people to go to jail. [*Why?*] I don't know. Simple.

3 BM. Her husband just died, she's crying. [*Die of?*] Car accident—that's what they claim, at least. Thinking of story on "Untouchables" or something.

Psychological Test Portrait

H: 14–4 Female

H has repeated the seventh grade because of behavioral difficulties. She is truant, fights when in school, and has temper outbursts. Her academic achievement is reported to be good. She lives alone with her mother, who has a chronic illness. She is a pretty girl who looks younger than her age, and related well to *E. H* worked with earnest deliberation and motivation in all areas of the testing.

Cognitive Functioning

WISC: Although there is little discrepancy between H's overall IQ of 90 and her Verbal IQ of 95 and Performance IQ of 86, there is extreme intertest (range from 4 to 17) and intratest variability. Her lowest scores are on Information, Arithmetic, and Block Design. Her academic knowledge—as seen in Information—is limited, and she has not progressed in her arithmetic computational skills beyond the simplest level. Block Design is lowered by her difficulty in completing the design within the time limit; she was not able to get time credits on Coding or Object Assembly either. Because accuracy is not at issue, it is possible that we have interference in her speed because of organic and/or dynamic reasons. There is some interference in her critical judgment (Picture Completion, 11, 12, and 15; Vocabulary, 10 and 24), the reasons for which are unclear at this point. Language usage and conceptualization are particularly inconsistent on Comprehension (10, in contrast to 13 and 14), Similarities (12, in contrast to 14), and Vocabulary (10, in contrast to 15). She displays good memory (Digit Span), ability to abstract on a verbal level (Similarities), and excellent awareness of social expectations and interactions (Comprehension).

B–G: *H* demonstrates difficulties in the B–G commensurate with an organic problem. She has problems in angulation (A, 7, 8), curves (4, 6), crossing (6, 7), and dots (1, 2, 3 and 5); rotates the paper (3, 4); leaves gaps (A, 2, 8); and alters her approach within a figure (1, 2, 3 and 4). Her overall placement of the figures on the page is confused. The gaps and intrafigure changes suggest the likelihood of states of *absence*.

FD: The drawings support the possibility of a perceptual-motor dysfunction in conjunction with an *absence* state. Her drawings are immature, stylized, and unable to communicate a real sense of body concept. In addition, there is the noteworthy break in the line on the right side of the heads, a very sketchy line used with the female, and a number of gaps in both drawings.

Rorschach: *H* is able to realize good percepts in the Rorschach using many *P*'s, some *O*'s, and most determinants and expressing more information about the world than was evident in the WISC. The only indication of organicity is seen in her slowed-down reaction time (III, VI) and vagueness of response (IX, 1 and 2). Her Rorschach suggests a higher intellectual potential than her achievement in the WISC.

TAT: *H* is able to respond appropriately to the card stimulus and to the instructions to tell a story. Strikingly, her language is superior on this task compared to the WISC.

Summary Statement of Cognitive Functioning: H achieves an average IQ, which has to be considered minimal for her potential as suggested in other tests. Her IQ score is lowered by perceptual-motor difficulties, slowed-down reaction time, and *absences*, as well as dynamically driven intrusions. In spite of great variability within and between tests, *H* is in good reality contact and has solid cognitive functions.

Dynamic Picture

WISC: Generally throughout the WISC there are few suggestions of dynamic concern. There is a sexual response to Information 16, which seems age appropriate. There is a hint that she is disturbed by questions related to body concept (Information, 14, 19; Comprehension, 11).

B–G: *H* was very distressed by this test. Her reaction seemed appropriate to the degree of difficulty she was experiencing due to perceptual-motor problems. She seeks explanation for her difficulties in the failure of her sensory organs to perform adequately.

FD: Although *H* shows difficulties in her motor execution on this task, there are also indications of problems in her body concept, feelings of fragility and of fragmentation, a sense of immaturity, vulnerable feelings related to a sense of emptiness, and difficulty in interaction with the world. Adequate sexual discrimination is portrayed on an immature level.

Rorschach: Again we see problems in *H*'s feelings about the integrity of her body (IX, 1 and 2). Some of these concerns seem age appropriate, particularly when she describes the effort involved in emerging (II, 1; VI, 1; VII, 2), which can also have sexual implications (I, 2). This emphasis on developing is in conflict with the wish to remain young (VII, 1). Although these concerns are well within normal expectations for adolescents, there is an additional concern peculiar to *H*. She perceives others in frightening terms (II, 2; IV, 1 and 2; IX, 3), attributing mysterious powers either to herself or to others. This seems to be related to her fear of expression of aggression, the intensity of which is hinted at (IV, 1 Inquiry and VIII, 2).

TAT: The normal adolescent conflict related to growing up hinted at in the Rorschach is not seen in the TAT. *H* wishes to remain childlike, as she portrays these roles with some feeling of security (1, 7 GF, and 8 GF). Her identification with adult experiences is fraught with danger stemming from arbitrary causes (5, 12 F, and 13 GF). In either child or adult roles, there seems to be little gratification.

Summary Statement of Dynamic Picture: *H*'s conflict between wishing to remain childlike versus growing up is heightened by her feelings of body vulnerability and poor self-esteem. These problems are exaggerated by her organic difficulties. In this perception of herself as fragile, she is fearful of danger from external sources.

Defenses

WISC: Defenses of suppression (Information), regression, impulsivity (Arithmetic), and negativism (Coding) may explain *H*'s poor performances on these tasks. Whatever may be the explanation for the difficulties, they certainly seem dynamically motivated, as *H* demonstrates her ability for concentrated effort in her high achievement on other tasks. Again in PC, seemingly for the dynamic implications of "missing parts," she uses projection for her failures (11–15, 20). Regression is seen in her inconsistent language usage, i.e., superior to immature formulations, as seen in the contrast between Comprehension and Similarities versus Information and Vocabulary.

B–G: *H* clearly attempts to use compulsive defenses to aid her in this task. Awareness of her difficulties in accurately producing the design is at times expressed through rationalizations.

FD: *H* in her drawings uses avoidance, denial, and regression (seen in the particularly immature male). The vacant eyes in both drawings is an extreme expression of denial of seeing, which in turn suggests the use of projection.

Rorschach: *H*'s defenses throughout the cards demonstrate a fluidity between undoing (I, 2 Inquiry; II, 1) and attempted denial (III, 1; VIII, 1 Inquiry; IX, 1 Inquiry and 3 Inquiry; X, 2 and 3). At times she also demonstrates compulsive attention to details (I, 1 and 2 Inquiry; II, 2 Inquiry; V, Inquiry), and the use of projection (I, 2; IV, 1; IX, 3).

TAT: It is clear that *H* intends to convey the impression of an obedient and complying child, and how she achieves this in the story context is through a regressive posture (1, 7 GF, and 8 GF). Card 12 F, however, demonstrates the nature of her fears and the negativism and projection she mobilizes.

Summary Statement of Defenses: *H* has a wide range of defenses at her disposal. She can utilize regression, denial, undoing, compulsivity, rationalization, and projection.

Affective Expression

WISC: There is no evidence that *H* was angry at different WISC subtests. She performed so poorly, however, that it appeared her energies were being used to contain her hostility toward the tests. On tests she liked (because she was able to do them easily) she expressed positive affect.

B–G: *H* was distressed at her difficulty in copying the designs, but again the main affective tone seems to be anger at her difficulties with the task.

FD: *H* seemed to feel comfortable at this task, and her drawings have a sense of pleasantness about them.

Rorschach: *H* performs the Rorschach with positive affect. Even when experiencing some kind of inner tension seen in long reaction times (II, III, and VI) or *m* (II, 1; IV, 2; VII, 2), *H*'s affect does not change. Although her demeanor during the Rorschach was friendly and pleasant, some of her responses (II, 1; VIII, 2; IX, 3) belie this equanimity.

TAT: Although *H* obviously enjoyed this task, there is no pleasure or pleasant feelings ascribed to the characters in the stories. This suggests that *H* enjoyed the opportunity to portray her feeling of victimization, as well as the opportunity to characterize parents as demanding or sadistic.

Summary Statement of Affective Expression: *H*'s overall affect was friendly but bland. There was little expression of any negative feelings, although her responses to the Rorschach and TAT clearly show her capacity for such feelings.

Summary

H is an angry girl who seems to resent the need to grow up and leave her childhood behind. Her conflict between remaining a child and becoming an adolescent is an exaggeration of the normal dilemma. Rather than experiencing this as her own conflict, she projects the reason (or blame) for her problems onto others. This leaves her in a position of powerlessness, and she can only feel anger at others' denial of nurturance and support for her.

In addition, she has obviously had a perceptual-motor problem, as well as experiences of *absence*, for a very long time. It is a testimony to her diligence and her intelligence that she has been able to accommodate her difficulties without special help. The problem, however, remains that her mastery over these organic difficulties is at the whim of her dynamic conflicts and defensive maneuvers. Therefore she can appear at one time to perform at a much higher level than at another time, when she appears regressed or quite delayed in her development.

Not only does *H* have her own sense of damage inherent in the above, but she also identifies with her chronically ill mother. This feeling of damage, along with her sense of others as mean, leaves her with a strong sense of deprivation. Given this sense of damage and the projection of demandingness or evil intent onto others, it is no wonder that she has behavioral problems at school.

Due to the wide fluctuation in her cognitive functions, the variability in her defensive maneuvers (from regression to projection), the failure in adaptive techniques, and her basic difficulty in relating to others, *H* is seen as a borderline personality with organic dysfunctions.

Recommendations are for a complete neurological examination, including EEG, and for intensive therapy. Therapy should address not only her conflicts and emotional difficulties but also her experience with her perceptual-motor and *absence* difficulties. With treatment, *H* has a good prognostic future.

Diagnosis

DSM III-R

Axis I:	312.00 Conduct Disorder, Solitary Aggressive Type
Axis II:	301.83 Borderline Personality Disorder with Paranoid Traits
	315.90 Developmental Disorders Not Otherwise Specified
Axis III:	None
Axis IV:	4-Severe
Axis V:	45-Serious symptoms

Psychological Test Data

H: 14–4 Female

WISC

Verbal Tests

	Scaled Score
Information	5
Comprehension	17
Arithmetic	5
Similarities	11
Vocabulary	8
(Digit Span)	(12)
Total	46

Performance Tests

Picture Completion	7
Picture Arrangement	12
Block Design	4 (5)
Object Assembly	9
Coding	8
	—
Total	40 (41)

	Scaled Score	IQ
Verbal Scale	46	95
Peformance Scale	40	86
Full Scale	86	90

Information

		Score
1.	Two	1
2.	Thumb	1
3.	Four	1
4.	Cow	1
5.	Heat it	1
6.	Grocery	1
7.	Five	1
8.	Seven	1
9.	Columbus	1
10.	Twelve	1
11.	Summer, Spring, Winter, Fall	1
12.	Purple	0
13.	Don't understand what you mean.	0
14.	[*giggles*] Takes my food, I eat.	0
15.	Because it's light	1
16.	Two lovers. [*smile*] Can't think of his name.	0
17.	Day the flag—they had a big parade a long time ago for the 4th of July.	0
18.	Something about delivery	0
19.	5'11" or 6'2"	0
20.	In Italy	0
21.	No	0
22.	No	0
23.	No	0
24.	1,200 miles	0
25.	No	0
26.	No	0
27.	Measure, uh, I think they use it for how high altitude is.	0
		—
	Total	12

Comprehension

		Score
1.	Put a Band-Aid on it	2
2.	Pay for it.	2
3.	Go to another store.	2
4.	Walk away.	2
5.	[*smiles*] Maybe yell or wave a white flag.	2
6.	Because wood is easily burned, and you could tear it down easier.	1

7. So they won't commit any more crimes, so they
   won't hurt anybody.   2
8. Before men? Because men are stronger, and little kids
   should have a better chance because grown-ups lived lives.   2
9. If mailing it, somebody could open mail and take
   money—check is easier.   2
10. Because you know where your money are going to.   1
11. See if anything's wrong with people—need a healthier
    person for majority of things they do.   0
12. Because it's soft, easier to be found.   1
13. To do a job a lot of people couldn't do—elect one
    person to do for them.   2
14. So next time they have faith in you.   2

                                                    Total   23

Arithmetic

		Score
1–3.		3
4.	2	1
5.	6	1
6.	14. Can't add so fast. [*counts on fingers*]	1
7.	7	1
8.	21¢	1
9.	14 [OT]	0
10.	16	0
11.	[OT] Can't think that one out.	0
12.	15¢	0
13.	[*gives up*]	0
14.	$1.35	0
15.	35¢	0
16.	Can't do.	0

                                                    Total   8

Similarities

		Score
1–4.		4
5.	Both round—have skin	1
6.	Both animals	2
7.	Both beverage—liquor-like	2
8.	Both instruments	1
9.	They burn	1
10.	Both measure	2
11.	Made of same thing. [Q] Copper.	0
12.	[*much thought*] Both same elements	0
13.	When put salt in water, it evaporates, so made of same chemicals—some water with salt	0
14.	Stand for almost same thing—freedom—like both sort of mean	2
15.	When start out and when you end	0
16.	No	0

                                                    Total   13 (15)

Digit Span

F 7 + B 5   Total Score   12

Vocabulary

		Score
1.	Something to ride on.	2
2.	Something to cut with.	2
3.	Something you wear.	2
4.	Something you read or write—mail to somebody.	2
5.	Something use to protect self when raining.	2
6.	Something put on sofa—make it look nice or be soft against back.	2
7.	Something hammer into chairs or tables—boxes to keep together.	2
8.	A stubborn animal.	2
9.	Can be used—something to put around you from animals.	2
10.	Something wear on your finger—a glass element—costs more.	0
11.	If join something, go with group of people to do certain things together.	2
12.	A card—like hearts.	2
13.	Something used to protect self—way back.	2
14.	Somebody who always bothers you.	2
15.	Somebody who did something to protect somebody else—help others—something dangerous and do anyway.	2
16.	Things you know that doesn't make any sense.	2
17.	Somebody who's always doing good deeds—superboy—true-to-life person.	2
18.	Play games with money.	2
19.	Highly explosive.	2
20.	Something look through that makes things bigger.	2
21.	Money.	1
22.	No.	0
23.	No.	0
24.	Something about a trip—like get in trouble.	0
25.	No.	0
26.	No.	0
27.	Like spangle banner?	0
28.	No.	0
29.	No.	0
30.	No.	0
	Total	39

Picture Completion

		Score
1.	Tooth	1
2.	Leg	1
3.	A ear [laughs]	1
4.	Mouth	1
5.	Whisker	1
6.	Hinge	1
7.	Nail	1
8.	One of spades	1
9.	Thing belongs here to keep together	1
10.	Two buttonholes	1
11.	One of fins other side	0
12.	Don't see nothin'—something to knock it in	0
13.	There's a spider—nothing	0
14.	His arm	0
15.	Other eye	0

16.	Don't see nothin'	0
17.	Nothin'	0
18.	Here either	0
19.	Not split—one like this	1
20.	Stars or something, because the sun set	0
	Total	10 (11)

Picture Arrangement

Time		Order	Score
A–D.			8
(Fight)		XYZ	
1.	9"	FIRE	6
2.	14"	THUG	5
3.	17"	QRST	4
4.	16"	EFGH	4
5.	21"	PERCY	4
6.	74"[*much examining before she starts*]	FSIHER	4
7.	30"	MASTER	5
		Total	40

Block Design

Time		Score
A–C.		6
1.	184"	0
2.	63" [*one half wrong way*]	0
3.	[*OT*]	0
4.	64"	4
5.	4'15" [*At time limit has center column by twos. Then recognizes 3 x 3 pattern. Finally gets it.*]	0
6.	[*at time limit has four correct*]	0
7.	Can't do.	0
	Total	6 (10)

Object Assembly

Time		Score
M	17"	5
H	37" [*hit-or-miss approach*]	6
F	63"	7
A	141" [*hit-or-miss approach*]	6
	Total	24

Bender–Gestalt

A. [*Distressed at ear on diamond—makes a line over it.*]
1. Can't hardly see. Don't know what's the matter with my eyes—lose track. [*Counts—moves from dots to circles.*].
2. [*No effort to count until nearly done—then counts visually.*]
3. [*Rotates sheet 90°. Begins with a circle, then a dot. Rest done with sheet in usual position.*]
4.
5. Same number of dots? [*Make it to look like it.*]
6. [*Well executed.*]
7. [*Real trouble with angles.*]
8. [*Trouble with angles and makes ears.*]

Figure Drawing

[*Starts with hair, then face, then body to feet on both drawings.*]

Rorschach

I.	6"

<table>
<tr><td>1. Looks like some kind of an insect. [W] [Describe it?] Okay. Looks like a, uh, like a spider. [examines more until 1'25".]</td></tr>
<tr><td>2. Looks like the shape of body. [center D]</td></tr>
</table>

Inquiry

1. Way body drawn. Things coming out of head there. Even though not straight legs could be coming out like on each side.

2. She shaped like a lady—can see her legs if move this—could see how her dress stops at—I mean starts rather—real short dress—right up to her—that—right there [*where waistline usually is*]. She's standing there.

3. Looks like bird, no a bat. [W]

3. A bat—way it's shaped—way it looks—bat always has his arms out. [*Arms out?*] Flying, he looks like he's flying.

II.   19"

1. Looks like a rocket [*usual top center d*], a little bit, blasting off in space—going to space—coming from here [*lower red*]. It's the rocket going up.

1. Looks like the fuel is coming down and it's startin' off, and it gets up to here. [*Fuel?*] Red makes it look like fire.

2. Two people with hands together. [W] Some kind of voodoo people.

2. Looks like got one hand behind their back and other going like this together.

III.   20"

Nothing.

58"

1. Don't look like nothin' except for one person standin' over here and one person standin' over there. Looks like they beating on something, drums or something.

2. This looks like a ribbon—a bow.

2. Way shapes up a little bit. [*Look as much like a bow if black?*] I don't know. Might. Probably would.

IV.   13"

1. Like some kind of monster.

1. Big, big legs—all furry—looks furry. Arms out like that—big feet—just looks like one. [*Frightening?*] Yes, because it's big and it looks furry. Way you look at it—it would scare you. Eyes and long nose with fur on it. Ugh.

		2. Scarecrow standing on a pole—a wood something.	2. Looks like big fat stick in middle of a yard, and they got the scarecrow hanging up like this [*demonstrates with arms up and hands dangling*].
V.	4"	1. Looks like an insect, too. That's all I see. [*keeps looking*] That's all.	1. Two legs—two antennas and wings—looks like back of him because I can't see the eyes. [*Q*] Yeah, yeah, but it looks like it's up in the sky.
VI.	45"	1. [*studies intently*] Looks like a bird is trying to get out of a hole or something, so he's flying straight up. [W]	1. Like a canyon or mountain—closed up on each side and little space where he just came out of. Birds—wings. Closed-in part looks like it's deep, deep inside [*center* di] and comes out to open.
VII.	8"	1. Looks like two girls with ponytails sticking straight up in the air.	1. [*Girls?*] Shape of faces with bangs of hair and something up is ponytail [*laugh*]. Looks like they're playin' with each other.
		2. Something trying to squeeze out from some rocks. That's all.	2. This is closed in. Looks like this, the fuel is here [*bottom* dd] and trying to push up—like with rocket [di]—rocks go up and out like—round rocks [*lower D's*].
		3. Looks like way back over the water when you look down here and you could see the sun. [*top of lower center* dr]	3. Like a horizon—sea goes way out. Can't see the sun.
VIII.	11"	1. Animals trying to crawl up and trying to hold onto something.	1. Don't know what trying to hold to—but can tell these are animals.

2. Looks like two animals trying to pull an insect apart.

2. If not an insect, something—see, it's ripping right here at the seams. Holding onto this [*top* D] and pulling this stuff [*blue center* D].

3. And looks like they're high up on some rocks.

3. Just looks like they're up on some rocks [*lower* D] shaped like rocks. Round, little bitty rocks here—think of it, they do look like they far away, and they're trying to climb up to the top. [W]

IX.   10"

1. Bleary part looks like somebody's insides.

1. Don't know what call it—oh yes, your lungs because fat on each side—round like. [*center* dr]

2. Somebody layin' down here [*lower red*] trying to hold this all up.

a. When look at it really looks like a cat [W]—like sittin' up so could see front part of him and two arms here.

3. And looks like two witches doing an evil spell, throwing their hands. [D]

3. That was upper part but then again don't look like witches—don't look like nothin'.

X.   9"

1. Looks like two bugs—I don't know—beetles or something.

1. Like they nibbling at something.

59"

2. Don't see nothin' in here. A spider with all the legs.

2. All the legs—little thing—all the legs.

3. Can't see anything in there—[2'] rabbit's face.

3. Two ears—and shape like it.

[*Where limits tested, H was able to identify an FC, bow on III.*]

TAT

1. That's a violin? He's frustrated and tired of practicing and just say—aah—and put hands on face, and before that he was practicing—finally he put it away. [*Doesn't like to work?*] Not on the violin. [*Why?*] Some people don't like some things—maybe he wanted to be outside playing.

7 GF. That's a doll baby—is that a book in her mother's hand? Looks like her mother's reading to her—before that she asked her mother to read to her—before that she asked her mother to read to her—or it might be a Bible, and her mother called her to read a Bible to her, and later her mother finished reading the Bible and told her to go out and play or go wash her hands for dinner. [*How did she feel?*] She looks like she have a bored expression on her face. [*Sits through it?*] Yes, because she's obeying her mother and knows it's right to sit and listen.

5. Looks like she's callin'—wait—looks like opened door and she's seen something frightening—somebody coulda got hurt—no, somebody got a heart attack, and she's seein' him lyin' on the floor—before that could've been calling to her husband to eat, and after that coulda called the cops and had a investigation—if he got hurt by some stranger or something or if he just had a heart attack. [*Which was it?*] He got hurt— just clobbered on head, and he was bleeding. [*Happens?*] Call cop. [*To him?*] Goes to the hospital. [*And?*] That's all. [*Get well?*] Mm-hmm—yes. [*Who did it?*] A burglar. [*Catch him?*] No, they never catch burglars, especially burglars like that because they don't really try to find people like that. All he did was get hit over the head and they took a few things. Nothin' worth value.

8 GF. Like a maid daydreaming on what she would like to have in life—like a little Cinderella sitting in the corner [LP]. [*Go ahead.*] Before she was goin' her work after that—she—somebody called her and she had to go finish all the rest of her work.

16. Turn over? [*That's the card.*] I don't see nothin' in here. It's dirty. [*laughs*]

3 GF. Looks like she's cryin'. Somebody downstairs made her mad—her husband may have—she went upstairs to her room—before that she had a argument—and he came up and apologized, said he was real sorry, so they made up.

12 F. [*laughs*] Looks funny. She looks like a witch—like a sadist, like somebody who always do something mean for nothing—I don't know what to make of that picture. Might be her mother—can't make nothin' of—[*Feel?*] Seem like her mother is always naggin' her—then again she looks so mean, I don't like her—I wouldn't like to know her either.

Psychological Text Portrait

J: 15–2 Female

J was referred after making a suicide attempt through drug ingestion. She called her friend who then called the police.

J is one of two children of divorced parents. She lives alone with her mother, as her brother is in college. She was appropriately in 10th grade and doing average work. No problems were presented in school, although it was found out that she had begun to isolate herself from friends in the previous few months.

She is an attractive girl of medium height with straight dark hair, and was wearing the typical adolescent costume of that time. She related to *E* with coyness, verbosity, inappropriate giggling, and variability of affect. Her nails were bitten down to the quick.

Cognitive Functioning

W–B, Form I: *J*'s even scores on Verbal and Performance do not tell of the extreme intratest variability. She achieves an average overall IQ, but is particularly deficient in the areas of concentration where she finds the task difficult. She herself states she has trouble: "I can't do anything with numbers," and this is born out in her poor scores in Arithmetic, Digit Span and reversals in Digit Symbol. This could be mistakenly thought of as a dyscalculia, but the evidence of her inconsistent performance suggests intrusions in her attention. In Similarities, she herself says that she has memory problems. Due to her at least average performance in Information, Comprehension, Similarities, and Vocabulary, there is no reason to suspect an organic reason for memory problems. She demonstrates very superior ability in her performance on Object Assembly in reconstructing the whole from the parts. One could speculate that this is related to a dynamic concern that summons up her ability to put forth concentrated effort.

Generally, *J*'s language is very good. There are only a few instances of regressed forms of communication (Comprehension, 7; Similarities, 8; Vocabulary, 6 and 7) that appear to be related to dynamic issues.

B–G: *J* copies the designs with effort and attention. She even corrects herself when she sees an error (Figure 1) but also is dissatisfied when it is inappropriate (Figure 3). This suggests inconsistencies in the accuracy of her judgment.

FD: Either *J* shows spatial misjudgment in her first drawing (female bust) or she chooses not to produce the body. There are stark discrepancies in size (hands versus head), in maturity (the head is as if drawn by an adolescent, the hands as if by a young child), and in differentiation (details are accorded to the eyes, yet the pupil is left blank). Further misjudgment is seen in leaving the marks on the cheeks of the drawing.

The male portrait is even more peculiar, with breaks in the line (nose, lips, chin, ear), a saw-like open mouth, strange placement of hair on the forehead, and the blank pupil again.

J's attempts to draw whole figures results in reasonably proportioned bodies. Her critical judgment is demonstrably faulty, as she does not correct the transparency and leaves a previously drawn line inappropriately on the female; on the male she does not complete a mouth, and she leaves the discrepancy in the size of the feet and the length and width of pants. On both the arms are left unattached.

Rorschach: *J* maintains the structure of the blot, achieving a high *F+* level. In addition, she makes use of many determinants and shows a variety of information. Disturbance is seen only in the idiosyncratic ideas and associations expressed in her language. Again, her critical judgment is often faulty (IV, 2; VIII, 1).

TAT: As in the Rorschach, *J* complies with the instructions and identifies the stimulus accurately. It is in the elaborations and content of her stories that idiosyncratic thoughts emerge. Also, there are unelicited intrusions of associations through singing and her comments.

Summary Statement of Cognitive Functioning:J's overall cognitive performance is superior to her average IQ score. She demonstrates excellent language, information, and perceptual integrative ability. These abilities, however, are severely curtailed by her thought disorder: her faulty critical judgment, persistent intrusions of idiosyncratic associations, and misuse of words.

Dynamic Picture

W–B, Form I: Information, Comprehension, and Similarities are remarkably free of the pervasiveness of the thought disorder seen in Vocabulary. The unusual failure on Information 4, along with the juxtaposition of words on Information 20, suggests a preoccupation with religious issues, which are sexualized. The response to Comprehension 7 is a personalized reaction provoked perhaps by fear. In Similarities 6, 8, 11, and 12, the dynamic is not clear. Concerns with aggression, primarily sadistic, emerge in her responses to Vocabulary 17, 31, and 34; Picture Arrangement—Taxi; Picture Completion 11, 14; and Object Assembly—Profile.

B–G: No dynamic material emerges in the Bender. She engages *E*, however, in associative asides as she works on her drawings. The content of these remarks implies her concerns with being strange and different and the lack of others' concern for her—indeed, their wish to harm her.

FD: One is startled by the tears and bizarre lines on the cheeks of *J*'s first drawing (the female bust). Although she may wish to convey sadness, the drawing is too disturbed to communicate any feeling of grief or depression. The suggestion of buttons and the childlike hands in a prayer position imply wishes for dependency.

Her second drawing, a male head, is in contrast to her later full-figure male. This male conveys strength and determination with a strong chin, phallic-like ear, and a razor-like mouth. These qualities can represent oral aggression.

Following her drawings of the head alone, she produced full-bodied drawings. There is obvious disturbance in *J*'s body concept. There is an amorphous feeling to the bodies, as well as a lack of interrelatedness of parts. (Also note that there are no ears.) The female drawing, relative to the male, has greater strength and activity, as well as an open mouth. The pony tail shaped like a phallus suggests a conflict in sexual identity, as well as having aggressive connotations. The female's hands, which appear mutilated, may be in response to aggressive implications. The reaching-out hands suggest the wish for interaction with the outside. The male drawing in contrast appears ineffectual and weak (as well as the mouth being undifferentiated). All of this implies that *J*'s self-concept is extremely inadequate, and to the degree that it exists at all, it is extraordinarily conflicted.

Rorschach: Sadistic aggression is expressed throughout *J*'s percepts (e.g., I, 2; II, 1 and 2; VIII, 1; X, 1, 5, and 6). Aggression is also expressed in themes of deadness (I, 1; III, 1) and damage (IV, 1; X, 4). All of this speaks to *J*'s primitive aggressive impulses toward others, which can be turned against herself, or emerge in a projected fear of what others intend toward her (Aside in II, Inquiry; VII aside). Pleasant responses only emerge in relation to ideas relating to being younger (Aside after V; IX), as well as oral expectations (IV, 2) and symbiotic merging (VI, 1). Conflict in sexual identity, as well as in the wish for and fear of sexual impulses, is suggested in responses to VI, 1 and 2; and VIII, 1. As a result of all of this, *J* may be as frightened as the Topsy in VII by her own image. Her self-concept would seem to be extremely confused and fragile. She therefore must feel very frightened or, even worse, dead.

TAT: As in the Rorschach, aggressive themes predominate in *J*'s stories. The aggression is sometimes toward others and sometimes toward the self. It emerges in her stories that relationships always include agression, with the exception of a little girl's clinging to her doll (7 GF) or the possibility of getting married (8 GF and 4). Indeed, she enacts with *E* a more childlike role in spontaneous singing, starting on Card 6 GF. Any oral gratifications such as alcoholism, however, lead to self-destruction. In contrast to the Rorschach, *J* addresses her feelings of loneliness (Cards 5, 8 GF) and emptiness (Card 16).

Summary Statement of Dynamic Picture: *J*'s dynamics, as portrayed in her responses, are primarily concerned with sadistic aggressive thoughts and impulses. Sexual drives are diverted into religious issues. Her own sexual identity is highly conflicted with both male and female attributes. Her self concept is so inadequate it seems barely to exist.

Defenses

W–B, Form I: *J* shows the capacity to utilize obsessive-compulsive defenses in many instances throughout the W–B. Intrusive associations and thoughts, however, mobilize ineffective or pathological defensive maneuvers. Thus she herself complains of forgetfulness, as well as demonstrating it in her blocking (Arithmetic; Similarities, 11; Digit Span; Digit Symbol). Intrusive concerns also appear in peculiar verbalizations, either of a too concrete or too syncretic nature (Information, 4, 20; Comprehension, 7; Similarities, 6, 8, 12; most of the Vocabulary).

B–G: Apart from the expression of her intrusive concerns, *J* manages to utilize compulsivity in achieving a good performance on the B–G.

FD: The major defense seen in *J*'s first two head drawings is avoidance of that which could represent libidinal drives. In addition, the focus on the heads suggests intellectualization. The hands in the female drawing held in a prayer-like way hint at the possibility of seeking divine protection. In the full-figure drawings, one can see unsuccessful attempts at primitive defenses of denial and avoidance. *J* excludes sensory organs, i.e., pupils and ears on both drawings, the mouth (on the male), and blunts the fingers on the female. The compulsivity seen in the B–G is absent here, and instead there is the intrusion of idiosyncratic slips (seen in the lines on the female's face and corner of the male's eye, line on the rear of the female, transparency of arm in the female, lack if integrity of the line on the male's body, and disproportionate legs and feet on the male).

Rorschach: To some extent *J*'s intellectual defenses hold together very well on the main performance of the Rorschach. Exceptions to this are seen in VI, 2, and VIII, 2. In the former (VI, 2) the religious emphasis suggests she may be flirting with a delusional system as a defense against her fears. In the second case (VIII, 2) her intellectualization fails and suggests, again, possible delusions about her body.

Obsessiveness is produced in her responses to Card I, 1 and 2; II, 1; IV, 2; and VIII, 1. She is able to maintain her compulsivity and elaborate good percepts (I, 2; III, 2; IX, 2). Regression also permits sustaining the original good percept (IV, 2; VII, 1; IX, 1, 2, and 3). In the Inquiry, however, her idiosyncratic associations intrude so that her percepts become more pathological.

TAT: *J*'s intellectual defenses enable her to comply to the test requirements and stimuli. The content of her stories, however, is again filled with idiosyncratic associations and peculiar verbalizations (with the exception of Card 1).

Summary Statement of Defenses: Although *J* has developed obsessive-compulsive defenses, they are too easily intruded upon by her idiosyncratic associations. Denial and avoidance are used on a childlike level and are not able to mask the push of her aggressive drives. Her defenses thus have lost their function in adapting to reality.

Affective Expression

W–B, Form I: *J* was relaxed and comfortable throughout this test in spite of intrusions of a self-derogatory nature. We assume from her performance that she felt she was doing well.

B–G: *J* was comfortable with this task, being talkative and friendly to *E*. Her only disturbance was demonstrated in her flood of associations.

FD: *J* accomplishes this task easily and comfortably. In the head drawings she portrays histrionic sadness and perhaps anger in the male drawing. The drawings of the full figure, in contrast, portray flatness of affect.

Rorschach: In spite of the disturbing (to us) elaborations of her percepts, *J* enjoyed this task. It appeared to be a cathartic experience for her. Affect in her percepts is expressed in a relentlessly aggressive sadistic way.

TAT: Although the content of the stories implies very unpleasant affect, again, *J* was comfortable with the task.

Summary Statement of Affective Expression: *J* maintained a superficial facade of feeling comfortable and at ease with *E* and the tests. The nature of her responses and asides, however, belied this facade and revealed the disassociated nature of her affects.

Summary

Given the referring problem of the suicide attempt, this protocol causes grave concern for the possibility that *J* could suicide or hurt someone else. She is driven by aggressive impulses of a sadistic nature whose only relief would be her own death. Although she is capable of using intellectual defenses of an obsessive-compulsive nature, these very defenses can be easily intruded upon by idiosyncratic associations, leaving her at the mercy of her impulses. Furthermore, of particular concern are the flaws in her judgment, the dissociative quality to her affect, her paranoid ideations, loss of distance, breaks in reality testing, implications of delusional experiences, and total lack of self-reflection.

Thus *J* is in immediate need of hospitalization for inpatient treatment. The diagnosis is paranoid schizophrenia.

Diagnosis

DSM-III-R

Axis I: 295.34 Schizophrenic paranoid, chronic with acute exacer-
bation

Axis II: 301.83 Borderline Personality Disorder

Axis III: None

Axis IV: 3-Moderate

Axis V: 20

We recommend immediate hospitalization for protection of J and others.
With good treatment and maturation, her prognosis is still poor.

Psychological Test Data

J: 15–2 Female

Wechsler–Bellevue, Form I

		Weighted Score
Verbal Tests		
Information		11
Comprehension		11
Digit Span		6
Arithmetic		4
Similarities		11
(Vocabulary)		(7)
	Total	43
Performance Tests		
Picture Arrangement		9
Picture Completion		9
Block Design		7
Object Assembly		15
Digit Symbol		10
	Total	50

	Weighted Score	IQ
Verbal Scale	43	97
Peformance Scale	50	102
Full Scale	93	99

Information

		Score
1.	Eisenhower	1
2.	Regulates temperature	1
3.	Trees	1
4.	Europe—next to the Virgin Islands	0
5.	Quart—2	1
6.	52	1
7.	Rome	1
8.	Tokyo	1
9.	5'5"	1
10.	Wright brothers	1
11.	South America	1
12.	I don't know.	0
13.	Circulates blood all over body	1
14.	Not sure—Shakespeare?	1
15.	Ten thousand—no, too much, I don't know.	0
16.	I don't know.	0
17.	Know it, but no.	0
18.	Africa	1
19.	Mark Twain	1
20.	Seat of the Catholic Roman Church, where the Pope stays	1
21.	Book of—wait—of Arabs, the Bible.	1
22.	No.	0
23.	Knew it once—something legal, but forget it.	0
24.	Don't know.	0
25.	No.	0

Total 16

Comprehension

		Score
1.	Put it in the mailbox	2
2.	Go to the manager of the theater	2
3.	So we won't get their bad traits	1
4.	Country can't be run alone—depends on taxes for free agencies	1
5.	Because more durable and more stylish	1
6.	Things can be built that profit more—oh, because it's harder to get	2
7.	Make a little fire—take a bunch of leaves and make it go until someone saw me	0
8.	To maintain justice	1
9.	If didn't have a license bigamy could be committed, and also prove couple was married	1
10.	Because can't hear and learn to speak by hearing words [*Is in good humor.*]	2

Total 13

Digit Span
 F 5 + B 4   Total Score   9

Arithmetic

		Score
1.	9	1
2.	4	1
3.	0	0

4.	10	0
5.	8	1
6.	34	0
7.	25	1
8.	0	0
9.	0	0
10.	0	0

Total 4

I can't do anything with numbers. I have to count on my fingers, even for easy ones.

Similarities

		Score
1.	Both fruits	2
2.	Both clothes	2
3.	Both animals	2
4.	Both vehicles	2
5.	Both give information—communication	2
6.	Both substances—chemical substances. My science is bad also.	0
7.	Both part of tree	0
8.	Both part of the human being—both found in same body —same source	1
9.	Both reproduce	1
10.	Both express feeling	2
11.	Both express feeling. I lose questions, forget what was just said.	0
12.	Fly is usually found around a tree if it's a fruit tree That's another problem—I forget from page to page when I'm reading—even what book it is.	0

Total 14

Vocabulary

		Score
1.	Fruit that's edible by man or any living thing.	1
2.	Animal in horse family—could be ridden.	1
3.	An individual or anything else collaborates with something else, they become—what could they become? They become a union or organization.	1
4.	A stone from rocks—used with a sign of wealth, I guess.	0
5.	Person or thing that's unpleasant, unbearable—creates disturbance.	1
6.	Coat—skin layer—hair layer of animals used for coats.	1
7.	Soft layer used as protection.	1
8.	English money, equivalent to a penny, I think.	1
9.	Means of making money when not sure, losing money, put into something, not sure get anything from it.	1
10.	Part of a pig. That fatty part used for eating or frying.	1
11.	Piece of metal used for keeping something together.	1
12.	Never heard of it.	0
13.	Change color by lightening it.	1
14.	Place where armor is stored.	0
15.	A tale.	1
16.	End of a hat.	1
17.	Place where, I think unjustly, place of execution.	1
18.	Something—said it's many people—of a few. People and not of one.	1
19.	Stay by one's self—alone.	1
20.	Fatty part of an animal—glycerine is—my brother's teacher is going to kill me	0

21. Part of a song.   1
22. Used to enlarge things that cannot be seen by naked eye.   1
23. No.   0
24. No.   0
25. Take out and replant. [Q] Oh, receding hairline—going back. [*laughs*]   1
26. Don't know. Is it some sort of complex, inflicted? Not sure.   0
27. Never heard of it.   0
28. No.   0
29. No.   0
30. No.   0
31. Planning some sort of harm on one's enemy. Destroying a vehicle by bomb or means of destruction that belongs to science.   0
32. No.   0
33. A flying animal.   0
34. Means of death. Japanese used to commit hara-kiri.   1
35. No.   0
36. Depilatory—no.   0
37. No.   0
38. No.   0
39. No.   0

Total   19 (20)

[*Frequent self-derogation.*]

Picture Arrangement

	Time		Score
1.	3"	PAT	2
2.	17"	ABCD	2
3.	11"	LMNO	2
4.	19"	JNAET	3
5.	14"	SALUEM	1
6.	21"	GEFHIJ	0

Total   10

Picture Completion

		Score
1.		1
2.		1
3.		1
4.		1
5.		0
6.		1
7.		0
8.		1
9.		1
10.	No hand holding the pitcher.	0
11.	I don't know if poor dear had an accident, but she's missing an arm.	0
12.		1
13.	The socket is missing.	0
14.	No eyebrows.	1
15.		1

Total   10

Block Design

	Time	Score
1.	22"	3
2.	40"	3
3.	15"	4
4.	OT	0
5.	120"	3
6.	OT	0
7.	OT	0
	Total	13

Object Assembly

	Time	Score
M	27"	6
P	22" [Aside: A snob.]	9
H	39"	9
	Total	24

Digit Symbol   Total Score   43

Bender–Gestalt

1. [*Asks if can go in a slant.*]
2. [*counts*] Little distorted, but anyway.
3. [*Dissatisfied, so repeated up in corner of page.*]
4. [*Presented upside down first.*]
5. Exact number of dots?

[*Likes to talk so much E cannot record all of her associations. J finds her associations interesting and likes them.*]

[*When asked what is going to be done with the tests, a question often repeated, E said they would be used to understand her better and help her. She giggled and said*] I know, send me to an institution. [*J would not elaborate on this. She spoke of another staff member.*] She wasn't bad except she was the coldest person I ever met in my life, but I ignored that.

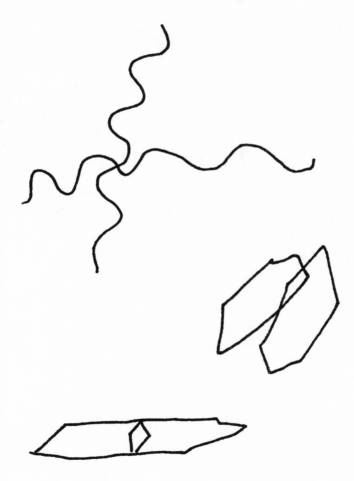

Figure Drawing

[*When asked to draw a person, J drew a female bust. When asked to draw the opposite sex, she drew a male portrait. E then requested a whole person, and J complied with a whole female, followed by a whole male.*]

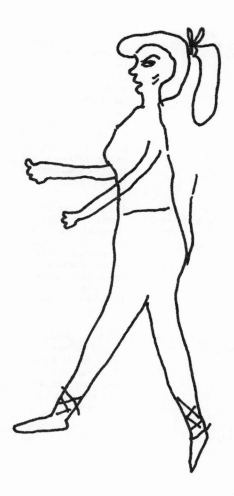

Rorschach

I.   3"

1. A lobster, a crab. [W]

1. The shape.

2. A rabbit or pig standing on a stand. [D] Center is a stand. [W]

2. Snobby rab-rab-pigs! Wild pig ready to jump on someone. Back is like hunched up together, fat—has extra large ears and this is the thing, you know, the nose, and that's all just an average pig.

II. 4"

1. A wild bull or a buffalo because it has the humps.

1. [*Humps? Head?*] Lost it in action—he's bleeding here—looks like blood, it's red. Not bleeding near head where it should be. [*Siren is heard from outside.*] One of these days they'll attack us at eleven and we won't know—we'll think it'll be the 11:00 siren—all the spies and everything.

↓ 2. Or another crab. Whole thing—little tails in the lower red projections.

2. I've never been too close to a crab. The things near the head— the things he projects [*points to* S]. Empty spot in middle, someone stepped on him— the middle fell out. [*Dead?*] I guess so.

III. 4"

1. A monkey—two monkeys.

1. Just looks like—tall, shaped like monkey's feet. Don't look like are alive—just looks dead—looks like something someone dug out of a grave.

2. A bow tie.

2. Shape. [*Q*] Yeah, could be black bow tie—this way is red bow tie.

3. Hip part of human skeleton. [*lower center shading*]

4. Two monkeys hanging from a tree. [*top reds*]

4. Swinging back and forth.

IV. 8"

↓ 1. This is depressing. A bat, exactly like a bat.

1. Flying around—wings, head—missing piece.

← 2. Two seals or sea horse.

2. Happy seals—cute little seals—look like expecting food or something.

V.	3"	1. This looks like a bat flying in orbit—flying around. No—nothing else. Just a bat.	1. Things up and wings—color not.
VI.	3"	1. Looks like two Siamese cats. This, hey, oh—	1. Purring away—look cute. These whiskers, and they're attached to each other and purring away.
		2. Looks like someone praying on a hill—man. This is hill, or like top of a cloud—hands folded together—hair is curly.	2. Man praying—a ray of sun coming down—a very holy picture. I see ray mentally, not here. Just see smudging of fingerprints.
VII.	7"		*[Repeatedly asks about other staff member]* Why did she ask so many questions and take so many notes?
		1. *[laughs]* Ever see *Uncle Tom's Cabin*—Topsy—when she gets scared? Two Topsys looking at each other.	1. [*What made look like Topsy?*] Big lips look like Negro's lips and scared—whenever I think of her, I think of braid in hair—they're looking at each other—maybe she's looking in mirror.
VIII.	3"	1. A cobra or some kind of cat on a hill ready to pounce on someone.	1. Cobras on hill ready to jump—don't see hill.
		2. Inside of intestines, like epithelial lining—inside winding of small intestines.	2. Once saw a movie, medical picture in color, and this is exactly what it looked like.
IX.	4"	1. Two clowns in a circus.	1. They're squirting water at each other because it's part of the act.

← 2. Old Mother Hubbard—a fat old woman.

2. Looks like she's mopping away—fat old back, typical. Once saw in children's books—pudgy—mop end sticking out—fat, pudgy face, small hat, and here's her dustpan and junk.

↓ 3. A weeping willow.

3. Very pretty—pink, big. Something you can picture in a fairyland.

X.   4"

↓ 1. Crabs in action.

1. Wild lobsters just look like everything is shot out.

2. Cat dancing in an alley.

Just looks like he's dancing.

3. Two crabs running up a hill or whatever they run up when in water.

4. A bagpipe.

4. In bad condition—but everything is intact. Sort of worn out—sort of half blown up because of shading—dark part is in, and light part is blown up.

5. Caterpillars biting a rabbit. A real scientific green—not much meaning.

5. Way they're twirled around and little eyes.

6. Hey, looks like wild rats.

6. In the park, running around.

7. Dachshunds.

7. Looks like something from an advertisement. Color just makes it look happier, but not the right color. None of these colors really mean anything, except in bats, because don't expect to see a red bat flying around.

TAT

1. I think he's being forced to play violin and knows he'll profit from it in future and trying to decide, should I practice or not. His conscience bothers him when he decides not and he's wondering what's so great about it anyway. [*What does he decide to do?*] He decides to play it, but he hates it so much.

5. Looks like she opened a door and found a dead person. She's terrified because probably a closely related person. Then she closes the door and calls the police. [*How die?*] A heart attack.

7 GF. Looks like the little girl is very troubled, and she always clings to that doll because she's very insecure, and the mother is trying to talk to her—tell her—talk things over. She doesn't need a doll to feel secure. There are other ways, and girl is not listening— maybe is, out of corner of ear, but trying not to show it. [*Still want to hold onto doll?*] I don't know. I'm not sure. I can't decide.

3 BM. Looks like an alcoholic and he's sort of drunk but still conscious and knows should stop drinking, but can't and just sits there for hours and hours. [*All?*] Well, he doesn't stop drinking and is found dead in his apartment.

16. I don't see anything really—never meant anything to me. I like blank paper. Leaves a lot to write on, and it's empty. It's empty.

9 GF. Looks like two girls, and one of them sees her boyfriend and her boyfriend is other woman's husband, and they're both looking and both love this man very much, but he kills himself and they're both shocked, as you can see on expressions on their faces.

2. She looks like a very lonely girl—very studious type. She's looking for friends, looking at people through corner of her eye. She doesn't trust them. She makes friends—but doesn't make friends with a human being, but made friends with a horse.

8 GF. I don't know. She looks like there's a party. She's secluded and doesn't want to join everybody else, is enjoying watching, but there's one man there that she really likes, but he's with someone else. She keeps admiring him—stay whole party and keeps admiring him and on the way home, she meets him and they get to know each other and get married.

3 GF. Oh, she looks like another alcoholic. She can't live with her husband, because she drinks too much and it's a bad influence on her children. And she has these terrible nightmares and is very confused, and all this makes her drink a lot and she's always drunk. [*Happens?*] She's put in an institution.

6 GF. I think—so she—she's a schoolteacher—looks creepy type—and he looks like another creepy teacher. Funny if I turned out to be a teacher—never know—always a big surprise. Once wanted to be a surgeon, but that depressed me—now be a social worker. And I think he wants to start an affair with her because he really likes her, but she refuses to because she's a very cold person and she—a horse is a horse, etc. [*singing theme from TV program*] Did she [*other staff member*] really expect me to answer those questions? [*I don't know what she asked, but I guess if she asked she expected answer.*] What was I up to? And she refuses to marry him, because she says we'll have a terrible marriage and not worth it. Just not very understanding person.

4. Oh, he's good looking—who's in background? Looks like he's going to war, and she doesn't want him to go to war because she knows he'll die. Oh, he's very good looking, but he's still determined to go, and he goes but he comes back and they marry.

13 MF. Did you ever see "Mr. Ed" [*a TV program*]? [*She sings the theme song and says it's the story of a horse who talks.*] Oh, what did he just do to her? I don't know. I think he's an unsuccessful husband as a husband and a businessman, and she's a very unhappy wife because he's a lousy husband, and they end up getting a divorce. [*Do to her?*] I don't know. Think they had a terrible argument—he runs out—never see each other again and have a terrible argument.

18 GF. Is this a man or a woman? I think it's her son, and they never had a real good understanding with each other. And they never have anything to say to each other—always turns out end up in an argument and he's—he is threatening to run away. Now she's really talking to him and trying. I don't think this really is a man—what is it? Hair does, but not body—trying to convince him to stay, and she guarantees they'll have a better life together. [*Believe her?*] No, he runs away.

5
The 16- to 18-Year-Old

Developmental Expectations

The growth spurts seen in the earlier years have ceased for the majority by this age. Physiological changes will continue to occur, but they will be far more slow and subtle. Identification and attachment to a group is the most important and critical aspect of social relationships now. There is less conflict with adults, except when the need to go along with the wishes of the group is threatened. Personal appearance becomes a preoccupation that is determined by the group.

Cognitive Functioning. Solidly into formal logical operations and secondary process, the 16- to 18-year-old has cognition almost equivalent to the adult. This opens up the possibility of planning for the future, and seeking avocations and activities possibly leading to interest areas for one's lifetime. Perceptual-motor coordination is well established by now; even awkward individuals are able to compensate for or cope with their difficulties.

Dynamic Picture. This age has achieved a reasonable sense of self, yet the security of this sense is still dependent upon the group. The individual by now recognizes areas of competence and difficulties in academics, athletics, social skills, and general acceptability. Individuation in self-concept apart from the group is part of the struggle and conflicts of this period. The comfort and security provided by being a member of the group create a conflict with the need to determine one's own independent identity. As the group has functioned to provide narcissistic gratification, this conflict can be particularly painful.

During this period, sexual identity and interest is evolving. Curiosity about sexuality is at its very height, and it can take the form of experimentation as well as being the interest of most peer communications. The adolescent who is excluded (or excludes himself) from the group also experiences pain and can adopt a more extreme appearance and/or behavior than the group members themselves tolerate. Excessive energy is placed in interactions with peers at this time. The intensity of these interactions can baffle adults as well as occasioning fear in the individual adolescent. In contemporary times, the pressure to have sexual experiences creates an additional conflict for the individual who does not want them or is afraid. This conflict is now heightened by the advent of the AIDS epidemic.

This age group is learning to use aggressive impulses effectively. This can lead to mild to extreme acts of aggression by the group when charged with the sexual excitement endemic to this age. These actions can be totally encompassed in the group or, on occasion, erupt to acts against others.

The greater capacity for mature thinking now permits this age adolescent to invest a great deal of energy in creative and productive pursuits. This can be done alone or with the group.

Defenses. By now the stabilization of the defenses leads to an integration into an organization that is called *personal style*. The psychological defenses are more internalized and therefore more reliable than they have been since the onset of puberty.

Affective Expression. Except for the periods when sexual and aggressive excitement is heightened, this is a time for the beginning of increasing modulation of feelings. Intense feelings are most often experienced in relation to one's peers, or in relation to conflicts with one's parents over issues of independence. There is a greater capacity now to recognize others' feelings and, therefore, to increase one's perspective on one's own feelings.

Normal Expectations on Tests

Intelligence Tests. This age is at the lowest end of the adult Wechsler. IQ scores, therefore, will be skewed (see Chapter 2) and may be somewhat higher than the actual capacity.

Bender–Gestalt. This should be accomplished according to adult standards.

Projectives. The figure drawings should be drawn with the standards for the adult form. Within the drawings, however, there will be additions of greater affective intensity to the figures, as well as specifics added reflecting the drawer's present peer concerns.

The number of responses, location, and forms of the percepts in the Rorschach should be more equal to adult standards. The content, however, will reflect the concerns of this age, including a greater *Fm* (than adult), demonstrating a greater inner tension; the possibility of C, reflecting the more explosive reaction to strong stimulation; and more percepts of reflections, revealing the preoccupation of this age with the appraisal of the self.

The TAT stories are expected to follow adult standards for the formulation of a story. These stories can vary from high drama to succinct avoidance of the affect inherent in the picture.

Representative psychological test interpretations and psychological test batteries for adolescents within this age range now follow. The raw test data from the psychological test battery follow the discussion of each adolescent, so that easy reference can be made to the examples selected for illustration of the interpretations. We include examples of adolescents diagnosed as having a reactive disorder, being mildly disturbed, moderately disturbed, and severely disturbed in order to demonstrate how a psychological portrait is developed. Each adolescent's tests are analyzed, interpreted, and concluded with an integrated summary.

As stated before, the summary is not a complete report, but represents the salient features leading to the diagnostic portrait.

Psychological Test Portrait

K: 16–0 Female

K's mother brought her for therapy because of concern over her defiant behavior. *K* is an attractive, well-groomed 16-year-old who lives with her mother, father, and older brother. She is doing well in the tenth grade of high school.

She explains her problem as being caused by her mother's intrusiveness in her life. *K* feels little support from her father and views her brother as the preferred child. She related well and worked with effort and cooperation. She seemed to enjoy the testing experience.

Cognitive Functioning

W–B, Form I: K attains a Bright Normal IQ of 115, with a Verbal Scale IQ of 105 and a Performance Scale IQ of 120. The range of weighted scores within each category (Verbal and Performance) are consistent. Although the Performance subtests are consistent within each test, the Verbal subtests show a great deal of intratest variability. This results in a lowered Verbal total score and could explain the 15-point discrepancy in IQ scores. This does not appear to be related to any problem in cognition.

K works attentively and with good concentration. There is nothing to suggest an interference in her cognitive functioning.

B–G: The Bender is a good example of accurate execution and organized placement of the figures.

FD: *K* refused to draw full figures, saying that she could not do it. Her first drawing is of the male in profile. The heads offer a clear differentiation between male and female and include all sense organs. They are well executed.

Rorschach: *K* makes good sense of the structure of the blots, giving 20 responses. This is an adequate number for this age. She makes use of all determinants in describing her percepts. She maintains a good form level, with *P*'s and an O (IX).

TAT: *K*'s stories reflect the TAT pictures accurately and are related with good sequential development.

Summary Statement of Cognitive Functioning: *K* is a bright adolescent with no disturbances in her cognitive functioning. The intratest variability in the W–B verbal area would suggest a higher potential. Overall she functions in a well-organized, accurate, and efficient manner.

Dynamic Picture

W–B, Form I: Although there are no idiosyncratic intrusions in the W–B, K adopts an immature stance in the Verbal portion of the test. Her language and conceptualizations can be childlike (Comprehension, 7, 8, 9, and 10; Similarities, 9; Vocabulary, 5). Occasional "I don't know" replies (Information, 5, 8, and 12) appear to stem from a need to portray herself in the interaction with E as dependent and naive (Comprehension, 7 and 9—" Don't know much about that yet"; Similarities, 9). When left to function by herself on the Performance portion of the test, she works with motivation and high achievement.

B–G: The Bender does not offer any dynamic interpretation.

FD: The large heads reflect a strong need for intellectual control on *K*'s part (see *Defenses*). She chooses to draw the male in profile, which is a more mature rendition, but the male looks more childlike than the female drawing. Her use of eyelashes on the male, but not on the female, gives him a more feminine mien. All of this suggests a still unresolved identity conflict.

Rorschach: *K*'s Rorschach percepts demonstrate expected adolescent concerns with introspection (VIII, 2), the body (III, 2; X, a), and sexual impulses

(VI, 1 and 3). Although *m* is to be expected at this age, K has more (5) than the usual, suggesting a greater amount of anxiety than usual. This appears to be related primarily to concerns about her sexual impulses. Again, although identity conflict is to be expected in adolescence, hers is heightened (VII, 1 and 2).

K's *FM* exceeds her sufficient number of *M*'s, speaking to some immaturity at this stage. In addition, the content of some percepts are childlike (II, 2; IV, 1 and 2) and can be seen as threatening (IV, 2; VIII, 1). She responds to this threat with anger (III, 1—"splattered liquid"; X, 4), as if she felt herself forced into such a position.

K presents the usual adolescent conflict between a longing to regress to childhood while wishing, and having, the capacity for good mature relationships. Mature interaction, however, is pictured as acrimonious (II, 2; III, 1). Even when she provides a positive *M* (VIII, 1), it is contradicted by the immediately following percept of fighting (VII, 2). Her good use of *C* and *c* (II, 1; V, 1 and 2; VIII, 2; IX, 1), though, demonstrates excellent potential for satisfactory interpersonal relationships.

TAT: K's TAT stories clearly present her conflict. Although she can conceive of positive mature relationships (10), there is the persistent threat through the stories of feeling pressured to grow faster (5 and 7 G) than she views her capabilities (1, 3 BM, and 2). She is in the midst of a struggle between independence and dependence (6 BM) and maturing and being nurtured (13 G). A few of the stories (1, 3 BM, and 3 GF) suggest she has not felt that there has been or will be sufficient nurturance.

Summary Statement of Dynamic Picture: K presents the tpyical adolescent dilemma of wanting to be mature and independent while longing to regress to a more childlike position. This struggle is complicated for her by her sense of neediness, as if she feels she is not yet ready to go on developing.

Defenses

W–B, Form I: Generally, K uses a good intellectual approach to the W–B. Specifically in the Verbal portion of the test she uses denial (Comprehension, 9), avoidance (Information, 5, 8, and 12), and regression (Comprehension, 7 and 9; Similarities, 4, 5, and 7; Vocabulary, 5). The use of these more primitive defenses seems to be aroused by the fact that E is asking questions. This certainly seems clear when contrasted to K's handling of the Performance items. E's questions may be perceived by K as a demand, inducing a more immature stance on her part (Comprehension 9 states this explicitly: ". . . don't know much about that yet.").

B–G: Similarly to her functioning on the Performance items of the W–B, *K* executes the Bender in an organized and accurate rendition.

FD: Both *K*'s refusal to draw the whole figure and the size of the heads she produces speak to a strong need for intellectual control. Her refusal to draw bodies is a way of avoiding anxiety aroused by impulses she experiences. Her rendition of the male as more immature and feminine than the female would seem to be an attempt to deny the threat of masculinity.

Rorschach: *K*'s good intellectual control is seen in her use of the structure and variety of determinants throughout the Rorschach. There are specific instances showing intellectual control over impulsive discharge (III, 2; IV, 1). Her excessive use of *FM*'s speaks, again, to her defensive strategy of regression when faced with the possibility that she may experience anxiety. In addition, we see frequent use of projection (III, 1; VII, 1 Inquiry and 2 Inquiry; VIII, 1 and 2 Inquiry) and distancing (II, 1 Inquiry and 2 Inquiry; IV, 1 and 2; V, 2 Inquiry; IX, 1).

TAT: *K*'s intellectual defenses permit her to produce accurate and sequentially organized stories. Obsessiveness appears for the first time in her protocol in response to the stimuli of 3 BM and 8 GF. She is able to avoid the aggression on 3 BM by ignoring the gun. Her initial response to 3 GF, "Wow! Who'd she kill?" is modified by her laughter, then by avoidance through "running" and subsequent "grief." Her laughter attempts to modify the aggression implicit in this story, as well as in her stories to 13 G and 5. She utilizes distancing in 13 G and 2, but loses distance when she interprets 5 as reflecting her difficulties with her mother.

Summary Statement of Defenses: *K* has good intellectual defenses that serve her well when she does not perceive interpersonal interaction as evoking aggressive or dependency needs. At such times she uses regression, avoidance, projection, and occasionally, obsessiveness and distancing.

Affective Expression

W–B, Form I: There is no indication of distress on K's part throughout the Wechsler. She seemed to enjoy the intellectual challenge of this test.

B–G: *K* also proceeded throughout the Bender as if she enjoyed copying the figures.

FD: Once *E* accepted *K*'s refusal to draw the whole person, *K* enjoyed completing this task. The heads themselves do not reveal any particular affect.

Rorschach: Although *K* enjoyed the demands of the Rorschach, her description of her percepts reveals a greater variety of affective experiences. There are many examples of the projection of anger and aggressivity (II, 2; III, 2; VI, 1; VII, 2; VIII, 1). Anger expressed through hostile impulses are seen in her "splattering" percepts (III, 1; X, 4). Anxiety is seen in her many *m*'s (III, 1 Inquiry; VI, 1 and 3; VIII, 2 Inquiry; X, 4).

The potential to interact with tact and sensitivity is seen in her *c*'s (I, 1 Inquiry; II, 1 Inquiry; VI, 1 Inquiry; VIII, 2). Her use of *FC* (II, 1 Inquiry) and *CF* (VIII, 2; IX, 1) indicates her potential and need to relate positively to others.

TAT: In spite of one instance of being "mad" (5) and one of "grief" (3 GF), *K* portrays the affective experience of the characters in her stories as happy or at least "not too unpleasant." This suggests the denial of her own anger and sadness.

Summary Statement of Affective Expression: K portrays herself as a person who feels pleasantly most of the time, with the one notable exception of anger at her mother. There are, however, strong indications of anger, hostility, anxiety, and feelings of helplessness.

Summary
K is an adolescent girl who is able to achieve a Bright Normal IQ, demonstrating good cognitive capabilities. She is struggling with the usual concerns of adolescence over independence versus dependence, insecurities about her body, and the pressure of sexual impulses. Also common in adolescence is her investment in introspection. Although her anxiety and distress over these concerns is excessive for her age, she copes with them primarily by the use of intellectual controls. When the anxiety mounts, she regresses to a more immature stance as a dependent and naive young girl. When faced with her projection of demands for growth and maturity, *K* intensifies her defensive maneuvers with denial, avoidance, projection, and distancing. This most often occurs when she experiences sexual and aggressive impulses or is faced with situations in which they are implicit.

Generally *K* expresses a positive affect, but she experiences anger and helplessness with rising anxiety in response to her perception of her mother and other adults as infantilizing and controlling.

Diagnosis

DSM-III-R

Axis I: 313.81 Oppositional Defiant Disorder (Mild)
Axis II: None
Axis III: None
Axis IV: 2-Mild
Axis V: 75-Mild

It is recommended that *K* begin psychotherapy. Her insistence on an immature stance will make the initial phases of treatment difficult. Her capacity to relate, her ability to introspect and her good intellect all point to a positive prognosis.

Psychological Test Data

K: 16–0 Female

W–B, Form I

		Weighted Score
Verbal Tests		
Information		10
Comprehension		10
Digit Span		9
Arithmetic		9
Similarities		11
(Vocabulary)		(11)
	Total	50
Performance Tests		
Picture Arrangement		12
Picture Completion		14
Block Design		14
Object Assembly		13
Digit Symbol		12
	Total	65

	Weighted Score	IQ
Verbal Scale	50	105
Performance Scale	65	120
Full Scale	115	115

Information

Score

1. Eisenhower   1
2. Glass object for measuring temperature   1
3. Tree   1
4. England   1
5. [*laughs*] I forgot.   0
6. 52   1
7. Venice?   0
8. I don't know.   0
9. 5'6"   1
10. Wilbur and Orville Wright   1
11. South America   1
12. Don't know.   0
13. Circulates blood through the body   1
14. Shakespeare   1
15. Don't know.   0
16. February?   0
17. Peary   1
18. Asia   0
19. Mark Twain   1
20. Home of Pope   1
21. Don't know.   0
22. Shakespeare   0
23. A writ—can't remember.   0
24. Study of something   0
25. Don't know.   0
                                                            ___

                                               Total   13

Comprehension

Score

1. Mail it.   2
2. I don't think I'd yell out. Go first and fast to head of movie
    theater—shouldn't cause panic.   2
3. Bad influence—you're judged by people you're with.   2
4. Law—support state and country problems. [Q] Finances—
    things like that.   2
5. Durable and comfortable—not all shoes are made of leather.   1
6. Location to be near work and transportation.   0
7. Wander until nighttime. Don't know what I'd have with me
    to attract someone at dusk—find a clearing.   0
8. Sad states of affairs if no laws to regulate people—for the
    country's and person's benefit—if the country is to run right
    must have laws.   1
9. Have to undergo certain tests—has something to do with
    population. [Q] Don't know—don't know much about that yet.   0
10. Can't hear sound of own voice and others. [Q] If can't hear,
    can't get picture of what saying—can mouth and hope it
    comes out right—can only see others' mouths.   1
                                                                                     ___

                                                                    Total   11

Digit Span

F7 + B4   Total Score   11

Arithmetic

		Score
1.		1
2.		1
3.		1
4.		1
5.	(*At 30" looked as if not going to answer, so E asked.*) 64	0
6.	(*had it correct, then changed*) 15	0
7.		1
8.	Can't do it. (40") $200	0
9.	72 yards	0
10.	96 (at 35")	2
	Total	7

Similarities

		Score
1.	Fruits	2
2.	Both clothing and inanimate objects. [*laughs*] Don't know why I stuck in inanimate objects.	2
3.	Both four-legged animals	2
4.	Both have wheels	1
5.	News—weather. [Q] Daily happenings that are important.	1
6.	Both contain moisture	0
7.	Both burn	1
8.	Sense organs	2
9.	Both unfinished form of the adult—of same classification.	2
10.	Show picture of the same thing—can both represent same thing or one can describe the other	0
11.	Aftermath of some action, result of . . .	0
12.	Both outdoors	0
	Total	13

Vocabulary

		Score
1.	Round fruit, usually red	1
2.	Four-legged animal shorter than horse, resembles horse	1
3.	Union. [Q] Coming together of objects or persons.	1
4.	Precious gem—usually used in marriage	1
5.	[*laughs*] What my mother calls me—annoying, nagging person or animal. [Q] Annoying more.	1
6.	Soft, fuzzy skin	1
7.	Comfortable foam seat	1
8.	Some kind of money. [Q] Don't know.	1/2
9.	To bet something—usually money	1
10.	Food that comes from a pig. [Q] Eaten raw causes trichinosis.	1
11.	Small steel, metal pointed object—to hold something together— also nail on your finger	1
12.	A type of tree	1
13.	To color something	1
14.	I think of tall building by school—the armory. [Q] Stone building—pointed towers—cannons outside—training there for army.	1
15.	Aesop's fables—type of ancient tale	1

16.	Edge	1
17.	Used in France—beheaded—two pieces of steel and one wood comes down	1
18.	Double	1/2
19.	Isolate	1
20.	Some chemical. [Q] Don't know.	1
21.	Segment—sort of paragraph of song or poetry	1
22.	Magnification instrument with a long eye piece [*goes into lengthy description*]	1
23.	Don't know.	0
24.	Usually tower on church—bell is there	1
25.	Draw back	1
26.	Some sort of handicap—not necessarily broken leg—could be a disease.	1/2
27.	Type of metal or pottery	1/2
28.	[*shakes head*] I'm going home and look it up.	0
29.	Flinging object—a machine like—	0
30.	Ornament	1/2
31.	Something dangerous having to do with the government	0
32.	Can't remember—have heard of eminent person	0
33.	[*shakes head no*]	0
34.	Chinese or Japanese suicide—matter of honor	1
35.	Don't know.	0
36.	Having to do with work—all I know.	0
37.	[*laughs*] No.	0
38.	No!	0
39.	Nope!	0

Total 24 1/2

Picture Arrangement

	Time	Order	Score
1.	7"	PAT	2
2.	10"	ABCD	2
3.	2"	LMNO	2
4.	19"	JANET	3
5.	21"	SALEUM	1
6.	35"	EFGHIJ	4

Total 14

Picture Completion

		Score
1.		1
2.		1
3.		1
4.		1
5.	Claw	1
6.		1
7.		1
8.		1
9.		1
10.		1
11.		1
12.		1

13. Filament		0
14.		1
15.		1
		—
	Total	14

Block Design

	Time	*Score*
1.	5"	6
2.	15"	4
3.	12"	4
4.	23"	4
5.	33"	5
6.	80"	4
7.	165"	3
		—
	Total	30

Object Assembly

	Time	*Score*
M	16"	6
P	38"	8
H	41"	8
		—
	Total	22

Digit Symbol   Total Score   50

Bender–Gestalt

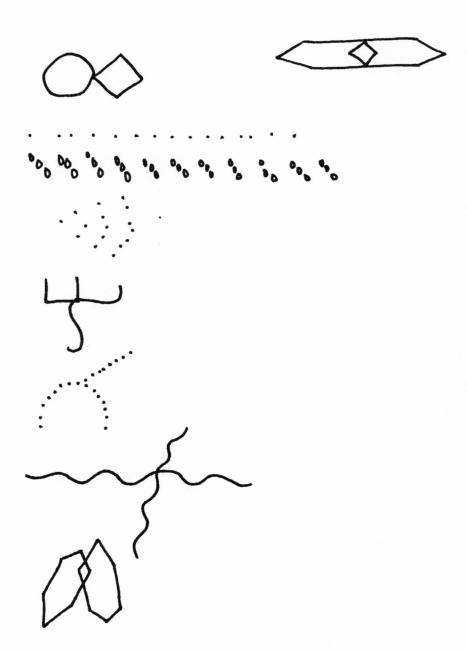

Figure Drawings

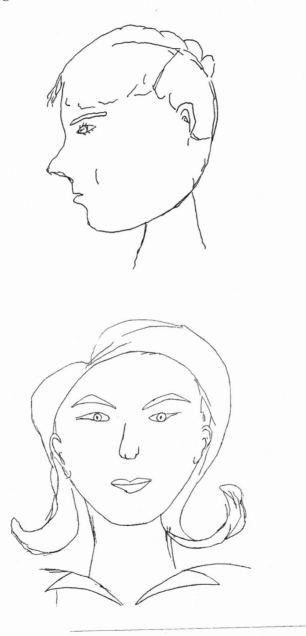

Rorschach

I.   1"

1. Crab. [Else?] No.

1. The shape of the claws reminded me. And this [shading] like sort of a colored shell that stands away, this middle part. These [lateral D's] are like the side claws but should be narrower. It's crawling.

II.

Can I turn it upside down?

3"

1. A butterly.

1. The larger part [*black*] is the wings. [Q] Because of the upper red antenna-like protrusions. The coloring reminds me of a butterfly and the shadings on the wings. Not that they're exactly that color. [Q] It is like some my brother mounted.

2. Two people yelling at each other.

2. They may be sitting down facing each other [*pointing to "knees"*]. It did remind me of two people yelling— like a cartoon. [Q] The shape of the mouths reminded me of yelling and these marks [dd's] like in a cartoon.

III.   5"

1. Two people fighting, looks like they're breaking things up.

1. I can't explain. They don't look exactly like people—it's just the outline. They are fighting. [Q] Because something has fallen against the wall and splattered [*red* D's]—a liquid.

a. A fly [Dr]. Have you ever seen one up close? Because of the big eyes—they are darker than the rest of the body. These things are what they walk on [*long* D's].

		2. Two skeletons.	2. We have a lot of skeletons in biology class—they remind me of those. [Q] Because of the lower jaw and the large back portion of the head.
IV.	5"	1. [*frowns*] A prehistoric archeopteryx [*spelled it for* E]. It's a bird with a very large wing span. It doesn't have feathers—a long beak. This is flying over something—an ugly bird! [*later tells E that it is a pterodactyl*]	1. [Q] The form—it's an underview. I saw one in a book. It has a long neck and head—it's ugly. There are no features—just skin covering the bone. [Q] Because of the grayish coloring. When there are feathers it has a perfect, smooth form.
		2. Some monster somebody dreamed up for a comic book. I'd say it's walking.	2. [Q] It looks exactly like one I saw in a comic book I was just reading. The eyes are here [*inner shading*]—if you saw it, you'd know what I mean. He's coming at something. The hands are out from the body.
V.	1"	1. A butterfly—definitely.	1. Because of the antenna and wings and perfect shape on both sides. [Q] It's flying.
		2. From either direction it's a butterfly. [*hands card back to* E.]	2. Upside down it looks like it's mounted—because it's the way my brother mounted them.
VI.	10"	1. A bomb exploding.	1. It starts here [*upper* D] in the smallest part—this looks like flames. [Q] The shape of flames and darkness on edges. The upper part is like a fuming cloud of smoke, and it would get larger as it goes up and sort of fades.
		2. A bird or animal	2. This looks like a bird because of the shape. It's flying up.

| | | 3. Or some sort of rocket taking off. | 3. Haven't you ever seen a rocket taking off? It jets out smoke and gas like this [D], and the upper part is just a rocket. |

VII. 5"

1. Two people about to kiss.

1. Would say boy and girl but they look like twins [*laughs*]. It doesn't look like they're talking, as their mouths aren't open. I included the necks. [Q] Because of the face and shape.

2. A dog and a cat about to fight.

2. Because mouths are open, and they're backing off that way. The mouth is snarling. [Q] They're too fierce to be people.

VIII. 5"

That's pretty.

10"

1. A panther stalking its prey.

1. They're on some rocks. [Q] Because of their sleek, smooth skin— their heads are down sort of low, and they have thin bodies. [Q] Looks like rocks because wouldn't be level ground because of the different colors and separations [S]. The choppiness gives that effect.

2. A reflection on a pool—of the setting sun.

2. It's just as it would be seen on the water—the way it shades into different colors—quite nice. [Q] It looks like shimmering water partly because of the breaks [S]. [Q] The reflection itself—the changing of colors and the rippling water.

IX.   10"

1. I don't see any-
   thing [*turns card*].
   Maybe a kaleido-
   scope, but that's
   all.

1. I don't see a kaleido-
   scope, just thought of
   that because of the
   shapes and colors.
   [*Looking through
   something?*] No
   [laughs]—just looks
   like three blots of color
   put on paper and
   folded [puts card down
   emphatically].

X.   2"

1. Spiders for one.

1. [*blue D's*] The many
   extensions and one
   color. [*Q*] No—not because of blue—I never
   saw a blue spider!

a. I see something else. A
   trachea and lungs—
   here are the kidneys.
   [*Q*] Because of the
   shape and location—
   the heaviness here [in
   "lungs"] and this tube-
   like structure.

2. Crabs for another.

2. Just the color of crabs,
   and also the shape and
   claws. They're crawling
   along.

3. Sea horses for a
   third.

3. The shape [*points out
   tail and head*].

4. Something splat-
   tered against a wall.

4. Because of all the ex-
   tensions. This [*pink D*]
   looks like semi-hard
   something that splat-
   ters like an egg and
   then drips down. [*Q*]
   Not actually an egg—
   just something.

b. An animal lying down.
   [*Q*] A bear—light-
   ness at edge of nose—
   shape.

TAT

1. This boy grew up with a longing to play instruments. He was blind and couldn't play and is just sitting there looking longingly at his father's or brother's violin. But in time I think he'll learn to play it. [Q] No, that's all.

3BM. This boy or girl had just been hurt one way or other . . . either had a fight or was hurt . . . is in his or her room crying or just feeling bad. I couldn't tell you what would happen. [Q] They're hurt mentally, not physically. [Q] I couldn't tell . . . it may or may not work out.
It's amazing what you can tell about a person from pictures.

10. I'd say these people separated for quite some time and they just found each other. They're embracing. [Q] I'd say it wasn't a willful separation—it was not a trip or that someone wanted to go away . . . maybe he went to the Army. [*Feeling?*] They're very happy . . . I just get that feeling . . . quite satisfied and content. They look as though they can't say anything at the moment. There it ends.
Whoever did these [the cards] is good.

13G. Oh, gosh! The only impression I get is . . . this woman going up the steps may be a nurse. She's going up the steps to help or see a patient. [*Thinking and feeling?*] She's hurrying. [*Before?*] Either the patient is in pain or . . . I guess that's it. [*Outcome?*] [*laughs*] This is like Ben Casey . . . she'll make him more comfortable—just ease his pain, I guess.

5. Wow! [*softly, then laughs*] This is just like . . . I was talking in the living room on the phone and everyone was yelling. The door opens—my mother comes in and says, "Get off the phone or I'll put my hand on the receiver this instant" [*laughs*]. [*Outcome?*] I get off the phone [*laughs*], but not willingly, of course. [*Feeling?*] Mad!

3 GF. Wow! Who'd she kill? [*laughs*] I get the feeling she's running from something. She's opening the door and walking out of the room. I'd say a relative just died and had just been pronounced dead, and from the looks of it I don't think she'd ever get over the grief of it. At that point she feels as though the world is coming to an end. [*Relative?*] Her parents. [*Both?*] One or the other . . . I'd say the one she's closest with.

2. I'd say this was a girl standing in front of a picture but not in it herself . . . a schoolgirl . . . that's all I can say. [*Before?*] She could have been learning about how people of different lands work and make a living. She may be learning about farming. [*Feeling?*] I think she'd feel they work very hard.

6 BM. The boy in the picture was the woman's son . . . and, of course, he has his hat and coat on. He's leaving. He has a determined but a sad face. The mother looks very forlorn and feels bad her son is leaving. [*Before?*] He was tied to his mother's apron strings too long and decided to try it on his own, I guess. [*Outcome?*] He won't make it at first, but after a while he will. I'd say it might involve a job.

7 G. [*gazes at arm's length, wry smile*] The girl looks as though she's getting a lecture. She plays with dolls too much . . . she doesn't do the things required of her, and her mother is telling her that. [*Feelings?*] Disgusted. She's not going to do it. [*What?*] Whatever her mother says . . . work . . . [*puts card down*].

8 GF. A very nice painting . . . I like it. I'd say it's raining outside, and this woman had just finished cleaning and no one was home. She had just finished looking out the window . . . she had turned around—I'd say, recalling something—and things . . . so . . . [*Like what?*] It could be either something pleasant or unpleasant—not too unpleasant . . . I think . . . longingly. [*Outcome?*] It's going to stop raining and she'll go back to whatever she was doing—housework.

Psychological Test Portrait

L: 16–0 Female

L was referred by her therapist for a differential diagnosis before beginning treatment. *L* had sought therapy because she had begun to fail in school and was unable to lose weight.

L is the oldest of three children who live with their mother after the parents' recent separation. The parents have reportedly had an unstable relationship for many years, with frequent fighting. She is an overweight girl who dresses in an immature style for her age. She cooperated throughout the testing and seemed interested in what the tests would reveal.

Cognitive Functioning

WAIS: *L* proceeded throughout the WAIS in a workmanlike way. She achieves a Superior IQ of 124, with a Superior Verbal IQ of 128 and a Bright Normal Performance IQ of 116. Her responses were always to the point, showing excellent use of language and concepts. Her strength is obviously in the verbal area, with her lowest score being in Arithmetic. In the latter test she gave answers unusually quickly to most of the items and seemed unwilling to take the time to work on the more difficult items; in other words, the lowered score does not seem to be the result of a problem with her computational ability. On the Performance test, in contrast, attention to accuracy took precedence over speed.

B–G: *L*'s Bender is well organized in the placement of the figures, and for the most part, the figures are reproduced accurately. There are indications of carelessness, perhaps related to too-quick execution.

FD: Although *L*'s figures were drawn quickly, resulting in simple figures, she does clearly differentiate the sexes. In spite of the speed of her sketching, she also makes adequately proportioned figures.

Rorschach: *L* was invested in achieving on the Rorschach, producing 47 responses. She utilizes the structure of the blots, attaining *P*'s and *O*'s. It is noteworthy that with all this effort she does not utilize color or shading. There is, in contrast, an unusually high number of *S* (6).

TAT: *L* tells well-organized stories to the TAT taking all aspects of the cards into account.

Summary Statement of Cognitive Functioning: L is a very bright 16-year-old whose primary strength is in the verbal area. She worked with effort and diligence throughout the tests, with a strong drive for achievement. When she does not feel challenged, she seemingly tends to do the task too quickly, resulting in carelessness.

Dynamic Picture

WAIS: The WAIS demonstrates L's cognitive functioning as essentially free of dynamic intrusions.

B–G: *L*'s Bender, with its minor slips and size variability, reflects the carelessness of her approach to this task. This suggests a dismissive attitude toward a task she may have considered unworthy of her effort.

FD: *L*'s anemic-looking people lack any substantiality. At best the sexes are distinguishable. There is no elaboration of any clothing. The male's head is tenuously connected to his body, and there is a lack of delineation seen in his missing eyebrows, fingers, and feet. This overall feeling of insubstantiality is seen particularly in the doll the female is holding, which appears to be suspended in air. These qualities of indefiniteness and insubstantiality convey the sense of *L*'s feelings of vulnerability and childlike dependency.

Rorschach: *L* produces percepts that indicate a need to make a symbiotic tie to another (I, 1; VI, 2, 3, and 5). Other examples of her feelings of immaturity are seen in the pervasive use of animal percepts as well as nonhuman *M*'s (I, 3; IX, 1 and 2). This wish for a regressive position carries with it a threatening potential seen in the F- obtained in I, 1, the frequent use of crabs with claws (II, 1; III, 2; IV, 4; VIII, 3; X, 2), the percept of "tongs" (VI, 4), and the "angry men" (VI, 5). As long as she does not sense a connection to another, she is left feeling incomplete (III, 6—an incomplete head; VII, 4—an incomplete canary; VIII, 5). These percepts are all seen in edge detail and space (*S*), reflecting an anger with her status. There is a lack of *C* responses, implying a difficulty in attaining satisfactory interpersonal relationships.

The nature of the emerging self as experienced in adolescence is translated by *L* into a wish for a rebirth or a new beginning (II, 3; VII, 3; IX, 4). The many phallic percepts (II, 1; III, 4; the handling of all of VI; VIII, 4; IX, 3; X, 4), as well as the fact that all of her *M*'s are male suggest that *L* may have a fantasy of rebirth as a strong and powerful male.

The percept in IV, 2, of "trees hanging" (*m*) with "spooky" aspects and "black shadows" (*C'*) reflect anxiety about strong suicidal impulses.

TAT: Most of *L*'s stories in the TAT describe unpleasant interactions between people. These interactions can be at the level of fighting (2, 3 BM, 4, 6 BM, and 10), or more dangerously, shooting by accident (8 BM and 13 MF). The only pleasant interactions are when it is a request from a child to her mother (7 GF), when a child is asleep (12 M), or when no one has "to worry about anything" (16).

An inability to make good relationships, as noted in the Rorschach, is seen in most of her stories.

Summary Statement of Dynamic Picture: L's cognitive functioning is free of any dynamic intrusions. Immaturity and difficulty in relating to others lead to a push for a symbiotic connection. The fear of phallic aggressiveness is countered by a wish for rebirth as a strong masculine self. The potential for suicide is of concern.

Defenses

WAIS: L's intellectual defenses function well for her throughout this test.

B–G: The Bender reveals in its careless errors a relaxation of her compulsivity.

FD: *L* mainly uses avoidance in drawing her figures, abandoning any obsessive or compulsive efforts.

Rorschach: *L*'s intellectual defenses permit good use of the structural aspects of the blots. Her pervasive defense throughout is regression, seen in the sparsity of human movement and in the numerous animal responses as compared to few human or humanlike responses. Avoidance of color and shading speaks to her problems in relating to others. Projection with potential agressive connotations is seen in I, 4; II, 6; and VI, 5. This defense is also seen in the arbitrariness of her locations in space, where she reverses figure and ground. Another frequent defense is oppositionalism, seen in the many *S* responses.

TAT: Again, *L*'s intellectual defenses allow her to produce an accurate accounting of the TAT pictures. Denial is used in countering the phallic aggressive implications of guns by stating that the gun "is broken" (3 BM), and that there is no intent to shoot (8 BM and 13 MF).

Summary Statement of Defenses: L has good working intellectual defenses. In addition, she uses regression, avoidance, projection, denial, and oppositionalism.

Affective Expression

WAIS: L seemed to enjoy the WAIS.

B–G: *L* applied herself to the Bender, displaying no distress over her careless slips.

FD: *L*'s drawings appear bland and affectless. She executed the drawings quickly and dismissively, which may have betrayed a disdain for the task or an anxiety relating to it.

Rorschach: *L* seemed to enjoy the intellectual challenge of the Rorschach. Her responses, however, are devoid of C, and affect expressed in the content reflects only dread (IV, 2; IX, 2) and anger (VI, 5; X, 2).

TAT: Most of *L*'s stories reflect angry and dangerous interactions between people. Her only pleasant content relates to children and "not having to worry" (16).

Summary Statement of Affective Expression: As long as L can utilize her intellectual competence, she seems to enjoy the tasks. Her expressed experience of interpersonal interactions contains unpleasant feelings.

Summary

L's superior intelligence and good use of intellectual defenses makes her school failure directly attributable to dynamic conflicts.

She is an unhappy adolescent who has a sense of isolation and distance from others. This seems to be related to her longing for a symbiotic connection to another. Fantasies of rebirth as a male point to a rejection of her femininity, resulting in a strong identification conflict. The fantasies of rebirth also contain a wish for a regression to a dependent and immature status. This may be her solution to perceiving males as aggressively threatening; her weight problem may, indeed, serve to protect her from acknowledging her femininity and sexual impulses. Her inability to realize satisfying relationships and her portrayal of relationships as bitter, angry, and dangerous leave her despairing, resulting in suicidal ideation.

Diagnosis

DSM-III-R

Axis I: 309.00 Adjustment Disorder with Depressed Mood
Axis II: 301.82 Avoidant Personality Disorder
Axis III: None
Axis IV: 3-Moderate
Axis V: 50-Serious

The recent separation of *L*'s parents has precipitated a serious adjustment problem. Of major concern is her depression and her suicidal ideation. Her good intellectual capabilities and defenses should enable her to profit from psychotherapy.

Psychotherapy at least twice a week at this point, is recommended. Prognosis is good.

Psychological Test Data

L: 16–0 Female

WAIS

	Scaled Score
Verbal Tests	
Information	14
Comprehension	18
Arithmetic	11
Similarities	16
Digit Span	12
Vocabulary	12
Total	83

	Scaled Score
Performance Tests	
Digit Symbol	11
Picture Completion	13
Block Design	13
Picture Arrangement	13
Object Assembly	11
Total	61

	Scaled Score	*IQ*
Verbal Score	83	128
Performance Score	61	116
Full Scale Score	144	126

Information

		Score
1–4		4
5.	Tree	1
6.	Coolidge, Kennedy, Eisenhower, Johnson	1
7.	Poet	1
8.	52	1
9.	South	1
10.	South America	1
11.	5'5"	1
12.	Rome	1
13.	Dark absorbs sunlight	1
14.	February 22	1
15.	Shakespeare	1
16.	Head of Roman Catholic church—where Pope is	1
17.	3,000	1
18.	Africa	1
19.	It's continual budding—cells keep splitting and keep adding—by fission.	0
20.	200 million	1
21.	112	0
22.	Creation	1
23.	200 Fahrenheit	0
24.	Homer	1
25.	Arteries, capillaries, veins	1
26.	Don't know.	0
27.	Goethe	1
28.	Don't know.	0
29.	Certain part of Bible, not included in Bible. It's like extra special book of things not in the Bible.	1
	Total	24

Comphrension

		Score
1–2.		4
3.	Mail it.	2
4.	You are known by the company you keep. You might be forced to do something really don't want to.	2
5.	Tell somebody immediately so the place can be evacuated, but don't scream 'cause there would be panic.	1
6.	Keep U.S. running—so can have parks, and schools and things.	2
7.	Do things at the moment they should be done, and don't wait until later on.	2
8.	So children can get an education and are not forced to work and do more than they are able to do.	2
9.	Check the moss, because it grows on the north side and from north can tell other directions to where you're going.	2
10.	Be unable to—learn to talk by mimicking and don't have a model.	2
11.	More populated—more people want to live there so taxes are higher—can get more than in the country.	2
12.	So it's legal—if no license anybody could consider themselves married, and society doesn't approve of that.	1

13. People who have least amount to say say more, but it doesn't
    make much sense.   2
14. Takes more than one incident to make a happening.   2

              Total   26

Arithmetic

			Score
1–2.			2
3.	1"		1
4.	1"		1
5.	1"		1
6.	15"		1
7.	1"		1
8.	1"		1
9.	15"		1
10.	8"	$10.50	1
11.	10"	Say $1.80	0
12.	4"	100	2
13.	5"	45	0
14.	5"	48	0
		Total	12

Similarities

		Score
1.	Fruit	2
2.	Clothes	2
3.	Tools	2
4.	Animals	2
5.	Directions	2
6.	Parts of body	1
7.	Both necessary for living	2
8.	Furniture	2
9.	Start of life	2
10.	Works of art	2
11.	Don't know—oh, both organic.	2
12.	Show of love—[Q] As far as parents go—parents have to do both.	0
13.	Living	2
	Total	23

Digit Span

		Score
F8 + B5	Total Score	13

Vocabulary

		Score
1–3.		6
4.	Season. [Q] Snow and ice—very cold.	2
5.	Fix something	2
6.	First meal of the day	2
7.	Material, cloth	2

8.	Cutting something, or could be piece of something	2
9.	Put together	2
10.	Hide	2
11.	Very large	2
12.	Quicken	2
13.	Group of words with subject and predicate	2
14.	Keep under control	2
15.	Start	2
16.	Think about	2
17.	Hole in a mountain	1
18.	To give exact directions	1
19.	At home	1
20.	Take in. [Q] To eat or something like that.	2
21.	End	2
22.	Be in the way of something	2
23.	Regret	2
24.	Place to go when in trouble	1
25.	Something doesn't have match. [Q] For example, shoes, if only one it's matchless.	0
26.	Apprehensive	1
27.	Disaster	2
28.	Strength	2
29.	Quiet, sedate	2
30.	Don't know.	0
31.	Feel for someone else	2
32.	Believable	0
33.	Area around a square	2
34.	Don't know.	0
35.	Secretive.	0
36.	Don't know.	0
37.	Don't know.	0
38.	Write something somebody else has written, copy and sign your name to it	2
39	Don't know.	0
40.	Don't know.	0

Total   57

Digit Symbol   Total Score   61

Picture Completion

		Score
1.		1
2.		1
3.		1
4.		1
5.		1
6.		1
7.		1
8.		1
9.		1
10.	Don't know.	0
11.		1
12.		1
13.		1
14.		1
15.		1

16.		1
17.		1
18.		1
19.	Don't know.	0
20.		1
21.	Don't know.	0
		—
	Total	18

Block Design

	Time	*Score*
1–2.		8
3.	10"	4
4.	35"	4
5.	15"	4
6.	20"	4
7.	35"	5
8.	48"	5
9.	100"	4
10.	90"	4
		—
	Total	42

Picture Arrangement

	Order	*Time*	*Score*
1–2.			8
3.		8"	4
4.	ATOMIC	15"	4
5.	OPENS	25"	4
6.	AJENT	10"	0
7.	EFGHIJ	25"	6
8.	SAMUEL	25"	5
			—
		Total	31

Object Assembly

	Time	*Score*
M	15"	7
P	22"	13
H	75"	7
E	170"	8
		—
	Total	35

Bender–Gestalt

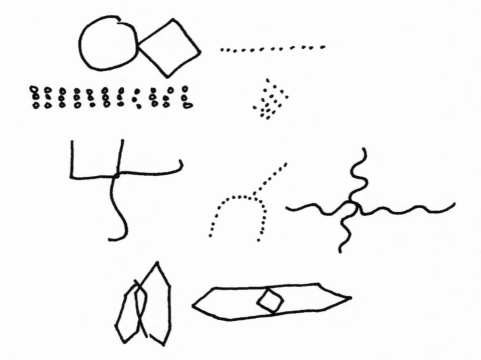

Figure Drawings

Rorschach

I.   1"

1. Two dogs back to back—profile, head and body.

1. [*Dogs?*] I don't know. [Q] Face attracted me first.

2. Frog.

2. Looks like a frog. [Q] Just had funny looking head.

3. These look like goblins, four of them [S's].

3. [*Goblins?*] White form and shape they were in.

4. These seem to be the heads of two people. That's all.

4. [*Heads?*] Reminded me of hippies. Seemed to be long-haired men. [Q] Way form was.

II.

Hmmm . . .

10"   ↓↑ 1. A crab. [Q] The red [*bottom*].

1. [*Crab?*] Claws and just looks like perfect picture of a crab.

→ 2. Two rabbits.

2. Looks like perfect pictures—ears and little nose.

↑ 3. Two snails coming out of shell [*top red*].

3. [Snails?] Shells seemed obvious—seemed like slithering out. [Q] Looks like a shell.

4. Overhead view of head of bird.

4. [*Bird?*] Like looking down and it's flying, and way beak was and head.

5. Duck—white, and there's the beak.

5. [*Duck?*] It's white and looks like a duck— wings were spread, and the head was obvious.

6. Two detectives— looks like Sherlock Holmes.

6. [*Detectives?*] Looks like old-fashioned detective with Sherlock Holmes cap and bent over.

III.   2"

1. Two dancers, more specifically fla- menco dancers, be- cause of heels on shoes.

1. [*Dancers?*] Grace to dancers—heels on shoes. [*Sex?*] Male— head and way legs are shaped.

2. Another crab.

2. [*Crab?*] Same as I said before—looks like perfect crab. Things outside of head and shell.

3. A butterfly—the red.

3. [*Butterfly?*] Wings.

4. Two ostriches.

4. [*Ostriches?*] Just body and neck—no legs—very long neck—just looks like ostriches.

5. Two hands pointing at each other.

5. [*Hands?*] Looks like two fingers—thumb and forefinger.

6. Two faces—nose, mouth. That's all.

6. [*Faces?*] Perfect shape of faces—eyes—slightly indented and nose—indented.

IV.   2"

1. Two feet—there and there.

1. [*Feet?*] Looks like big Army boots with feet in them. [*Army boots?*] Big and heavy and klutzy looking.

2. Two cliffs and a tree hanging off each cliff.

2. [*Tree and cliff?*] Just looks like spooky thing, thing like see in movies with trees just hanging there. [*Spooky?*] Black shadows.

→ 3. Two heads of two wolves, mouth, nose.

3. [*Wolves?*] Long noses, ears and mouths—looked exactly like wolves.

4. Another crab—eyes and things over there.

4. [*Crab?*] Because of eyes and shell. [*Q*] Shape of it. And way shadowed in—just looks like shell.

V.   1"

1. A bat.

1. [*Bat?*] Wings and feet.

2. Two crocodiles—their mouth. [*Q*] Part of head—mostly mouth.

2. [*Crocodiles?*] Mostly because of mouths—very, very long.

3. A butterfly [*W*]—whole thing upside down. No more.

3. [*Butterfly?*] Just whole thing—wings, head, tail.

VI.   2"

1. Two Indians— faces and feathers [*heads only*].

1. [*Indians?*] Looks like two old Indians— feathers in hat. [*Feathers?*] Way shaped, kind of frilled.

2. Two weasels front to front.

2. [*Weasels?*] Perfect out- line of heads—bodies just kinda blended in with heads.

3. Two wolves stand- ing back to back. [*Q*] Nose, mouth [*heads only*].

3. [*Wolves?*] Heads, strik- ing long noses, mouths.

4. Pair of tongs—ends seem to curl around.

4. [*Tongs?*] Could see handle and tongs kinda curving at top.

↓ 5. Two angry men standing back to back—eyes, nose, mouth. That's all.

5. [*Men?*] Shape of heads and could tell angry by way eyes made.

VII.   1"

1. Two Indians—like Indian boys. [*Q*] There and there.

1. [*Indian boys?*] Feathers and head. [*Feathers?*] Shape. [*Boys?*] Faces look young, heads are smaller.

2. Two heads of bears. [*Q*] There and there—nose, eyes and mouths.

2. [*Bears?*] Because looked big and nose prominent and mouth.

3. A harbor [*S*] and opening up into ocean.

3. [*Harbor?*] Seemed to be surrounded by land and opened up into larger body of water.

→ 4. Outline of bird— here's head and beak—just seems to fade into rest of picture. [*dropped card*]

4. [*Bird?*] Looks like a ca- nary. [*Q*] Head round and tiny beak.

VIII.   1"

1. Two gophers climbing mountain. [*W*]

1. [*Gophers?*] Mountain very obvious, and just looks like gophers.

2. Butterfly [*blue*].

2. [*Butterfly?*] Wings, head, tail.

		3. Crab [*gray except for extensions*].	3. [*Crab?*] Mostly the eyes—I saw them first and then the rest of the body fell into place.
		4. Two hands.	4. [*Hands?*] Fingers. [*Q*] Just the way it was— more like claws, I guess. Very pointy.
		5. Heart—there in the white.	5. [*Heart?*] Just in shape of heart.
IX.	14"	1. Two dragons facing each other with smoke coming out.	1. [*Dragons?*] Way bodies shaped, with smoke coming out of noses. [*Smoke?*] Very faint— not like hot fire, but smoke.
		↓ 2. A ghost [*D*].	2. [*Ghost?*] Just looks like ghost, and eyes very big and looked questioning—kinda frightened. [*Q*] Because half dark and half light, and just looked frightened.
		3. A worm [*pink*].	3. [*Worm?*] Looks like big worm—could see body and dents—like starts of sections of worm. [*Worm?*] Lots of little feet—that's all.
		4. The head of a fetus. That's all.	4. [*Fetus?*] Didn't seem completed formed— some of it—eyes—but head not completely formed yet.
X.	6"	1. Two spiders [*blue*].	1. Two spiders with lots of legs.
		2. Two crabs but look like they are fighting, but have legs as if animated.	2. [*Crabs?*] Thingies on top and looked angry— angry expressions. [*Q*] Eyes, mouth. [*Animated?*] Real crabs don't have legs but looks like legs like something would do in a cartoon.

3. Head of a rabbit.	3. Looks like rabbit— eyes, nose—very plain and ears.
4. Two snakes.	4. [*Snakes?*] Shape.
5. Wishbone. That's all.	5. [*Wishbone?*] Shaped exactly like a wish- bone.

TAT

2. What do you want me to tell you? She's in love with the guy running the plow. She's very upset she can't meet him, because the maid or whoever she is doesn't want them fraternizing. The story turns out that they have a fight and never get to see each other anyhow after they do get together. Is the idea for me to get as close to the real story as possible?

3 BM. Looks like a little boy and he's very upset, and a gun—looks like a toy gun beside him is broken. One of his brothers or sisters broke it, and he's very upset. It ends up mother makes the brother or sister who broke the toy apologize for it.

4. Well, that's a married couple and they just had a fight, and she's trying to convince him to listen to her side of the story but he never listens—thinks he's right and wants to go away, and she's trying to hold him back and ends up where he storms out of the house.

6 BM. Well—that's a son and his mother, and the son wants to get married. He's been living at home all his life and she's playing on his sympathy, telling him that she's a lonely old woman and how can he do that to her. Turns out that he'll go off and get married, and the mother will resent it the rest of her life.

7 GF. A little girl and her mother, and she has no brothers or sisters and she gets very lonely, so she asks her mother to play with her with the doll, so the mother is. And that's all.

8 BM. Hmm . . . The man on the table is the boy's father. The boy shot him, not really on purpose, but more as a threat and the gun really went off. Now they're operating on him and he's waiting. And the father comes through the operation and lives. [*Then?*] That's it.

10. Man and wife, and they had a big fight and now they're making up, and each one is telling the other that it's all their fault and they're making up.

12 M. A father and son—the son is sleeping, and the father just went in to kind of look at him while he's sleeping. That's all. [Q] That's all—some parents just like to go in and see kids sleeping—maybe that's the only time they see them quiet.

13 MF. More? A lot more? Umm—the lady in bed is dead, and the man standing over her is a robber and he pulled his first robbery job—when she saw him she screamed very loud, and he got frightened 'cause he didn't want the police to be called or the neighbors, so he shot her, but he didn't mean to shoot her. [Q] It was just out of panic. Now he's very upset about it. That's all. [*Happen?*] He turns himself in. [Q] Well, if he turns himself in, it gives him a better chance with the judge.

16. [*Laughs*] Oh come on, you have to give me a story . . . OK—it's a fantastic snow storm [*smiles*], and the snow is twenty feet high and nobody can go anywhere or do anything, but everybody's happy because they don't have to work and can just enjoy nature the way it is—snow and the season, without having to worry about anything that's going on.

Psychological Test Portrait

M: 16–9 Male

M has a three-year history of delinquent behavior (burglary and drug abuse), which has brought him before the court on three occasions. Each time the court dismissed the charges in favor of the father's promise to handle him. At the last hearing, the court recommended that the parents seek placement in a residential facility, and this occasioned the evaluation.

M is at grade level in spite of spending more time out of school than in school. This was possible because he would always show up for exams and pass them. The principal, therefore, felt justified in promoting him.

M is a tall, handsome, neatly dressed young man. In the testing he was cooperative, eager to please, and strongly motivated to achieve. As he put it, he wanted "to be smarter than others so that I can con them." Anxiety was expressed through his compulsive talking, the content of which exposed an immature and naive conflict between rebelling against the rules of authority while seeking acceptance from his family and adults around him. *E* needed to limit the extent of compulsive talking in order to complete the tasks.

Cognitive Functioning

W–B, Form I: *M*'s Very Superior IQ of 129 is reflected in the precision of his language, conceptual thinking, memory, and ability to concentrate. His Verbal IQ of 135 demonstrates his excellent intellectual functioning; his Performance IQ of 114 is lower because he does not achieve maximum time bonuses, although he is well able to accomplish the tasks accurately. This lowered speed of performance may be an indication of intrusions in *M*'s concentration and effort (two errors in Coding). In addition, his approach to the Profile (in Object Assembly) may be indicative of a perceptual-motor problem. He could not recognize the object from the pieces of the Profile until he suddenly achieved an insight into a perception of the whole; at this point he was quickly able to assemble the pieces.

B–G: *M* strives for accuracy in carrying out this task in spite of his comments as to how difficult it seems to be for him. He achieves a reasonable facsimile of the design, but each design contains evidence of lapses in his efforts at accuracy. Again, this may be due to intrusions in his thinking and/or the possibility of perceptual-motor difficulty.

FD: *M*'s excellent effort at concentration, expressed in precision and detail, fail in this task. Instead he exaggerates certain features, resulting in bizarre details in an overall vague (incomplete legs) rendition. His male figure conveys the intense alertness that he himself has.

Rorschach: *M*'s productions in this task do not live up to his demonstrated superior intellectual ability. This seems to be due to the particular meaning that the Rorschach had for him. His circumscribed use of body details results in percepts that are constricted (II, 1 and 4; III, 2; IX, 2). Generally the content of his responses is childish (III, 1; IV, 1; VII, 1). He is able to see the commonly perceived responses, but he often adds idiosyncratic elaborations (IV, I; V, 1 and 2). His perceptions are rendered in good form, but sometimes his selection of the area of the blot is arbitrary.

TAT: *M* complies to the demands of this task and is accurate in his identification of the pictures. As in the Rorschach, however, he intruded his own idiosyncratic interpretations and elaborations throughout.

Summary Statement of Cognitive Functioning: *M* is intellectually gifted in spite of his problems with idiosyncratic intrusions in his thinking and minor perceptual-motor difficulties. He can concentrate and attend well when academically challenged. On more personally significant tasks, he produces more immature ideas than one would expect at his intellectual level.

Dynamic Picture

W–B, Form I: There is remarkably little dynamic material on the W–B. The exception is the investment he puts in Comprehension 18, which reveals his astuteness as to society's social expectations. This allows him, as he says, to "con" others into seeing him as conforming. This provides the framework for his grandiose fantasies that he can enact his aggressive needs against society's rules with impunity. This is seen in the allusion to aggression (Comprehension, 2; Vocabulary, 17 and 33; Picture Completion, 12).

Due to his demonstrated superior abilities, we speculate that the lack of time bonuses on the Performance was due to preoccupation with something other than the task at hand and/or his difficulty in perceptual-motor coordination.

B–G: There is no obvious dynamic material expressed in *M*'s productions on this test. As in the Performance on the W–B, we can only speculate that some other preoccupations permitted him to accept the lapses in accuracy seen in the figures. *M*'s manner of approach to copying the figure, as well as the accompanying expressions of concern over the difficulty he experiences, suggests an underlying feeling of impotence and inadequacy when faced with this perceptual-motor task.

FD: The drawings express *M*'s problems with his own body image. The bodies on the drawings are vague and undifferentiated, suggesting a lack of confidence in relating to his own body. In addition, this lack of confidence is seen in the incompleteness of the figures. It is as if he does not feel securely anchored to this world. The emphasis on the sensory organs (in the face and the hands), particularly on the male, suggest a hypervigilance on his part in relating to the world. More importantly, he seems to feel he has to relate with an aggressive stance, expressed in primitively razored teeth and fingers. The overall difficulty in his body concept is also expressed in the accompanying verbalizations as he draws. He seeks directions from *E*, as if this would give him the structure to enable him to perform the task.

Rorschach: *M*'s responses confirm what we had already speculated about in the previous tests. The predominant dynamic concern for him is in the area of body integrity. He expresses an unusual preoccupation with body parts and distortions in the organization of human figures throughout the test (I, a; II, 4; III, 2 and 4; IX, 2). Related to his sense of a damaged self is the concern with aggression, which he experiences as both internal (III, 4) and projected out (III, 2). His perceptions of distorted and damaged bodies throughout not only suggest his feelings of body disturbance in his body integrity and self-image but could also be related to feelings of disability stemming from an organic basis. In addition, there is an extreme emphasis on spelling out the mirror image of the cards, suggesting a symbiotic longing (X, 4). Therefore the immature nature of the content of his percepts could stem from organic problems and symbiotic needs. In the midst of all of this, there is still evidence of a young man struggling with adolescence: themes of emerging (II, 4), feelings of too-large body parts (IV), and concern over sexuality (II, 2; IX, 2). His emphasis on looking (I, 1; III, 4; IV, 1; VIII, 1), although expected for this age, is exaggerated.

TAT: The stories to the TAT cards concern themes appropriate to a younger child. *M* portrays his characters as focused primarily on one issue, conflict with their parents. His heroes have no autonomy and are responding to, or because of, a parental action or lack of action. In the two instances where this theme is not repeated, the main character engages in either violent aggression or drug abuse (Cards 12 M and 16). Obviously, these two extreme forms of behavior represent *M*'s consuming conflict—to be a child with directing parents, or alone and at the mercy of one's impulses. His sexual identity is confused (3 BM), and his sexual impulses are frightening (12 M), connected as they are with aggression.

Summary Statement of Dynamic Picture: The predominant dynamic theme in *M*'s record is repetitively a concern about his body integrity. He expresses feelings of low self-esteem, insecurity, and inferiority. In addition to normal adolescent concerns, he is excessively fearful of his sexual and aggressive impulses and needs for dependence.

Defenses

W–B, Form I: Generally in the Wechsler, M is able to use intellectual defenses well. This is strikingly demonstrated in his very superior scaled score of 18 on Comprehension. He attempts to impress E with his knowledge (Information, 10, 16 and 19; Similarities, 5; Vocabulary, 8). Other defenses are seen in his projection of control onto the external world of authority to contain the impulses he is unable to defend himself against (Information, 23; Comprehension, 2 and 9; Similarities, 11) and negation of his dependence needs (Comprehension, 7). His lowered Performance score may possibly be attributed to resistance and/or negativism, but is probably more likely the result of a perceptual-motor dysfunction.

B–G: Compulsivity is utilized well by M in this task. Undoing is seen in his verbal self-derogating comments as he tries to alleviate his own perfectionistic demands. Perhaps his poor evaluation of his performance is the only way he can mobilize himself to concentrate on the task.

FD: As in the B–G, M attempts to undo his difficulties in doing the FD's by asserting they represent a "goof." Thus, through a fairly unsuccessful humorous attempt, he tries to rationalize the troubles he is experiencing. He also projects onto E his need for direction ("Tell me specifically how").

Rorschach: M's main defenses in the Rorschach are distancing and a pseudointellectualized approach utilized in his efforts to make potentially dangerous ideas inanimate (II, 3 and 4; IV, 1). Aggressive ideas can be somewhat inhibited in this fashion, and sexual ideas are totally avoided. The unusual childlike quality of the content speaks to his use of regression, again as a way of not dealing with more threatening ideas. He also stresses unusual views that can be an attempt to deny voyeuristic impulses or, more likely, a developing reliance on projection (III, 1; IV, 1; IX, 2). The Rorschach ends on a naively optimistic note, as if to deny the conflicts expressed before.

TAT: As in the Rorschach, M uses regression, which is seen in the unusually childlike content of his stories. In the stories he projects the source of any difficulties onto parents or other authority (Cards 1, 3 BM, 5, and 7 BM). His pseudointellectualized approach comes into effect when he wants to assert his own autonomy, and he rationalizes that he can do so by being smart and conning others (Cards 1 and 7 BM). His arbitrary linking of all the stories at the end (Card 6 BM) is an attempt to minimize and perhaps deny all of which has preceded (as in the Rorschach). The content of the final story portrays naive wish fulfillment.

Summary Statement of Defenses: M relies primarily on intellectualization and projection. Regression to a more naive, childlike stance appears at times, including distancing and unsuccessful rationalization.

Affective Expression

W–B, Form I: M was challenged by the demands of the intelligence test. His need to be perfect led him to experience a great deal of anxiety at times. His only relief seemed to come through minimization and denigration of his achievement. Throughout he conveyed his need to please E in an immature way.

B–G: In spite of working diligently at this task, M expressed a great deal of distress and anxiety.

FD: Again, as in the B–G, M is upset by the demands of this task. He attempts to handle his anxiety by introducing a humorous explanation, which is not successful and comes across as bizarre.

Rorschach: M feels he must achieve on the Rorschach. He works very hard but is always unsatisfied with his responses. He feels it is important to let E know that he recognizes the colors in the cards (II; VIII; X, 2 and 4), but it is as if he wants to deny that they have any affective meaning. This suggests an ongoing attempt seen in his other tests to unsuccessfully detach or distance himself from his affective experiences.

TAT: As in all the other tasks, M works hard but is obviously made anxious and uncomfortable by the nature of the test. He is explicit about feeling imposed upon in Card 3 BM. When he is made uncomfortable by what he sees, he interprets E's question as a demand to describe his feelings.

Summary Statement of Affective Expression: M makes unsuccessful attempts to distance himself from his affective experience. His primary feelings therefore are revealed as discomfort, anxiety, and dissatisfaction with himself.

Summary

M's pathology exceeds the normally expected turmoil of adolescence. The wish to return or, indeed, remain a young child conflicts with his age, physical growth, and the pressures of his adolescent impulses. This is perhaps exaggerated by his organic dysfunction in perceptual-motor coordination, which leaves him feeling inadequate, damaged, and with a poor body concept. This does not fully explain, however, the discrepant nature of his performance throughout the testing.

Rather, we see evidence of primitive defenses (denial and projection), that are unsuccessful in coping with wishes emanating from the separation-individuation stage of development. Thus there is a great longing on M's part to merge with another and for dependence on another whereas he must actively assert his independence via his pride in his psychopathy. The latter appears to be the only means by which he can acquire a facade of being grown-up. Indeed, M feels rather empty inside and, therefore, very unsure of himself.

M presents the picture of borderline personality with organic dysfunction specifically in the perceptual-motor sphere. Recommendation is made for residential treatment because of his parents' inability to cope with him. Not only does he obviously need a therapist, but it is recommended that he be assigned a therapist who could understand the nature of his perceptual-motor problems.

Diagnosis

DSM III-R

Axis I: 312.90 Conduct Disorder, undifferentiated type, severe
Axis II: 301.83 Borderline Personality Disorder
Axis III: None
Axis IV: 4-Severe
Avis V: 40

Psychological Test Data

M: 16–9 Male

Wechsler–Bellevue, Form I

	Weighted Score
Verbal Tests	
Information	13
Comprehension	18
Digit Span	14
Arithmetic	13

Similarities	15	
(Vocabulary)	(11)	
	——	
Total	73	

Performance Tests

Picture Arrangement	12	
Picture Completion	13	
Block Design	11	
Object Assembly	12	
Digit Symbol	11	
	——	
Total	59	

	Weighted Score	IQ
Verbal Scale	73	135
Performance Scale	89	114
Full Scale	132	129

Information

		Score
1.	Kennedy	1
2.	Measures temperature	1
3.	Tree	1
4.	England	1
5.	2	1
6.	52	1
7.	Rome	1
8.	Tokyo	1
9.	5'4"	1
10.	Wright brothers—Orville & Wilbur	1
11.	South America	1
12.	In miles? About 5,000? No, couldn't be. About 2,000.	1
13.	Pumps blood through system	1
14.	Shakespeare	1
15.	194 million	0
16.	February 12. Either his or Lincoln's.	0
17.	Byrd	0
18.	Africa	1
19.	Samuel Clemens	1
20.	Center of Catholic Church	1
21.	Don't know—also religious center of Moslem religion	0
22.	Don't know.	0
23.	Exact meaning—should I say what it is?—not sure— law can't lock you up without evidence to back up charge.	1
24.	Don't know.	0
25.	No.	0
		——
	Total	18

Comprehension

		Score
1.	Put it in mailbox.	2
2.	I guess report it to manager. I know you're not supposed to yell fire, because it's against the law. [Q] Start a panic.	2

3. Have a bad influence on them.   2
4. To support government functions and programs.   2
5. Best material—wears better, is flexible and durable.   2
6. More populated, be at a premium.   2
7. Couldn't say "look for somebody," could you? Could look at side of tree, see where sap is—supposed to be on north, but not sure—if he is way out. Sun is in east in morning and west in afternoon, so know direction, and if know direction, should go—can get out.   2
8. Set a code by which people have to live, so certain people won't take advantage of each other.   2
9. Because a license is proof that you're married and certain rights need proof for, and so people don't go around marrying everyone they see.   2
10. Because they can't learn words because can't hear them.   2

Total   20

Digit Span

Score

F 8 + B 7   Total   15

Arithmetic

Score

1. 9   1
2. 4¢   1
3. 17¢   1
4. 9   1
5. 8   1
6. 36¢   1
7. 28   1
8. 600   1
9. 9   1
10. 46   1

Total   10

Similarities

Score

1. Both fruits   2
2. Both clothing   2
3. Both animals   2
4. Vehicles   2
5. Media of information   2
6. Both made of similar basic elements   1
7. Both from trees   0
8. Both human sense organs   2
9. Both beginning of life   2
10. Both done by artists, works of art   2
11. Both things given you for something you've done   1
12. Both forms of nature   1

Total   19

Can't think too good today. Don't feel well. [*Went for water. Needs perfect score. Accepts reassurance.*]

Vocabulary

		Score
	[*Very anxious. Tension in voice and movements.*]	
1.	Fruit	1
2.	Animal	1
3.	To enlist. [Q] I know what it means—it's so easy—more this—to bring together.	1
4.	Precious gem	1
5.	Um, um, person who's a bother or a pain	1
6.	Skin from fur-bearing animal	1
7.	Pillow—soft cushion—soft something	1
8.	English monetary unit	1
9.	It's exactly what it says. [Q] To take a chance, risk what you have.	1
10.	Meat—pork	1
11.	Long thin—cross out. Used to join two pieces of wood.	1
12.	Type of wood	1
13.	To dye, paint, color	1
14.	I know, but hard to explain. Large gymnasium—exactly like Jamaica Armory—play basketball.	1/2
15.	Like a story—with a moral	1
16.	Brim of hat edge	1
17.	Machine for slicing people's heads off	1
18.	More than one	1
19.	[*mild stutter*] To hide away to be alone	1
20.	Explosive chemical	1
21.	Verse of song	1
22.	Machine used to enlarge—greatly enlarge things like bacteria	1
23.	It's an Italian word—motor scooter. [Q] I don't know.	0
24.	Part of church—upper part where bell is	1
25.	To fade away	1
26.	Disease or malady—trying to think of word	1
27.	Type of metal	1
28.	Weighted to keep it steady	1
29.	Like a labyrinth	1/2
30.	Ornament or bead—shiny	1
31.	Spying—work for government and spy on another government	1
32.	Inevitable—bound to happen	0
33.	Animal like a praying mantis—insect—it eats its mate	1
34.	Japanese form of suicide	1
35.	Some kind of castle or house	0
36.	I know—can't think of it.	0
37.	Don't know.	0
38.	No.	0
39.	No.	0
40.	Don't know—has to do with medicine—thing they say is aseptic	0
41.	Is that related to flaunt?	0
42.	No.	0
	Total	31

Picture Arrangement

	Time	Order	Score
1.	4"	PAT	2
2.	12"	ABCD Easiest	2

3.	8"	LMNO	2
4.	51"	AJNET	2
5.	49"	SAMUEL	3
6.	72"	EFGHIJ	3
		Total	14

Picture Completion

		Score
1.		1
2.		1
3.		1
4.		1
5.		1
6.		1
7.	Nothing.	0
8.		1
9.		1
10.		1
11.		1
12.	Head not connected to shoulder. Nose is broken—could be the way the guy draws it, though!	0
13.		1
14.		1
15.		1

[*Does them very quickly, except where can't get it.*]

| | Total | 13 |

Block Design

	Time	Score
1.	17"	3
2.	12"	4
3.	6"	5
4.	21"	4
5.	46"	4
6.	109"	3
7.	228"	0
	Total	23

Object Assembly

	Time	Score
Man	18"	6
Profile	33" [*Confused re: hairpiece and nose; suddenly sees the whole very quickly.*]	8
Hand	56"	7
	Total	21

| Digit Symbol | | Total Score | 47 |

Bender–Gestalt

Am I a genius? [*He would like to have the results discussed with him, which he will.*]

A. [*He starts right away. Rotates paper to do the square.*]
1. [*Does it right away. Careful, well done.*]
2. [*Carefully done.*] Can't do these. [*Erases—was going up at slant and redoes it. Quickly rejects it and becomes frustrated, yet works at it conscientiously despite self-derogatory comments.*]
3. [*Well executed.*]
4. I can't do these. [*Is uncertain and puts on extra dot.*] It never comes out like it is on there.
5. [*Done carefully. Counts, well-organized approach but with much distress, sighing, etc., because it is not precise.*]
6. Oh, no! [*Moves to bottom of sheet for room. Making the curve seems to upset him. Rotates sheet as crosses the line.*] Now I lost it. [*Though he is doing well. The paper is turned 90° now, so he is always drawing in left-to-right direction.*]
7. Should I use back? [*Whatever you like. Does so.*]
8. Oh, thank God. [*Rotates paper for each new line so is always drawing in a left-to-right direction.*]

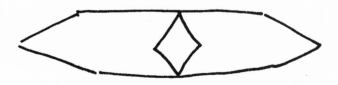

(*continued on next page*)

Bender–Gestalt

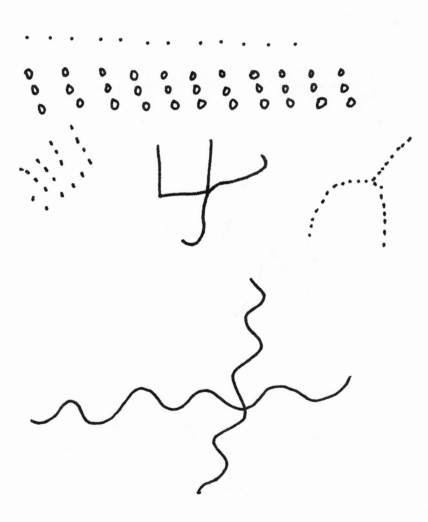

Figure Drawing

Person—whole person? [*Yes.*] Supposed to be a drawing or how person looks, etc.? [*Any way you want to draw it.*] I knew that. I knew. How do you want it? [*Any way.*] Yeah, I wish there was a particular way so I could know what to do. Tell me specifically how. [*Very distressed. He has a real need for direction. Drawing becomes expansive. Then he erases several times.*] No good either. [*Repeats each time before he erases. Finally continues, has a vague outline, puts in features, examines own hand to make sure of fingers. Adds extra finger on right hand.*] Oh! I blew that! [*Erases again and repeats. Leaves left hand with only 4 fingers. He erases the outline of the head to correct it. Grins as he makes top of head and ears.*] That's it. I don't know how to make legs, so I'll leave it. Actually I better make legs, or can't tell what it is. Yeah. Made it pretty good. I left out tail. Looks like kind of person who would have a tail. If I saw someone who looked like that, wouldn't surprise me if he had a tail. He has horns and claws. [*starts to put on tail, mildly, joking, then*] No, I won't.

Woman? [*Erases on head—does it piece at a time.*] I don't know how to do hair. This one's not gonna be good. [*Works intently throughout.*] She should have horns, too, if he does. [*Why?*] Figured be a goof. I figured what kind of a sight is she gonna make if I put horns on. Just threw it on because eyes look like should have horns. They look pretty evil, though. I put 'em on because thought it would be a goof—I'll change, then—no, I'll leave them.

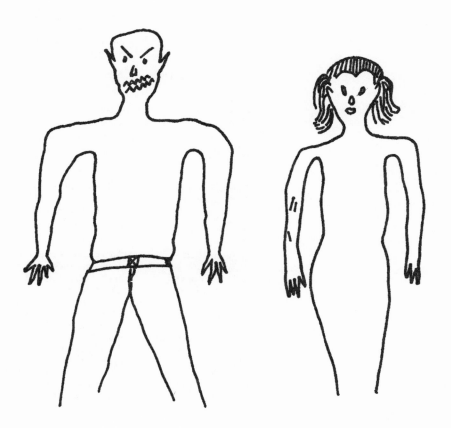

Rorschach

These will be used against me to see if I should go to an institution. I haven't been in school for three years. Just come occasionally to take the tests. I do well and pass. I was able to con them all—great!

<table>
<tr><td></td><td></td><td></td><td>*Inquiry*</td></tr>
<tr>
<td>I</td>
<td>30"</td>
<td>1. Whole thing looks like a mask.</td>
<td>1. Colored like a mask would be—two eyes and where mouth would be, and these two things stick out like a mask would be with things that stick out [*side* D].</td>
</tr>
<tr>
<td></td><td></td><td></td>
<td>a. Tiny claws like—body in center. Now see something else—a man with wings, two legs—human shape—like a bat with human body.</td>
</tr>
<tr>
<td></td><td></td>
<td>2. Or could look like a bug or a bat—body, wings.</td>
<td>2. Just a bat with wings sticking out—in a fly-ing position, but doesn't look like it's moving.</td>
</tr>
<tr>
<td>II.</td><td>20"</td>
<td>↓ 1. Head of a prehis-toric animal—horns, eyes [*center bottom* D].</td>
<td>1. Nose, too.</td>
</tr>
<tr>
<td></td><td></td>
<td>↑ 2. Another here like a lizard head [*center top* D].</td>
<td>2. Eyes, tip-nose—shaped like it tapers down.</td>
</tr>
<tr>
<td></td><td></td>
<td>3. Head—statue of caveman carved out of rocks—big, tremendous jaw [D].</td>
<td>3. Color of like rock and texture of rock—like somebody carved the face into rock.</td>
</tr>
<tr>
<td></td><td></td>
<td>↓ 4. Animal face—beak, wing on its head; wings all over [dr].</td>
<td>4. Also coming out of the rock—not rock, just animal's head coming out of the rock.</td>
</tr>
<tr>
<td>III.</td><td>7"</td>
<td>1. Batman. Two eyes like mask over face—rest of face, but blocked off—if just look at it quick, see two eyes and that's all [*bot-tom center* D].</td>
<td>1. Batman—first came to my mind. Some kind of mask Batman wears. Two black things over eyes—but looks evil—goes around doing evil things instead of good things like Batman does.</td>
</tr>
</table>

2. Two heads, neck, strange, distorted body—out of shape—because has head. Attached is a body alone doesn't look like body. There's two of them facing each other.

2. These two things—this could be strange-looking woman, strange head, looks more like a dog's head, though could be either one—either a woman or a dog.

3. This looks like a fish—two of them—two of everything, actually [*side* D].

3. [*Fish?*] Fin on back—fin up further and fish head up here.

4. Looks like could be tonsils, looking down somebody's throat—really doesn't look like anything, but that's something, so—[*center* D].

4. [*Tonsils?*] Two red things looking down, and see only that. Impossible to explain without getting all involved and everything—shading and color.

5. This could be somebody's windpipe and stomach [*upper* D].

5. Kind of thing you'd see in textbook—windpipe coming down and stomach.

IV.   4"

1. This one's groovy. A big giant—two big, tremendous feet—very little arms. Those things hanging down here are arms. Head with ears stick out. If don't look too closely has eyes, but if look close doesn't have eyes. Big tremendous tail that trails along behind it, that swings along behind it, that hits people with. This is made of stone like in horror movies—things that walk around and steps on buildings—knocks people down, rips up Empire State Building—steps on people. That's it—big giant, any way you look at it.

1. [*Q*] Color and texture looks hard. Has both feet off the ground—maybe balances on tail and jumps forward.

V.	18"	1. Big tremendous bird—prehistoric bird with antennas or horns coming out of its head. Two feet—that stick out like a bird's stick out when it flies.	
		2. Alligators on both sides. See head and jaw and snout and has its mouth open—rest is covered by bird.	
VI.	11"	1. This part is good. Looks like head of fox or wolf.	1. [Q] Head—spine— spread skin out flat. [Q] Mostly head looks like—fur, grey kind of color—fox or wolf is.
VII.	9"	1. This looks like girls' heads. Same two little girls' ponytail—wind blowing it—standing up—looks exactly like little girl like in comic strips—Little Lulu or somebody.	1. Looking at each other.
		2. Looks like another monster. Looking at his profile, eye— one eye only—and nose, and this big horn it sticks people with or other monsters—I don't know. Bottom doesn't look like anything.	2. Has that eye over there and that nose here— could be an animal— prehistoric animal—just a face.
VIII.	14"	1. Groovy colors. Two panthers— four legs and a tail, and it's walking. [*covers half*] Rest just looks like ink blots. Nothing else there.	
IX.	17"	1. A skull or head, but all pointy, so must be a skull. No, could be skull of a man with a long chin [*bottom* D].	1. Doesn't look much like a skull—just part looks like long chin. Looks like skull. Rest looks like a mistake.

2. This looks like a very skinny man standing in profile. Can see head and neck clearly—rest isn't clear, but comes down like shadow—too long to see a guy out of it, but head very clear. [di]

3. Not really looks like it—but guy with a machine gun and other guy with machine gun, and they're shooting at each other. Hat on, long pointed hat like a funnel—kind of hats that wizards wear, like in *Wizard of Oz,* hats like that, wave wands and cast spells.

X   7"

1. Two gray animals with antennas facing each other. Look exactly like two little gray animals—kind of animals I've never seen before.

2. Rabbit with two green things that come out of its face.

2. Don't know what green things are.

3. Two crabs.

3. Crabs—all those legs and arms, things that crabs have.

↓ 4. Two more crabs, or shell animal that lives in ocean. Those two pink things aren't anything—just like holding everything together. Everything is attached to that. So many things—everything's attached to everything else in this.

4. They look like regular little crabs. Shaped like it—color doesn't mean anything.

5. Two yellow
things—sunbeams
look like things
that have legs and
go jumping
around—move
around—made out
of sunlight.

5. [*Sunbeams?*] Because
yellow. Really don't
look like anything.

TAT

1. Kid's looking at the violin. Supposed to be practicing but hates it—doesn't—want to practice on violin. Like he was left there and they said practice. Just sitting there looking at it and thinking, now I gotta practice. Doesn't look like—kind of kid who'd want to play violin. Would rather be outside playing with friends, baseball and something like that. . . . [Q] Probably pick up violin and play it horrible. He'll have to play because can hear him outside and have to hear him practicing. [Q] Probably end up practicing, but will never play violin because he hates it but has to practice for an hour. [*Feel?*] Thinks now will have to pick up and start practicing because can't sit there and look at it too much longer. [*Feel about others outside?*] His mother and father who want him to play the violin—thinking of—if he's smart, a way to scheme way out of it. If smart and good talker won't have to take up the violin. Cheat. Then he'll be like all those other kids who have to play an instrument—just play because they have to practice, never for own enjoyment. [*Cheating selves?*] If they like it, they'll play—maybe years later will like it, but when a kid, don't appreciate it then. Looks like his parents picked out the instrument and the music he'll play and things like that, and he resents it.

3 BM. These kids are so young. Boy or girl—has hair like boy and legs like girl. Let me know. Looks like a girl—doesn't look like has pants on—she looks like she's crying? I don't know why. Make up a story why she's crying? In her grandmother's house. That's mean to do—you'd write for no use—was grandmother and wolf there and scared. Maybe mother punished her—won't buy her a toy—I don't know. I can't think of why girls cry. I can't see face. I don't know what thinking of—maybe she's sick. I don't know. [*Alone?*] Yeah—and the door's open. She looks like she's being punished for something.

5. [*laughs*] A good one. No, actually not what thought it was. Look at room now. A den, not a kid's room—reminded me how mother used to stick her head in my room on some pretense to see what I was doing. She'd sniff, "What's that horrible smell," and I'd say what do you mean, horrible smell. It's a cigarette. That's what I'm smoking. That's exactly what it looks like. [*How did you feel then?*] Umm—I don't know. I just felt I'm gonna have to con her—annoyed stuck her head in—and they'd have to believe me, so all they'd do is walk away and not do anything. [*What do you want them to do?*] Not to stick head in door. Not to stick head in door. [*How did it feel they did nothing?*] That's what I expected them to do. I knew, what could they do. They did exactly what I expected them to do. Nothing. What they're supposed to do. Nothing.

8 BM. [*laughs a bit*] Hah. This one looks pretty stupid. [*Why?*] Obviously this guy got shot—operating on him, holding light over, and he looks like in pain and there's this big gun in the picture [*fingers card*]. Definitely looks like a gun, and I don't know what that kid's doing in picture—suit and tie on, goes to prep school. Looks like doesn't belong in picture, just blocking the view of the guy lying there. [*Happens?*] I don't know where he was shot, why he was shot. Stupid picture. Maybe out hunting and got shot accidentally. Kid looks like doesn't want to watch. Weak stomach and with back to it all. [*Know the man?*] Yeah. Maybe father or a relative. [*Get well?*] Yeah, probably.

12 M. These pictures are so strange. Looks like someone lying there, and this kid's putting hand up like to touch her or put hand over mouth. Doesn't look like he belongs there doing it. I could make up some foolish thing—all seems so illogical. Doesn't seem like kind of thing that happens. Can't tell what he's gonna do. Strangle her, punch her

hard over mouth. He's doing it so sneakily. Must be something wrong he's gonna do. And she's asleep. Feet up on bed, so not just tiptoeing past. Probably his sister or something. [*Q*] Don't know. So many things could possibly want to do. Maybe wants to rape her, or kill her, definitely doing something he shouldn't be doing. I could make something up. He's gonna grab her, she'll scream, and he'll kill her. Want me to make something else up? That what you want? Should I think of something else? I don't know what he's doing. Is that good enough? [*Said with tension and annoyance. Need to comply conflicting with anger at the demand.*]

16. [*occasional slurring throughout the TAT as if drugged*] No picture—these get less and less logical, harder and harder to figure out. More and more strange. I don't want to make up a story. I don't even know what kind of story to make up. I'll have to pretend was a picture there. I'll just describe it like it was a picture. All right? This big dark room, dimly lit. Can't see people in it, all hazy. About seven, eight people there, all lying around, some on chairs, some lying on bed, some on floor propped against the bed. About four or five have long pipes in their hands. All pretty stoned looking. Looks like feel beautiful. Victrola playing in background. Middle of room big cannister. Every so often go over, fill pipe, and smoke another pipeful. Two people talking softly to each other. Can tell everybody in picture pretty stoned. Looks like groovy place to be at. Every once in a while doorbell rings, and people come in. Hello, how are you, they'll fill pipe and smoke. [*Do these people ever feel good normally?*] Yeah, but always feel better when high. [*Why always need to feel better?*] Don't need to. Like to.

7 BM. Guy's a criminal, younger guy. Guy talking to him is his lawyer, and like in court, and you know, telling him what's up, what's happening. Comforting word now and then. Kid's on trial for something he did. [*Do?*] I don't know. Lotta things he coulda done—didn't murder anybody, or rob a bank, maybe forgery. People who do armed robbery are hardened criminals, those who do forgery are clever, smart maneuver, and generally get off. Kid looks like comes from a good family, so will surely get off. Not a degenerate like Puerto Rican. Judge doesn't know, good home, good middle-class people or rich can get away with it. Or maybe judge dishonest and give him money, but most aren't and this one probably isn't either. This kid has tie on. It is unfair. Could get good judge, an easy one or hard one. Always better off to come from good home. If father a businessman, not a truck driver, father can talk to judge on judge's level—make promises—always helps. This kid's father would go up and stick up for his own son. [*Father feels?*] What did I do wrong, where did I make my mistake? [*Father's fault?*] Well, maybe after third bust father says nothing more I can do for him—then the kid's getting it. Unless judge says what kind of father are you—don't help own son, or judge could agree with him. If I was kid and my father said it, I'd figure he'd stick up for me and if he didn't stick up for me it's my own fault. I couldn't con him into sticking up for me—if I did get punished. [*Should you be punished?*] If I did anything wrong, should be punished. I'd know I should be punished, but I wouldn't want to go to jail. I lied in court, made promises I haven't kept. My father made promises he didn't keep.

6 BM. Guy looks pretty old—I don't know anything about him. Doesn't look like anybody I know. Looks like a normal, well-adjusted, everyday dull person. Looks like mother who got old. Father not there, maybe he died. Mother sad, faraway look in her eye. Handkerchief in hand. Looks like sad occasion. Something horrible happened. [*Do they help each other?*] Probably. Looks like kind of person could be very comforting to his mother. Like kind of person who turned out well in the end. Like all these pictures were of him growing up.

Psychological Test Portrait

N: 17–7 Male

N was referred for differential diagnosis by his therapist, who had seen him once a week for six months. The therapist became concerned about his increasingly idiosyncratic behavior and verbalizations.

N is the middle of three children who live with an overprotective mother and an alcoholic father given to violent rages. Academically he is achieving adequately in the eleventh grade.

N is an attractive 17-year-old who is neatly groomed and conservatively dressed. He presented with a basically flat demeanor. In spite of obvious anxiety and overt expressions of anger at stressful points in the testing, N carried out all the tasks. He requested that the door of the testing room be left open because he felt more comfortable that way.

Cognitive Functioning

WAIS: N achieved an average IQ of 100, with no discrepancy between his Verbal IQ of 99 and his Performance IQ of 100. There is, however, a great deal of variability in his inter- and intratest scores. The fact that he was able to achieve more difficult items while failing easier items points to a greater potential than his average IQ scores indicate.

N's highest scores are gained in tests tapping his fund of knowledge, abstract reasoning, attention to details, and awareness of interpersonal interactions. His low scores are obtained on tests of social expectations, defining words, integration of spatial perception with motor execution, and a visual-motor rote task. His responses to Comprehension present difficulties in scoring because of the confusion in his language (Comprehension, 6, 8, and 9), reflecting confusion in coherent thinking. Impulsive concrete associations (Vocabulary, 4, 6, 7, 8, 13, and 25) lower his scores in Vocabulary, as well as seemingly throwaway responses that have no relation to the word (Vocabulary, 12, 14, 16, 17, 27, and 33). Peculiar language usage appears sporadically (Information, 19; Comprehension, 4; Similarities, 12; Picture Completion, 8). There is the suggestion of difficulty in perceptual-motor integration in his lowered performances on Block Design and Digit Symbol.

B–G: N's Bender figures show that he worked diligently to reproduce the stimulus figures; however, he is unable to peform accurately on this task. There is variability in size of figures (A to 2, and 5 to 8) and in pencil pressure (each figure in A, 3, and 8). Difficulty in making angles is seen in flattening out the line in 7 and producing ears on 8. In addition, difficulty in contact between two figures is seen in A, where an adaptive effort was made by using a line to join them. Also he shows a problem in crossing on 6 by making a large curve to cross and then extending the line.

These difficulties, in conjunction with the lowered scores seen above (Block Design and Digit Symbol) in the WAIS, indicate a problem for N in perceptual-motor integrated functioning. He shows, however, an ability to recognize and correct for his errors.

FD: Both drawings by N show an attempt to disguise the figures, in spite of making a clear differentiation between male and female. In the male drawing his attempt at a caricature distorts the proportional relationships in the body, and in the female drawing he antiquates the woman but is able to give the figure the proper placement and proportions. In both drawings the lack of shoulders may again represent his problems in perceptual-motor functioning.

N shows in caricaturing the male an interest and knowledge of politics that would suggest the impression mentioned above (Cognitive Functioning, WAIS) of a higher intellectual potential.

Rorschach: The majority of N's responses demonstrate a W approach to the Rorschach cards. His use of determinants, however, is meager. There is no shading, one FC, one FM, and a limited number of responses (11). In spite of four P's in which the form level is adequate, generally the form level is a minus or, at best, vague. This suggests an inconsistent and constricted perception of the world as it is.

As seen in the WAIS, N's use of language is peculiar. He produces associations that reveal a similar incoherence in his thinking and language production.

TAT: Unlike the WAIS, N is able to tell coherent stories that are appropriate to the presented pictures. His language is adequate, and he does not produce unrelated associations. There are, however, instances of awkward language (7 BM and 13 MF), conceptual confusion (3 GF and 4), and ideas of self-reference (6 BM and 13 MF).

Summary Statement of Cognitive Functioning: With the exception of N's performance on the TAT, there are many indications in the tests of N's cognitive difficulties in language production, incoherence in his thinking, and problems in perceptual-motor functioning.

Dynamic Picture

WAIS: The predominant dynamic seen in N's WAIS is the need to counter his low self-esteem by displays of a potpourri of information that may or may not be correct in response to the question (Information, 20; Comprehension, 5, 8, 9, and 10; and Vocabulary, 33). This need frequently leads to loss of credit in that he "spoils" his responses. It further leads to his portraying ideas of grandiosity (Information, 20; Comprehension, 3, 4, and 9).

A preoccupation with aggressive fantasies intrudes into his responses to Comprehension, 3, 4, and 11. The structured nature of the WAIS may have enabled him to limit his associations of an aggressive nature.

B–G: The Bender does not reveal any dynamic considerations.

FD: In both drawings, N's need to caricature the male and female figures suggest his fear of exposure. The most striking feature in his drawings is the exaggerated teeth and mouth in the male and the donkey, reflecting strong oral aggression. Another striking feature in this drawing is the contrast between the wide-open eyes on the man and the malevolent eye on the donkey, suggesting a conflict between innocence and malice. The shortened tie and limbs may speak to castration fears, emphasized by the inclusion of a dagger.

Excessive shading and scribbled lines in both figures point to N's extreme anxiety and tension related to body concerns. His fears seem to be related to sexual impulses, seen in the expressed castration anxiety in the male drawing and the closed-off quality of the female, with a basket covering the genital area.

Rorschach: N's first seven responses to the first six cards of the Rorschach are simplistic, suggesting his feelings of vulnerability and fragility when faced with the unstructured nature of this task. His labeling tiny projections as "feet" (Cards I and VII) and even "false feet" (Card VI) underscores his feeling of not being securely grounded. His angry comments (Card III Inquiry; Card VII Inquiry) support the interpretation of the distress he experienced at whatever his task aroused.

His initial response to Card I of "ink smeared all over" indicates sadistic impulses that seem to threaten him, as his perception of a villain on Card X reiterates. An essential conflict between good and evil is represented in his two-faced person on Card IX.

The expression of N's dynamics in the Rorschach are limited because of the need to defend excessively against the obviously threatening associations the cards elicited.

TAT: The striking dynamic theme to emerge in N's TAT stories is the sense of a righteous self, suggesting his need to feel omnipotent. This belies the underlying sense of loneliness and sadness (3 BM, 7 BM, and 3 GF) leading to suicidal impulses (14). It is obvious that he is overly concerned with his sexual impulses (7 BM and 13 MF) and perhaps sexual identity (see slip in 9

GF). His aggressive impulses (5, 6 BM, 7 BM, 8 BM, 9 GF, 12 M, 13 MF, 14, 3 GF, and 4) would appear to be a preoccupation. These aspects of N demonstrate his difficulties in relating to others, such as family or friends.

Summary Statement of Dynamic Picture: N presents the picture of a very disturbed adolescent still struggling with strong, unmodulated sexual and aggressive impulses. He feels himself to be fragile and vulnerable to dangers from internal as well as external sources. This precludes his ability to make satisfying interpersonal relationships.

Defenses

WAIS: In spite of compliance to the demands of this test, N treats the questioning in Information as if he were under attack when he is concerned that he does not know the answer. He becomes defensively aggressive and returns the attack (Information, 14, 17, 20, and 24). In Comprehension his attempts at intellectualization lead him to assume a lecturing stance that is moralistic, judgmental, grandiose, and self-righteous (Comprehension, 3, 4, 6, 9, 10, and 11); this is also seen in Similarities 12. There is also an obsessive tendency in many of his responses (Information, 13, 19, and 25; Comprehension, 8 and 9). In contrast to this defensiveness, he responds to Vocabulary by giving associations (Vocabulary, 4, 6, 7, 8, 13, and 21) rather than definitions.

He becomes concrete in his inability to understand proverbs (Comprehension, 7, 13, and 14), and because he is able to demonstrate abstract reasoning in Similarities, it is assumed that this concreteness is serving a defensive function. This concreteness can become bizarre at times (Similarities, 10; Vocabulary, 25 and 33).

B–G: The Bender does not reveal any defenses.

FD: The major defensive effort in the FD is N's avoidance of representing the human body in both drawings. The ideational component expressed in the male drawing is replete with obsessive detailing.

Rorschach: N's W approach to the Rorschach demonstrates his need for control. Obsessive defenses are seen in his delineation of form and detailing of parts. He imposes arbitrary ideas onto the percept in his effort to create a W. This most often results in an F–(I, 2; II—"that comes from wings"; III, use of upper reds; and IV—"any extra it might have"). On Card VI, probably in denial of the threat of castration anxiety, he has his longest reaction time and perceives an amorphous shape. In response to the first six cards his percepts are generally regressed.

The use of projection becomes most evident when he sees a two-faced person—"right is good, left is bad" (IX)—and an angry villain (X). It would appear that the Rorschach is so stressful for N that he must defend against his discomfort by demeaning the test and E (I, IV, VII, VIII, and IX).

TAT: The structure of the TAT appears to cause less stress for N than the Rorschach did, but he does lose distance and on occasion personalizes the cards (6 BM, 13 MF, and 3 GF). Instances of avoidance are seen in his deceitful answer to his mother (1) and avoidance of identifying dangerous objects (3 BM and 8 BM). He denies interest in activities with sexual connotations (7 BM and 13 MF). He uses obsessiveness to defend against distressing ideas of depression (3 BM and 14), danger (8 BM), and sex (13 MF). Projection is seen in the portrayal of the person ending up a "bum" (3 BM), in the threat of danger (6 BM and 9 GF) and his attribution of playing around (7 BM). There is a strong righteous and moralistic sense that appears in his stories (7 BM, 13 MF, 14, and 3 GF).

Summary Statement of Defenses: N conveys himself as a judgmental, righteous, and moralistic person. In order to maintain this stance he utilizes denial, avoidance, obsessiveness, and projection.

Affective Expression

WAIS: N appeared to feel very put upon by the nature of this test. On occasion he retorts with annoyance, but generally he is able to perform without undue affective intrusions.

B–G: The Bender did not elicit affective responses from N.

FD: N, if anything, seemed to enjoy his drawings. It is only in the content that we see his disparaging expressions.

Rorschach: This test clearly provoked N to express anger in demeaning comments to E about the test. In the use of determinants it is noteworthy that C and c are missing. The last two cards in their content suggest that he experienced fear in reaction to the stimuli.

TAT: In contrast to the Rorschach N appeared to be more comfortable with the TAT. He does demonstrate annoyance (5 and 14) and anxiety (6 BM, 7 BM, and 13 MF) on occasion.

Summary Statement of Affective Expression: Although N complied to all the testing requirements, he exhibited little pleasure or satisfaction in his performance. Rather, any emotions he expressed were of anger, discomfort, and anxiety.

Summary

N is a seriously disturbed adolescent who is able to achieve an average IQ with evidence of higher potential in spite of signs of a perceptual-motor dysfunction. His thinking, language usage, and conceptualizations are often peculiar, distorted, and self-referent. His defenses are limited to denial, avoidance, obsessessiveness, projection, and regression. There is an inordinate sense of body vulnerability, with castration anxiety as well as a poor self-image. All of this seems to be compensated for by a drive to omnipotence and grandiosity in which he is judgmental and self-righteous. All of this leaves him without the ability to relate to others.

There is a sense throughout the testing of an active paranoid system with delusions. He seems to be living in a present reality, as well as with a delusional construct intruding into his reality at times. His preoccupation with good and evil with an omnipotent moralistic sense seems to be his effort to contain unmodulated sexual and aggressive impulses. He experiences dangers from within as well as from without.

Diagnosis

DSM-III-R

Axis I:	295.32 Schizophrenia, Paranoid Type
Axis II:	301.22 Schizotypal Personality Disorder
	315.90 Specific Developmental Disorder NOS
Axis III:	None
Axis IV:	4-Severe
Axis V:	50-Serious Symptoms

Due to the severity of N's disturbance, he is at risk for impulsive suicide. Treatment must be geared to developing a degree of trust and relatedness to the therapist. This can only be obtained through frequent therapy sessions per week or a day treatment program. Prognosis is guarded.

Psychological Test Data

N: 17–7 Male

WAIS

		Scaled Score
Verbal Tests		
Information		12
Comprehension		7
Arithmetic		8
Similarities		11
Digit Span		9
Vocabulary		7
	Total	54

Performance Tests		
Digit Symbol		7
Picture Completion		13
Block Design		7
Picture Arrangement		13
Object Assembly		9
	Total	49

	Scaled Score	IQ
Verbal Score	54	99
Performance Score	49	100
Full Scale Score	103	100

Information

	Score
1–4.	4
5. Plants in South America, not right name . . . sap.	1
6. Taft. No, sorry for Taft. Cleveland, Harding, Kennedy, Johnson.	0
7. Author	1
8. 52	1
9. South	1
10. Located in South America, above, below the equator . . . or is it above?	1
11. 5'6"	1
12. Rome	1
13. Reflected. Light is reflected from the clothes and no heat is absorbed. [Q] Dark-colored clothes absorb white light; light-colored clothes give it off. Dark-colored clothes are much hotter to wear, light are not.	1
14. *(shakes head)* February 12? Don't know. Only remember my own.	0
15. Shakespeare	1
16. Located in Rome, where Pope and his bishops live and whoever else.	1
17. I'm supposed to remember? Takes about 6 hours to get there by plane, the plane travels *(mumbles about rate)* . . . 2,000 miles.	0

18. Located in Africa, North Africa, right? Hope I'm right.   0
19. Budding. Water or moisture gets to the yeast. [Q] Had it in school, I should know . . . I've been left back so many times in biology. Reproduces by asexual reproduction. *(mumbled)* It's hard to explain. There's a name for it. Asexual reproduction *(enunciated carefully)*. Yeast rises by budding. It expands and separates.   0
20. New York City has 8 million, so somewhere between 2 billion and 250 billion. [Q] Leave it at 2 billion. I don't go around counting people; I'm not the census.   0
21. Two for every state . . . 100, if you don't count Puerto Rico, Guam, places like that. I don't know if they have senators.   1
22. Beginning of the world, beginning of life   1
23. 170 Fahrenheit   0
24. Excuse me! Never heard of that.   0
25. I can't tell you. What do you mean by vessels? I'm confusing it with cells. Ohh, veins, arteries, capillaries. For a change somebody else does the writing. [Q] In school I do so much writing, and lately I write when I have free time—about my photographs, short stories, poems, verses, when no one's in the house and everything's quiet and I'm watching TV.   1
26. The Moslem Bible   1
27. Say it again—I have no idea.   0
28. *(smiles)* Got me there.   0
29. I have no idea.   0

Total   19

Comprehension

Score

1–2.   4
3. Drop in the mailbox . . . open it. If it's nothing special, put a stamp on it. It's a moral thing. Unless it's something special. [Q] A top secret envelope. The government would consider you a spy if you turned it in. Russia would kill you for finding it. I'd keep it as a souvenir. . . . I've found money on the street a few times, without an envelope. Eighty dollars all together. I found most of it all at once, about forty dollars, all in corners in the same area of the sidewalk. I found some; then I went back and found the rest.   0
4. They're a bad influence. They divert you to things you don't want to do, you were brought up not to want to do. But I don't believe it. If you know right, you can be with them and not do what you don't want. They can go out and kill a person or rob a bank, and you don't have to. I talk a lot, don't I?   0
5. Go up and tell the person who is the attendant and they'll take care of it. Won't tell them. [Q] The people, they'd panic.   2
6. The first taxes were made to support you, the economy, the government. To pay politicians, government. Always get back one-third in tax returns, sometimes nothing. [Q] File tax returns. Form A or B; A is harder, B is easier. You file before the deadline—or else.   2
7. [N *repeats*] Would say was—I don't know—never heard of that one.   0
8. In the 1900s—since the 1800s 'til the 1920s, well, maybe 'til the depression, children were used as cheap labor, under poor lighting, poor heating, unsatisfactory conditions. Since there

was a depression they had to work. Where else were they
going to get money? The laws were made to keep the factories
only for people at the age limit. At 14 you can get working
papers, but not as a factory worker. At 17 or 18, you can be
a factory worker. What time is it?   1
9. I'd use the sign of the river—rivers flow up not down, to
south not north—moss on the trees, pointing to the north,
the railroad tracks, which way the train runs, and the sun.
It comes up in the north and sets in the south. [Q] Where
it's first the brightest, it sets in the opposite direction. Like
in Japan, the land of the rising sun, it comes up in the east,
sets in the west. It should be that it comes up in the west
here, sets in the east.   1
10. Born deaf? Has to do with ears right? Never heard the
sound of someone talking. Never get response from other
person when they talk. They wouldn't understand what
others say . . . except from reading lips, making hand
signals, writing on paper.   1
11. There's a higher rate of insurance, less space in the city.
In the country there's more space, lower risk of robbery.
The city is high risk, high rates of insurance, a high-risk
area. In the country you can have a normal life.   1
12. If people ever get divorced or remarried to another woman,
the law says you're not allowed 'til you're divorced. For
regulation.   0
13. Excuse me! Saying? I never heard of it. Since brooks are
shallow, lot of rocks and fallen trees make lots of noise
when water travels over. I really don't understand the saying.   0
14. Once? *(shakes head)* No idea.   0
                                                                        ___
                                                          Total   12

Arithmetic

	Score
1–2.	2
3.	1
4.	1
5.	1
6.	1
7.	1
8.	1
9.	0
10.	1
11.	0
12.	0
13.	0
Total	9

Similarities

		Score
1.	Both fruit	2
2.	Clothing	2
3.	Ummm . . . tools.	2
4.	Animals	2
5.	Direction	2

6.	Parts of the human body	1
7.	Matter	0
8.	Furniture	2
9.	Hmm . . . egg and seed—both embryos. I don't know . . . living things. [Q] Embryos.	2
10.	They have meanings, sentimental meanings. You can put up a statue of George Washington and write a poem about someone you love and it means the same thing.	0
11.	*(lowers head, sighs)* Items.	0
12.	Values. [Q] You're valuing what they've done for you. You're giving them what they deserve, so I used the word value.	0
13.	Nature.	1
	Total	16

Digit Span

F6 + B4   Total Score   10

Vocabulary

		Score
1–3.		6
4.	Season	1
5.	Fix	2
6.	Food	1
7.	Clothing	0
8.	Bread	0
9.	To put together	2
10.	Cover up	2
11.	Large	1
12.	Hard head . . . stubborn . . . I'm using street language.	0
13.	Words	0
14.	Simplify	0
15.	Start	2
16.	Go on	0
17.	Shack	0
18.	Point out . . . like an area.	2
19.	Civilized	0
20.	Take in	0
21.	Destroy, get rid of	0
22.	Disturb	1
23.	I have no idea.	0
24.	Hmmm . . . a quiet place.	0
25.	*(frowns)* No matches—wait! Sorry. That's the dumb way. A book without matches . . . uneven. A twin, person who doesn't look like you, clothing that doesn't match.	0
26.	Not to do something. [Q] Many reasons. If you don't think it's good.	1
27.	Crowd	0
28.	I have no idea.	0
29.	Peaceful	2
30.	I have no idea.	0
31.	To understand	1
32.	I have no idea	0
33.	Area. If each side of a circle is 2, then 4 times 2 = 8 is the perimeter, of the square.	0

34.	I have no idea.	0
35.	*(shakes head)* No idea.	0
36.	*(shakes head)* No idea.	0
37.	*(shakes head)* No idea.	0
38.	*(shakes head)* No idea.	0
39.	*(shakes head)* No idea.	0
40.	*(shakes head)* No idea.	0
	Total	24

Digit Symbol Total Score 40

Picture Completion

		Score
1.		1
2.		1
3.		1
4.	Antenna—handle	1
5.		1
6.		1
7.	Bridge	1
8.	One of bolts from neck	1
9.	Person	0
10.		1
11.		0
12.	Paw prints	1
13.	Southern California	1
14.		1
15.		1
16.		1
17.	Pinky	1
18.		1
19.	Don't know what you call where foot goes in hanging down from saddle when you ride a horse.	1
20.	*(shakes head)* I don't see anything. Oh! Logs on ground not covered with snow.	1
21.	Don't see a thing. Her ear?	0
	Total	18

Block Design

		Time	*Score*
1.		14"	4
2.		8"	4
3.	*(at end mixes blocks up)* I did it for you.	10"	4
4.		8"	4
5.		12"	4
6.		60"+	0
7.		41"	4
8.		85"	0
9.		120"+	0
10.		120"+	0
		Total	24

Picture Arrangement

	Time	Order	Score
1.	1"	WXY	4
2.	1"	PAT	4
3.	5"	ABCD	4
4.	6"	ATOMIC	4
5.	20"	OPENS	4
6.	17"	JNAET	2
7.	25"	EFGHIJ	6
8.	20"	SALMUE	2
		Total	30

Object Assembly

		Time	Score
M	Little boy or girl? Can't tell. A bellboy.	20"	6
P	Profile of a woman, a woman's face.	48"	9
H	Hand.	80"	7
E	Elephant *(said before assembly)*.	100"	8
		Total	30

Bender–Gestalt

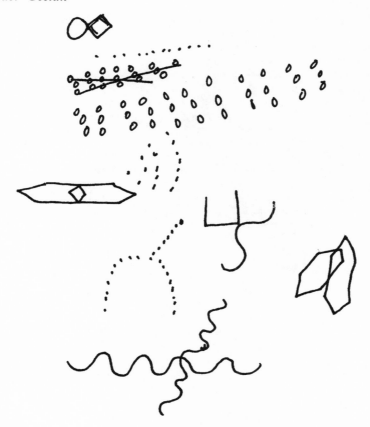

Figure Drawings

Rorschach

I.

                                What am I sup-
posed to say?

    12"   1. Ink smeared all over. [Q]

1. [Q] Because it is. I don't know what you mean. The shape.

2. A bat—I used to do these in elementary school. It feels funny to say what they mean. I don't know why they use ink blots.

2. [Q] The shape again. The whole thing. [*points to parts*] Wing, tail, it has four feet—front feet, back feet.

II.   4"   1. It's a butterfly.

1. [Q] The shape. [*names parts*] Antenna, head, wings, two things, I don't know what they're called that come out from the wings.

III.   1"   1. A frog. [W]

1. [Q] The shape. [*points to parts*] Head [*center D*], body, front legs, back legs [*using upper side reds*].

IV.   1"   1. [*grimaces*] A waterbug.

1. [Q] [*sighs*] The shape again. But it looks more like a mess. [*points to parts*] Head, big feet, small feet, any extra it might have.

V.   4"   1. A bird.

1. I know what I said, what did I say? A bird. Because of the shape. (Points to parts) Wings, tail (bottom D), beak (top D).

VI.   22"   1. [*leans over card*] Amoeba. It doesn't look like anything. It has shape but doesn't look like anything.

1. What did I say? Amoeba? Right? It's a matter of no structure, an amoeba just moves around, like jelly, it has no shape. No, this has shape, it looks like an amoeba because it has no structure. [*points to parts*] Front [*top*], false foot—pseudopod, is that how you pronounce it?

VII.	1"	1. Two people.	1. [*Q*] [*sighs*] The shape. They're facing each other. [*smirks*] They look like Indians. [*points to parts*] Features, head, hair, nose, body, torso. They're sitting on two rocks. Let's get on to the next one. Let's finish them. They're so stupid, these blots. They make you feel so low-graded.
VIII.	20"	1. A mess! [*with disdain*] Just joking. They're animals. You're writing down everything I say? Every little thing?	1. [*Q*] The shape. [*Q*] There's more. There are two animals climbing up the hill, trying to meet each other at the top. [*points to parts*] Hill, paws, head.
IX.	17"	1. A person who's two-faced. . . . What would you say if I asked you?	1. [*Q*] The right's the good side, the left side the bad. [*Q*] It's folded in half. [*Q*] Well, in the Bible, I was taught that when Christ died, he turned his face to the right. So right is good, left is bad. The face is in the middle [*green D*], the outside world is around him.
X.	11"	1. A villain with long hair.	1. [*Q*] It has an angry look. [*Angry?*] The shape. The way they designed it. It's the last one. [*smiles*] [*Q*] It's a villain with a mustache and long hair [*red D*], wearing a hat [*top*] of course.

TAT

1. How will I say it? A boy who doesn't want to play the violin. He's looking at it. He's bored. He doesn't want to play it. He stands there, staring . . . his time's up. He says to his mother, "I'm finished." He's thinking, "I got away with it." [*Q*] He got away without practicing. He doesn't want to play the violin. [*Q*] His mother wants him to grow up and play violin. [*Q*] I was thinking . . . it's just a plain picture. The kid, he's about 11, doesn't want to play violin. It's hard to make up a story.
2. What can I tell you? I have nothing to say about it. She's looking into the future. She's thinking what would happen if she didn't go to school. She'd have to be working hard, wouldn't have a good education, wouldn't get a good job. [*Q*] I don't know. She's just

thinking. She doesn't feel sad, she doesn't feel happy. [*Q*] Her and her husband. [*points to background*] That's what she's thinking. [*Old?*] 17.

3 BM. Lonely. Has no one to talk to. Seems like . . . the person's crying . . . doesn't know what to do . . . has a problem, doesn't know what to do . . . lonely. [*Q*] A problem in the house, streets or job. [*Q*] At the job, the person doesn't know what to do. Just been fired. [*Man or woman?*] Can't tell from here. Could be a man. There's some debris on the floor. [*Q*] Things will get worse . . . the person may become a bum . . . live a miserable life.

5. Are there a lot of them? Are we gonna do them all? [*Q*] Well, they're not too exciting, telling stories about picture. The lady in the picture sees someone in the room. She heard a noise. She's shocked by what she sees. They broke a window. [*Q*] Someone's in the room. She didn't expect it. She's shocked . . . a window's broken. [*Q*] The person was playing around in the room. Her son, maybe, daughter.

6 BM. The lady's worried about what will happen to the man. The man has a problem. He has to go and do something. The lady's worried about a mistake he might make, doesn't want him to go. [*Q*] He has to leave on a dangerous trip. She doesn't want him to go. [*Q*] He may have an accident. Car accident, plane, maybe. [*Q*] He's sad. He doesn't want his mother to feel worried. [*Q*] He loves his mother. He doesn't want her to worry. [*She?*] He's her son. She loves him. She's worried and sad. It's the same with my friends and family. It seems like all these cards are about my family, things that are happening to me.

7 BM. Father and son are having a fight. The son is angry at what the father is saying. He doesn't want to hear what he's saying. [*Q*] School. He wants him to wake up early go to school early. Finish school. Do his homework. Pass his tests. [*Son feel?*] He feels angry. He doesn't want to hear. He's able to do it, but he has problems of his own. It's hard to do all at once. [*Q*] In the house, outside in the street, with friends. [*They don't get along?*] He gets along. But him pains . . . in the neck, in the as . . . rear. [*Q*] They play around too much . . . more than he does. It bothers him. He doesn't do a lot of things they do. [*Q*] Smoke, drink, dance, stay out late at night. [*He doesn't?*] No, it's just his style, his personality.

8 BM. Looks like a person who's worried about somebody. The person's having an operation. He's wondering if this person's gonna make it, be OK, recoup, be better after what happened [*points to background*]. [*He feel?*] Worried. [*Q*] A patient and two doctors. [*points to gun*] I have no idea what this is—anything from the barrel of a shotgun to a stick holding the light up. Could be anything. Maybe the patient was shot by somebody and they're trying to take the bullet out.

9 GF. I don't know what I can tell you. I have no reason why the lady wants to be up a tree unless she's a little screwy. The second lady is running away from something . . . she's a rich lady. The lady in the tree is her maid . . . she has a towel. She's wondering what is happening. [*Running from?*] Somebody. Somebody who's after her. Somebody who wants to hurt him, her. One is scared . . . the lady running; one is confused . . . wondering what is happening.

10. [*laughs*] Two people caring for each other. One is a male, one is a female. They're thinking about each other, caring about each other. [*Thinking?*] How much they love each other. [*Q*] Boyfriend and girlfriend. [*Old?*] Twenties. Looks like they're embracing. [*Feel?*] That's a nice question. Looking for the right word. They feel . . . happy with each other.

12 M. Hmmm . . . looks like a priest. The person in the picture is very sick. The priest is giving . . . the person's very sick, he might die, giving him last rites. [*Q*] Of a disease. [*Old?*] 17 or 18. [*Feel?*] Very sick. [*Emotions?*] Happy the priest is there.

13 MF. I knew there'd be something like this. [*Q*] These kind of pictures. Here we have a man—it looks like he just finished. . . . He looks very sad; someone just died. [*Finished?*] He just finished having sex with the woman. Didn't really want to answer this way. [*Q*] It's hard for me to tell you these things. The other way . . . she died in her sleep. She was very sick of high blood pressure attacks. [*Old?*] 40s. [*Q*] Husband and wife. [*Q*] He wakes up. He's gotten up. Gets dressed. Goes to work or goes home. [*Related?*] Anything from boyfriend and girlfriend to prostitute from the street. [*Why hard to talk?*] I think I won't stop. In bio class, we're talking and talking, we don't

stop. My friends like to talk about it. My friends like to talk about sex with girlfriends. I'm not like that. I'm different. I don't like to talk about things that are private.

14. I can't believe people get paid for this. He's looking out the window, staring, thinking of things he'd like to do, things that have happened to him in the past. [Q] Waiting for a job, looking for an apartment. He's in between jobs, apartments. . . . There's another part . . . he's ready to jump out the window. [Q] He did something he shouldn't have, in the streets. [Q] He robbed somebody and it's bothering him. . . . He killed somebody. [*Feel?*] Very unhappy. [*Old?*] Twenty or up. Still, could be sixties. He has no facial or body features.

3 GF. It's a nice drawing. It's one of the best yet. The woman just finished doing something wrong. She wishes she never did it. She's sad, she's crying. She wishes she could repent. [Q] Stole something. [*Feel?*] She's stoned . . . something happy comes and then you think about sad things . . . I never got drunk, but my father did. He'd say, "I wish I did this, I did that." [*Her feelings?*] When you feel happy, then you think of bad things. You sit and wonder. The bad conquers the good.

4. The man is annoyed at the woman. She wants to plead with him. She tells him that "I'm sorry." He doesn't want to hear. He says, "Leave me alone. I don't want to be bothered." [Q] She spent too much of his money. She doesn't have to do it. He just says, "Leave me alone, don't bother me with problems of the house."

6
The 18- to 21-Year-Old

Developmental Expectations

Physically, to all outward appearances, this age group now appears to be adult. Psychologically, preoccupations are primarily concerned with separation. First, the individual now struggles to attain his own identification distinct from the group and from his parents or family. Second, the individual who leaves home struggles with the separation from home and high school. If he remains at home to go to school, this separation conflict may be delayed; however, if the high school graduate enters the job market, he faces new stresses in a non-protected environment. The contrast between being on top (as a senior in high school) to the bottom of the heap (as a freshman in college or an entry-level worker) can be fraught with difficulties in adjustment.

By 21 years of age these struggles should be resolved, so that the young adult has a more confident sense of self, his values, and his future plans.

Cognitive Functioning. By now the potential for adult cognitive processes has been reached, and a cognitive style has been established.

Dynamic Picture. In the process of the establishment of identification, the individual at this time is preoccupied with introspective pursuits relating to values, relationships, career choices, and the definition of self. He no longer has the sense of security provided by his identification with the group and can therefore suffer from feelings of depersonalization and isolation. This particularly seems to peak around 19 years of age.

Although a solid sexual identity has been achieved, the individual pursues different relationships in the attempt to clarify his own interest. Sexual fears have been reduced through the achievement of greater control over one's impulses; aggressive impulses similarly have come under greater control. By 21 years of age the preoccupation with the self is over, and the individual is free to invest his talents and energies into pursuing a career, finding a mate and, hopefully, enjoying himself.

Defenses. The process begun during the 16- to 18-year-old period continues with further consolidation and integration of the defenses, leading to the establishment of the personality picture.

Affective Expression. Due to the preoccupation with the self, this is a period of time when feelings can be extremely painful, sad, and/or one can feel withdrawn. At moments of clarification and insight there can be good feelings, at time reaching euphoric intensity.

Normal Expectations on Tests

Intelligence Tests. At this time the performance on the Wechsler should be consistent across all areas.

Bender–Gestalt. This should be accomplished according to adult standards.

Projectives. The figure drawings should be drawn with the standards for the adult form. Either a profile or front view is acceptable.

The number of responses and determinants of the percepts on the Rorschach should be equal to adult standards now. The content of the responses may reflect specific interests or areas of study (anatomy, geology, art, and so on).

The TAT stories are expected to follow adult standards for the formulation of a story.

Representative psychological and test interpretations and psychological test batteries for adolescents within this age range now follow. The raw test data from the psychological test battery follow the discussion of each adolescent, so that easy reference can be made to the examples selected for illustration of the interpretations. We include examples of adolescents diagnosed as having a reactive disorder, being mildly disturbed, moderately disturbed, and severely disturbed, in order to demonstrate how a psychological portrait is developed. Each adolescent's tests are analyzed, interpreted, and concluded with an integrated summary.

As stated before, the summary is not a complete report, but represents the salient features leading to the diagnostic portrait.

Psychological Test Portrait

O: 18–8 Female

O was evaluated as part of the intake procedure to determine whether she needed treatment. She had come to the clinic because she felt she could not shake off the sadness over her parents' recent death. Her parents were killed in an automobile accident four months prior to her seeking treatment.

O is a recent high school graduate who is working in a clerical position in an office. She has recently moved in with her oldest sibling, a married sister. She is the youngest of four children. In addition to her sister, she has two older unmarried brothers.

She is an attractive, plump young woman who wears her hair in a stylish fashion. She presents herself with a pleasant, quiet demeanor.

She attended inconsistently to the testing requirements, sometimes seeming motivated and at other times disinterested. She maintained her pleasant demeanor throughout.

Cognitive Functioning

WAIS: O performs on the WAIS at an across-the-board average level with a Verbal IQ of 104, a Performance IQ of 94 and a Full-Scale IQ of 100. There is very little intertest variability, but her intratest scores show occasional variability. The fact that she is able to achieve the correct answers on some items in Block Design and Picture Arrangement after the time limit suggests a potential for a more consistent performance than her actual scores show. Although she is able to abstract well (Similarities, 12), the content of some questions leads to concreteness in her thinking at times (Comprehension, 7, 11, 13, and 14; Similarities, 8 and 12; Vocabulary, 25). In summary O demonstrates average abilities across all areas of cognitive functioning.

B–G: O's Bender reflects many instances of visual-motor difficulties (A, 4, 6, 7, and 8). She has ears (A, 7, and 8), leaves gaps in connections between lines (7 and 8) and figures (A and 4), and overextends lines (7 and 8). Her difficulty in drawing angles is particularly noticeable in A, 7, and 8.

These difficulties may well explain the loss of credits on timed items in the WAIS Performance tests (Block Design and Picture Arrangement).

FD: O's figure drawings are clearly differentiated sexually. There is a notable discrepancy, however, between the disproportionate rendering of her female figure and the good proportions of the male figure. The too-large head, missing lower jaw, misplaced breast lines, unfinished skirt, and missing legs and feet on the female drawing all suggest dynamic issues.

Rorschach: O makes good use of all the blots, including good form and many determinants. Her achievement of 23 responses, with many details as well as two originals (V and IX), suggest a better than her achieved average intellectual potential.

TAT: The TAT stories told by O have proper sequences, reflecting the pictures as depicted.

Summary Statement of Cognitive Functioning: O shows an average intellectual ability with evidence for higher potential. She has good language usage and good memory, and she is reality oriented. In spite of evidence of a perceptual-motor difficulty, she has managed to compensate well.

Dynamic Picture

WAIS: The WAIS does not reflect any dynamic issues.

B–G: There are no dynamic issues revealed in O's Bender figures.

FD: O clearly defines herself as feminine, as seen in her figure drawing. The too-large head and lack of its completion, added to the lack of legs and feet, suggest a sense of insecurity and need to rely on intellectual control. In both drawings the hands are hidden, which can reflect an unwillingness to reach out to others.

Although the boy is adequately proportioned and completed (except for a hand), his stated age of 12 and immature appearance may reflect O's wish to perceive males as more childlike and dependent.

Rorschach: Similarly to the large head on O's female drawing, her excessive need to achieve *W*'s speaks again to the push for intellectual control. At the same time, the small number of *M*'s suggest O's unwillingness to accept her mature status as an 18-year-old. This conflict is reflected in an inner tension and anxiety seen in the great number of *m*'s. Although O has an excellent ability for interactions with others (*FC*'s) and the capacity for fun and spontaneity (*FM*'s and *CF*'s), she chooses to spend a great deal of energy in introspection and self-reflection (*FK*'s). This and the depressive feelings (seen in numbers of *C*'s) would appear to be the result of an inability to come to terms with the mourning of the recent loss of her parents.

The content of her percepts shows feelings of her wish to come through the darkness into the light (Card II, 1).

TAT: O's mourning of her parents' recent deaths is implied throughout her TAT stories. Almost half of O's stories deal with the potential for suicide (3

BM, 14, and 17 GF) or actual death (10, 12 M, and 13 MF). In contrast, her other stories speak to good and caring family interactions. There is a suggestion of a regret over the loss of a caring and/or structuring parent (1, 7 GF, and 12 F).

Summary Statement of Dynamic Picture: The projectives reflect O's overall healthy inner status with concerns appropriate for her age. She struggles, however, with a need to resolve her preoccupation with her intense sense of loss, a loss which occurred before she was ready to establish her own independence.

Defenses

WAIS: O's response to the WAIS is almost completely free of any defensive maneuvers. There is the suggestion of projection on authority for the sake of control and limits (Comprehension, 5, 8, and 9; and Similarities, 12). Otherwise she proceeds in a straightforward way.

B–G: The figures produced on the Bender show O's efforts to compensate for a perceptual-motor difficulty.

FD: The disproportionate size of the female figure's head suggests the need for the use of intellectual controls on O's part. In addition, the hidden hands and missing legs suggest the use of avoidance in interpersonal interactions.

Rorschach: O's good intellectual defenses are seen in her achievement of W's, the F+ level, and the good use she makes of structure and determinants. Within her intellectual control there are evidences of regression (VII, 1; VIII, 2; IX, 1 and 2). Avoidance is seen only in her dealing with the sharp stimulus of the red on II (1) and III (2 and 3). She handles the softer colors of VIII, IX, and X with good intellectual control. Her reaction to Card IV suggests a phobic response, which is handled by criticizing the concept and gaining distance from it. This may also explain the blocking on the name in Card V (1).

TAT: O's stories are noteworthy for the use of denial when confronting suicidal impulses (3 BM, 14, and 17 GF). There is one instance of the projection on the adult for control (Card 1) as was seen in the WAIS. She also uses fantasy of a happy future (Card 2 and 16).

Summary Statement of Defenses: O generally utilizes good intellectual controls throughout the testing. There is evidence at times for the use of denial, projection, and fantasy.

Affective Expression

WAIS: O does not express any affect throughout the WAIS, maintaining a bland compliance. She never seems either upset or particularly pleased with her efforts.

B–G: The Bender was completed by O without any affective comments.

FD: O's pictures show a female and male with bland expressions on their faces. This is true in spite of her comment to the female "Let's have her smile!" and she erases the mouth in an attempt to draw a smile.

Rorschach: O seemed to enjoy the Rorschach. She reached to the lighter-colored cards with pleasure (VIII, 2; IX, 1, 2; X). She also conveyed pleasure in her description in her second response to Card V. This pleasurable affect is in contrast to the depressive feeling elicited by dark stimuli in Cards I (2), II (1), V (1), and VI (2).

TAT: As seen in the previous tests, there is a paucity of positive affects in O's TAT stories. They are best described as bland. Quite in contrast are her repetitive themes of death and suicide (3 BM, 10, 12 M, 13 MF, and 17 GF), suggesting her underlying depressed feeling.

Summary Statement of Affective Expression: O's predominant affective mood is one of blandness. In spite of the capacity for pleasure and enjoyment, when she expresses any feelings they reflect unhappiness.

Summary

O is a young woman who has a basically healthy ego organization. She has the capacity for caring interpersonal relationships, good use of her cognitive skills, and a good sense of self, and she is reality oriented. There are occasional glimpses of creativity, as well as suggestions of a higher intellectual potential than she achieved.

At this point in time she is reacting with sadness and depression to her recent losses. Thoughts of suicide and death preoccupy her, and therefore she is in need of help. Her overall bland presentation appears to be her current way of coping with her mourning.

Diagnosis

DSM-III-R

Axis I: V62.82 Uncomplicated Bereavement
Axis II   V71.09 No Diagnosis
Axis III: Healthy
Axis IV: 6-Catastrophic
Axis V: 70-Mild

O seeks treatment at this time for her sadness. Her good introspective abilities and awareness of the source of her distress make her an excellent candidate for individual psychotherapy.

Psychological Test Data

O: 18–8 Female

WAIS

		Scaled Score
Verbal Tests		
Information		10
Comprehension		9
Arithmetic		12
Similarities		12
Digit Span		9
Vocabulary		9
	Total	61

Performance Tests		
Digit Symbol		12
Picture Completion		9
Block Design		7(10)
Picture Arrangement		8(11)
Object Assembly		9
	Total	45 (51)

	Scaled Score	IQ
Verbal Score	61	104
Performance Score	45 (51)	94 (102)
Full Scale Score	106 (112)	100 (103)

Information

	Score
1–4.	4
5. I don't know—thinking what rubber is—gum.	0
6. Eisenhower, Kennedy, Johnson, Truman	1
7. A writer	1
8. 52	1
9. Guessing . . . south.	1
10. South America	1
11. About 5'4"	1
12. Rome?	1
13. Gee—I don't know. They are warmer? Maybe because heavier?	0
14. February 22	1
15. Shakespeare	1
16. Where the Pope lives	1
17. I don't know—no idea. Guess? Mileage maybe 2,000 miles.	0
18. Israel—closest. Where's Israel? My geography is very bad.	0
19. By putting it in the cooking? I don't know process.	0
20. I don't know. 160 billion people?	0
21. Two from each state	1
22. I don't know—never heard of it, the Bible.	0
23. Gee—I don't know.	0
24. Don't know.	0
25. Don't know.	0
26. Don't know.	0
Total	15

Comprehension

	Score
1–2	4
3. Drop it in the letter box.	2
4. Cause they're bad. [Q] They say, "Tell me who your friends are and I'll tell what you are." Guess if you hang around with bad, you get bad.	2
5. Guess I'd report it—and they'd do whatever is needed. [Q] The people who are head of movie—the manager. Guess there's a fire box—you'd ring it. If I see manager before box, go to him. If I see fire box first, go to box.	2
6. Support the city. [Q] Suppose people couldn't go into regular hospital, they would have to go to city hospital. Who would be paying for city hospital? To help yourself, it comes down to.	1
7. I never heard of it before. [Q] I could only think of ironing clothes. Do it while iron is hot. [*Other meaning?*] Do it while you can. If it's a good thing do it while you can or the opportunity might not come again.	2
8. For going to school? [Q] Everything would be out of hand with the kids growing up—if they had their own way—wouldn't go to school. [*Repeat Q*] I don't know how to say it. They have to have some discipline—system—at end they'll feel they've accomplished something. [Q] Thinking why there are regular laws. Why are there just child labor laws? Nothing sold to minors, under 18 years old. Wouldn't that be considered a child labor law?	0
9. Uh, keep walking. [Q] No compass or flare? Give a holler to see if anybody nearby. [Q] Keep walking.	0

10. I don't know. [Q] They can't hear very good, not at all. Can get across what they want to say. Can't hear regular pronunciation. Get used to your lips, sound of a word.   1
11. Taxes I guess—higher taxes. I knw there are higher taxes in city for house—higher than Westchester or Island.   0
12. I don't know, just has to be. [Q] Guess to be registered with the state of New York and not just the parish priest. A notice for the estate, to keep things in order.   1
13. Brooks like where water is coming into it? [Q] Kids are near the brook, throw rocks in maybe. There are fishes in it. Noise is in water from rocks.   0
14. One week away doesn't make a vacation. You can go away— it doesn't mean a vacation. [Q] Could go away for business, family. Just because you have it, doesn't mean it couldn't be a vacation. I don't know, thinking of what to say. Bird, one bird is around, doesn't mean it is summer yet.   1

Total   16

Arithmetic

	Score
1.	1
2.	1
3.	1
4.	1
5.	1
6.	1
7.	1
8.	1
9.	1
10.	1
11.	2
12.	0
13.	1
14.	0
Total	13

Similarities

	Score
1. They are both sweet. They are both fruits.	2
2. You usually wear them together. Are clothing.	2
3. Both tools.	2
4. Animals	2
5. Like east and south. Two different directions.	2
6. Senses.	2
7. Need them both to exist.	2
8. Together, to be used at the same time.	0
9. Uh—for planting? Or when you're gonna conceive a child? Both round. Produce egg each month, there's a seed planted.	1
10. Both remembered? A statue made of a person to be remembered, and a poem you remember when you read it. For remembrance of a special person.	1
11. They both could destroy something. Alcohol could destroy by excessiveness. Wood, if it is put on fire, could destroy a person—anything.	0

12. They're just the opposite. They are both necessary if you're bringing up children. Need to praise and should be punished for doing wrong.   1
13. I could think of lots of things, but not for this one.   0
                                                                   ___

                                                    Total   17

Digit Span

                                                                   Score
F6 + B4   Total Score   10

Vocabulary

                                                                   Score
1–3.   6
4. A season. [Q] Time of year when it's cold.   2
5. To fix   2
6. A meal. [Q] something to eat in the morning.   2
7. Clothing, material   2
8. A piece of   1
9. Together. [Q] To get together, to group   2
10. To hide   2
11. Huge, big   2
12. To slow down   0
13. A sentence is like a complete thought   2
14. To schedule   2
15. To end, stop   0
16. Think   2
17. I don't know.   0
18. In honor of—to designate the statue   0
19. Family, home   1
20. To get, to gather   0
21. End   2
22. To disturb. Interfere, like.   1
23. To dislike   0
24. The thing inside the church. The altar.   1
25. To be without matches is matchless. Like if you had shoes or socks and one of them is gone.   0
26. Not wanting to do something   2
27. I don't know. Thinking of Calamity Jane.   0
28. I heard it used so many times. Something you're supposed to have. Like goodness.   0
29. Change   0
30. I don't know.   0
31. To have feeling. To have understanding, softness.   1
32. Changeable   0
33. I don't know.   0
34. No.   0
35. The bus? No.   0
36. No.   0
                                                                 ___

                                                    Total   35

Digit Symbol   Total Score   63

Picture Completion

		Score
1.		1
2.	Tail	1
3.	Nose	1
4.		1
5.		1
6.		0
7.		0
8.		1
9.		1
10.		1
11.		0
12.		0
13.		1
14.		1
15.		0
16.		0
17.		1
18.		1
19.		1
20.		0
21.		0
	Total	13

Block Design

	Time	Score
1.	5"	4
2.	30"	4
3.	8"	4
4.	8"	4
5.	10"	4
6.	10"	4
7.	26"	0
8.	120"	0 (4)
9.	120"	0
10.	90"	0 (4)
	Total	24 (32)

Picture Arrangement

	Time	Order	Score
1.	7"	WXY	4
2.	7"	PAT	4
3.	13"	ABCD	4
4.	42"	TMIAOC	0 (4)
5.	82"	OPESN	0
6.	42"	JNAET	2
7.	75"	EFGHIJ	4
8.	50"	SAMEUL	0 (4)
		Total	18 (26)

Object Assembly

	Time		Score
M	17"		6
P	50"		9
H	86"		7
E	130"		8
		Total	30

Bender–Gestalt

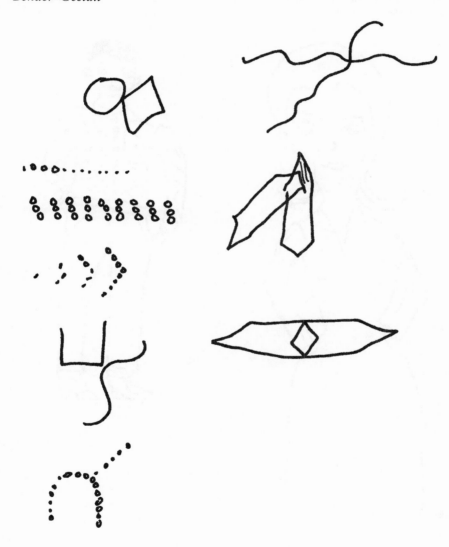

Figure Drawings

Any person? [*stops at head*]

[*Female*] A little weird! [*laughs*] I'm not an artist. Not anything looks like she has . . . [*Reminds you of?*] A girl. Looks pretty awful. I don't know, like she's got nothing to do. Got hands in pockets—just staring. [Q] At nothing. [*erases mouth*] At least let's have her smile. About 19.

[*Male*] Whole body too? [*legs first, head last*] I'm no good at this! Looks like he has a girl's blouse on—let me make more checks. [*She is wearing checked blouse.*] [Q] Like a little boy—small! Mischievous. Pretty good looking. Twelve years old. Not doing anything. Let me fix the collar [*fixes shoes*].

Rorschach

I.   6"

1. A butterfly.

1. The little—looks like it has wings. The center part looks like the body of the butterfly [Q] This looks like the face. I don't know—just the shape of the whole picture. [Q] Big—in size, the wideness.

2. Something spilling on the floor, maybe.

2. Something spilt. Any number of things. [Q] Gravy—over the floor, all over. [Q] Maybe because it's dark.

II.   15"

1. It looks like a tunnel—hmm—it's a small tunnel where, let's say, a car is going through. [D]

1. I was looking at the black streaks. [*rubs finger along side* D] Like you are just coming out of the tunnel, 'cause you see the light over here. [*points to center* S] Here's a car on the bottom. [*center bottom*] [Q] The tunnel is dark, looks wide enough, it's inside.

2. Looks like two animals putting their hands together. [W]

2. Yeah, they're putting their hands and their feet together. Like they're dancing or something. Head, nose, mouth, neck, hands, feet.

III.   20"

1. Two people. They look like they're gonna play the drums. Legs, hands, and a face.

1. That looks like something for them to play with, I just thought of a drum. They're probably women because it looks like they got high heels on, got pants on, too. [Q] This is the pants, and this is a jacket. They're probably some kind of performers.

2. Some decorations on the wall. [*center red* D]

2. This looks like a bow here, some sort of decoration. Shaped just like a bow—little knot in middle.

3. This looks like some sort of bird hanging from a string.

3. The round front part of the bird, the wing, the face. It's hanging from a string, a decoration, must be made of paper.

1. Maybe the two people are pulling something. They're bent over, have their hands on a piece of black thing. Must be heavy. They're pulling something along together, yeah.

IV. 5"

1. It looks like a giant [*laughs*] with very big feet.

1. Looks pretty big, awkward. You're looking up at him—that's why the top looks so small. He looks like a big monster. That sounds awful. [Q] Like something you would see on those weird pictures on TV.

2. Don't know what else it could be. Some kind of leaf maybe. Looks like it is all crisp now.

2. When it first falls off the tree, it gets very crisp. Looks like it's splitting right here. It's crinkly like. [Q] Maybe because it's broken. It must be crisp in order to start breaking.

V. 24"

1. It looks like—what do you call it? One of those birds that fly in the sky. I'll think of his name, in a minute. You know, when people die on the desert, the kind of bird that comes around the body.

1. This is the wings, this is the face. Guess this must be little feet, like. It's black and shaped like that bird. Flying in the air, just like the bird.

2. Once you see the
picture one way,
it's hard to visual-
ize another way.
Two things it could
be. This here [*cen-
ter* D] could be one
of those half doors
that swing open,
and that could be a
bunny behind it.

2. There's a darker line in
the center. I think of
doors swinging open. It
looks like legs showing
outside the door. This
looks like a bunny,
with the ears up here. If
she were to come out,
doors would swing out
towards you. [*Bunny?*]
The round face.
Probably a person in,
like, a bunny cos-
tume—'cause it looks
like a girl. [*Q*] In a
barn or saloon.

VI.   42"

↑↓ 1. I really don't know
what it could be. If
I hold it this way,
it looks like maybe
a scarecrow's
jacket on a pole.

1. Sleeves, no head, arms,
uneven jacket, all un-
even like. [*Q*] This
looks like zipper of
jacket—a little white
down here, looks like
the neckline . . . a
raggedy jacket. Just
looks like a scarecrow's
jacket.

↓↑ 2. If I hold it upside
down this looks
like one of those
sticks—poles like
where an Indian
tribe has one of
their flags, uh—
their sign.

2. Those feathers on the
pole, like in the hat, all
different colors. [*Q*]
Usually two-toned, I
know it's black and
white. [*Q*] Pole goes
down to the ground.

Is is all right to see part of it? You must be tired
of writing.

VII.   22"

1. You'll laugh if I tell
you. This part
looks like breaded
shrimp. Like fan-
tailed shrimp—like
Chinese food. The
body is soft, and
the tail here. I
don't think of any-
thing else.

1. [*Breaded?*] They're big
looking—puffy look-
ing. It has the—uh—
any kind of shape when
it's breaded.

VIII.   22"

1. These look like
two cats over here.

1. Four legs, the little
face, the skinny body.
[*Q*] Like a house cat.

2. This maybe could be a dress. [*lower center* D]

2. Like a little ballerina dress, the two-tone, and it's short. Shaped like a flair dress. [Q] Sleeveless, neck up there. The pink and orange color.

→ 3. This could be like clear water, the grass on the ground—like a reflection—he's looking in. It's clear, you can see the whole thing.

3. Ground is where he's walking on, climbing—not using the pink part—I think of it as being one color, like grass. [*Water?*] 'Cause it's split in half—clear, like. Could be like a mirror. Don't know why I thought of water. [Q] Something he is climbing on.

IX.   17"

1. Ah—you know those colored animals you put on a baby's wall—plaques—two different colorful animals together on a plaque.

1. Face, blond hair, green dress, like dancing dolls. [Q] The bottom is there just to make the picture colorful, like, just there. [Q] Face was funny, though—Animal, like, like a big long nose, like a beak here. [Q] They are close together, like—arm of dress, skirt.

2. That's the only thing—see the center part here—reminds me of my toothbrush [*laughs*].

2. My toothbrush is green, thinner on top, gets thinner and thinner.

X.   15"

1. Looks like a birthday tablecloth.

1. Usually has pink, yellow, and blue. [Q] The background where it is white—big enough to have all these things on it.

2. Like birds.

2. The birds are the yellow. [Q] This is their tail. Shaped like a tiny bird, a robin or a canary.

3. Orange and green is like leaves, maybe, 'cause the bird is there.

3. The colors—like the shape, one here and one here. Orange and brown—turning colors.

4. The green would be grass—where the birds would be.	4. [Q] The color, I guess. Just where the deep green is. [Q] No, I don't know what the blue or pink is. It's usually there [*refers to the "tablecloth"*]

TAT

1. Doesn't look like he's very happy that he has to play his violin lessons. [Q] Well, ah—he probably—his mother requires him to take violin lessons. He doesn't like it. He'll probably sit and sulk about it. [*Practice?*] Maybe eventually after he's thinking about it. I don't know whether he'll be happy about it. [Q] He will continue, guess his mother tells him what to do.

2. Well, really I don't see much. He's plowing the field—assuming that's his wife over there. She looks as though she's going to have a baby. The other girl looks as though she's envious of her. Maybe the girl is her sister. Maybe she'd like to be in her position instead of going to school. Has books in her hand. She'll look for the same satisfaction that the couple has.

3 BM. What is that on the floor there? Evidently the girl is unhappy, and she's crying about it. It's a knife or a gun, I think. Perhaps she has intentions of hurting herself. [Q] Family, if she's married, it may be her husband—I don't know, could be lots of things. She wishes she was married—maybe somebody hurt her or something. I think that's a knife. Maybe that got her disgusted that she even thought of it. [Q] I think she'll be OK—she's about 24.

4. Ah, looks like he's going away. Perhaps he sees somebody he knows, and she doesn't want him to go to her. She wants to hold him back. Doesn't look like it's a home. Wouldn't have that picture in a home. Perhaps they're in a dance hall. He doesn't want to dance. He wants to walk away. [Q] I think he'll go away.

6 GF. The man in back looks like he startled the young woman from behind. He looks older than her. Perhaps he wants to introduce himself to her. Maybe she was startled by his forwardness. [Q] Maybe he found her pretty, interesting, and attractive. [Q] In somebody's home at a party. [Q] They'll meet and be friends. He looks too old just to strike up a conversation. [*Startled?*] Maybe he said something to her? Just introducing himself to her when no one else did.

7 GF. The little girl is holding her doll. Mother is reading her a story. Looks like she's daydreaming about what the mother was reading the story about. Could be she'd not interested in story, and she's wandering somewhere else. [Q] Mother will realize she's not paying attention and will stop. The little girl will go out to play.

9 GF. Girl down below looks like she's going out, doesn't look too happy about it. Going out to a party. Looks like she's got a much different dress on than the other girl. The other girl looks like she wishes she was her going out. Or perhaps she's bringing something to her, a purse or a stole. Probably sisters. She's hiding behind tree, looking down on other one. [*Unhappy?*] No smile, anxious, maybe they had an argument, sister and her. [Q] They'll forget it.

10. They look like they're consoling one another. Perhaps something happened to them and they were unhappy about it. They look like they are comforting one another. [Q] Could be dancing? Maybe one of their children is very sick. Perhaps it is very serious and it's hopeless. [Q] Child will pass away. She's 39, he's 41.

12 M. Looks like a man, that he's very, very sick. And the other man looks like he came to give him some kind of a blessing, or just to see whether he's awake or not. [Q] Looks like he's gonna die. [Q] A priest, maybe a doctor. [Q] Must have been—not a long illness. He's dressed, got hurt badly, maybe a heart attack. He's maybe 27.

13 MF. Looks like a lady's in bed. Looks like maybe she's dead. He found her dead. Very upset about it. Looks like he's gonna cry. Looks like she died in her sleep, like. [Q] Probably husband and wife—could be very sick, maybe. Guess he'll call somebody. He has hand over face.

14. Looks like a man or a young fellow in his dark room, with hand on the windowsill. Looking out the window when it is very light out. Perhaps he just awoke and he goes to open up the window, or just to sit, or to look out. [Q] Don't think anything is going to happen. He'll probably turn on the lights after he's finished looking out. Young? Looks slender. Looks like a nice day outside, with light in the room.

12 F. It looks like a very old grandmother in the back. Like she's wide awake for her age, you might say. Could be her daughter. Maybe they're watching somebody. They're both staring. The grandchild is doing something. Maybe they think he's very bright, seem to be staring. Thinking, I would say, hand like this. [*Happens?*] Nothing, the little child is playing or will stop. They are noticing her. That's all.

17 GF. Looks like it's a sunny day out. There's a bridge. Some kind of factory. Ships underneath the bridge, loading. There's the girl up on the bridge, looking into the water [Q] I don't think she'll do anything. I don't think she'll do anything. Just going across the bridge and staring in the water. [Q] She'll probably walk away. She's thinking the water is pretty with the sun shining on it.

11. Looks like some kind of forest with a bunch of rocks in it. Looks like there's some kind of bug or animal walking through the dirty garbage up there. Nothing's going to happen, just a mess. Maybe it's a dumping area.

18 GF. It looks like another lady must have fell against the staircase and fainted. She must look very weak to this other lady, who's holding her up. Looks like the other lady is older than this lady. Maybe her mother, the one who fainted. She'll probably take her in and put her on the couch. She'll try to bring her back to herself. She feels very sad, she's wondering how it happened. Mother is probably old and weak.

16. Any kind? I see a house and two trees beside it, one on each side. Grass in front of house, sidewalk, street with one or two cars passing. Maybe about four people sitting out on the porch, just talking. Two people there are visiting. Perhaps they're talking about dinner for next night, what's good to eat. Thinking about that—what they like to eat. [Q] Everyone will go home to their own home, like.

Psychological Test Portrait

P: 20–6 Female

P sought treatment because of her feelings of inadequacy and concerns about her appearance. She feels herself to be too fat, although she appeared to be of average weight. She had recently graduated from college and was worried about her future. She feels inadequate to make a decision as to what career she should pursue. She is concerned about her relationships with men and women and feels rejected by her peers.

P is single and lives with her parents and younger brother. She attended a local college while living at home. Her parents have fought continuously over the years but have never separated.

It was rather startling to E when P arrived for testing dresed in a man's suit and wearing a wedding ring. She explained that wearing the ring made her feel good.

She hoped the testing would be of help in understanding her problems. She cooperated and was anxious for the results.

Cognitive Functioning

WAIS: *P* achieves a Bright Normal IQ of 115 with a Bright Normal Verbal IQ of 118 and an Average Performance IQ of 108. With the exception of Block Design (which may have to do with motivational factors; see *Dynamics*) she performs fairly consistently across tests, but there is intratest variability (Comprehension, Similarities, Vocabulary, and Picture Completion). She functions adequately in the cognitive areas of language, abstract conceptualizations, social understanding, and perceptual-motor fucntioning.

B–G: *P* reproduces the Bender designs adequately. Her organization of the figures, however, is very poor. This suggests poor planning on her part.

FD: *P*'s figure drawings are well proportioned and of good size. She does differentiate the sexes adequately, although the male figure appears effeminate.

Rorschach: *P* produced 39 responses, a high number of *R*'s. She took into account all aspects of the blots, using an array of determinants. Her *F+* percentage is good. All of this achievement points to a higher intellectual potential than she achieved on the WAIS.

TAT: *P* tells adequate stories to the TAT cards. Her stories are concise, sequentially organized, and related to the pictures. They are well articulated.

Summary Statement of Cognitive Functioning: *P*'s having graduated from college at the relatively young age of 20 suggests earlier successes in her schooling. This cognitive achievement is seen in her Rorschach performance, in contrast to the Bright Normal level attained in the WAIS.

Dynamic Picture

WAIS:: One dynamic in *P*'s WAIS performance appears to be her attempt to involve *E* verbally in the Performance items where one is left on one's own. This is in contrast to the Verbal section of the test, which is interactive. Additionally, *P* responds to items that are available to her but does not make the effort to tackle items that are more difficult for her (Similarities, 6, 7, and 9; Arithmetic, 11; Information, 22 and 25; and Block Design, 6). This indication of a lack of motivation for achievement is in striking contrast to her having graduated from college at a relatively young age.

B–G: There is striking contrast in the size of *P*'s Bender figures (A versus 1 and 2), which implies a labile moving from constriction to expansiveness.

Otherwise they are carefully reproduced. Her seeming lack of motivation on the WAIS is contradicted here by her efforts to draw the figures correctly, as seen especially in figure 6.

FD: *P*'s figure drawings indicate her own clear-cut sexual identification, although the expression on the male's face is softer than the female's. A sense of a lack of stability and security is suggested by the insubstantial hands and feet on both drawings. Her difficulty in representing the arms suggests a feeling of passivity, and the buttons on both drawings refer to an immature dependency need. There are unexplained extraneous lines on the female's bodice and face.

Rorschach: The content of *P*'s Rorschach percepts are primarily concerned with immature oral needs. These needs are expressed through regressed dependency (I, 2; II, 1; VIII, 1 and IX, 1) or through oral sadism (III, 1) or oral aggression (IX, 3). There is also a strong concern about body integrity (I, 5; III, 4; X, 3). Difficulties in female interactions are suggested in two responses (I, 1; VII, 1). There is some indication of sexual identification confusion (X, 1).

There is evidence that *P* has some insight into and understanding of her problems (IV, 3; VII, 4) with some anxiety in relation to her oral needs (IX, 1).

TAT: The primary dynamic theme in *P*'s TAT stories is one of low self-esteem (1, 3 BM, and 4). Additionally there is difficulty in relating to others (4 and 18 GF). This perception is explained in her final story (16) by the fact that others only pretend to care.

Summary Statement of Dynamic Picture: The most salient dynamic issue with *P* is her immature oral dependency and oral aggression needs. With this is an underlying concern over body integrity. These dynamics lead to a lack of self-esteem with expectations of failure. Interactions with others are problematic in her inability to trust that others can care.

Defenses

WAIS: *P* performs the WAIS with little evidence of any defensive efforts. The one exception is her response to Comprehension 4, in which she denies the intent of the question and becomes judgmental. An instance of projection is also seen in her associations on Picture Arrangement (6 and 8).

B–G: If *P* is presented with defined and contained figures (A, 7, and 8), she copies them in proportion, although constricted. When presented with on-going sequences (1 and 2), she becomes expansive and relies on the edge of the paper to provide limits. In figure 6 she expands and distorts the crossing A curve and has to repeat her efforts. Even in the repetition there are erasures and extensions; this suggests that she has to seek control from external sources, which is related to the dependency needs referred to above (see *Dynamics*).

FD: *P* draws very tiny hands and feet in both drawings, suggesting a defense against aggression through minimization. Similarly, in feminizing the male drawing and making him shorter, she would seem to be minimizing any masculine threat. We do not know the meaning of the markings on the face and bodice, the seeming attempts at extensions of the hair, the distorted right hand, and the addition of a tiny projection on the back of the left hand on the female, but they are deliberately drawn. At least, they serve to mar the overall drawing of the female.

Rorschach: The defensive picture presented by *P* in the Rorschach is of paranoia. The excessive numbers of edge detail profiles (I, 3 and 4; IV, 4; V, 3; VI, 3), the tiny human interior detail (VIII, 3), the rigid intellectual constriction represented by maps (III, 3; VI, 4; X, 6) and the grandiosity in one percept ("King/Queen of the Underworld," X, 1) are all commensurate with a person relying primarily on paranoia as a defensive posture to the world.

She is quick to regress (I, 2; II, 1; III, 1; VIII, 1; IX, 1) when faced with affective stimuli. In spite of this, she maintains intellectual defenses to utilize the structure of the blots well.

TAT: In her stories, *P* makes use of the TAT pictures as depicted. The interaction of her characters, however, reflects the paranoia seen in the Rorschach. Her female characters are rejected by a man (3 BM and 4) or deserted by death (18 GF). The females are left bored (7 GF) or withdrawn and lonely (16). The only story that represents a positive relationship (10) ends with a sarcastic "That's that."

Summary Statement of Defenses: P is reality oriented and uses intellectual defenses well. Her primary and maladaptive defense is paranoia with projection, grandiosity, rigidity, and distrust. Affective stimulation can produce regression.

Affective Expression

WAIS: *P* works throughout the WAIS with seemingly no affective reactions.

B–G: The expansion and constriction of the figures drawn by *P* suggest affective lability.

FD: The faces on *P*'s drawings are devoid of affective expression, although the female looks unpleasant.

Rorschach: *P*'s productivity in the Rorschach clearly showed her enjoyment of the task. The content of her percepts, however, suggests that the Rorschach offered her an opportunity to express negative paranoid feelings and oral needs, from which we presume she experienced catharsis.

TAT: In contrast to the Rorschach, *P* did not seem to enjoy the TAT. The feelings expressed by her characters are primarily unpleasant, culminating in her statement, "build a wall that will never be broken around herself" (16).

Summary Statement of Affective Expression: In structured situations, *P* performs matter-of-factly. The projectives, however, permitted a discharge of negative and lonely feelings.

Summary

P is at the typical crossroads for late adolescents moving into adulthood. Two months prior to coming for treatment she had graduated from college, and she is now faced with performing in the adult world.

Her wish to enter treatment is valid. Her feelings of inadequacy are based upon a poor self-image, low self-esteem, and a lack of a sense of body integrity. These concerns have intensified her strong oral dependency needs and longings; this in turn has increased her fears for her future. She has limited and somewhat rigid defenses of projection and regression that justify her fears and intrude upon her interpersonal interactions. She has little trust in others and even less trust in herself. She is, however, reality oriented and has good intellectual defenses and is motivated for change.

P is very much in need of treatment to help her develop a capacity for a trusting relationship. This would provide the basis for her to relinquish her present stance of oral dependency and projection as a protection against the challenge of the real world.

Diagnosis

DSM-III-R

Axis I: 309.28 Adjustment Disorders with Mixed Emotional Features

Axis II: 301.00 Paranoid Personality Disorder

Axis III: Healthy

Axis IV: 3-Moderate

Axis V: 65-Mild to Moderate

With a combination of individual and group therapy, *P*, with her strong motivation for help, should be able to move in the direction of more independence and more rewarding interpersonal relationships.

Psychological Test Data

P: 20–6 Female

WAIS

		Scaled Score
Verbal Tests		
Information		15
Comprehension		15
Arithmetic		11
Similarities		12
Digit Span		11
Vocabulary		14
	Verbal Score	78
Performance Tests		
Digit Symbol		14
Picture Completion		11
Block Design		9
Picture Arrangement		12
Object Assembly		11
	Performance Score	57

	Scaled Score	IQ
Verbal Score	78	118
Performance Score	57	108
Full Scale Score	135	115

Information

		Score
1–4.		4
5.	Plant. [Q] Tree.	1
6.	Eisenhower, Truman, Coolidge . . . and FDR.	1
7.	Poet—American	1
8.	52	1
9.	South	1
10.	South America	1
11.	5'3"	1
12.	Rome	1

13.	Retain heat more	1
14.	February 22nd	1
15.	Shakespeare	1
16.	Where Pope resides	1
17.	Paris to New York? I think, 1,500—wait, either 1,500 or 3,000, I'd say 3,000	1
18.	In Africa	1
19.	Fermentation—carbon dioxide—gives off . . . rises.	1
20.	Approximately 170 million	1
21.	Two times 50 is 100.	1
22.	I don't know.	0
23.	100° . . . 132° F.	0
24.	Homer	1
25.	Arteries, veins, and—pulmonary	0
26.	The Bible for Muslim religion	1
27.	Goethe	1
28.	Uh . . . study region where people come from and culture that evolves.	1
29.	Ancient Egyptian—rule . . . rules.	0

Total 25

Comprehension

1–2.		4
3.	Mail it.	2
4.	[*long pause*] No reason why they should—depends on individual—supposed to be bad—against the law, criminal can get into trouble associating with them. [Q] So you won't get into trouble.	1
5.	Tell the manager, be calm, don't get excited.	2
6.	Benefits that the government offers—must pay taxes.	0
7.	To act immediately . . . upon the stimulus—go ahead with plans or ideas that are important at the present time and lose their meaning as time goes on.	1
8.	To protect child against big businessmen and exploitation by paying low wages, etc.	2
9.	Climb a tree . . . see a path . . . try to remember direction.	1
10.	Can't hear words—don't know how they sound.	2
11.	In urban area, demand is more than supply.	2
12.	Record keeping, it's a law.	2
13.	People who have nothing to say, the ones who are aware or not, will scream louder about their ideas and feelings.	2
14.	Experience should not be generalized into entirety.	2

Total 23

Arithmetic

		Score
1.		1
2.		1
3.		1
4.		1
5.		1
6.		1
7.		1
8.		1

9.		1
10.		1
11.	I don't know.	0
12.		2
13.	I don't really know.	0
14.		0
	Total	12

Similarities

		Score
1.	Fruit	2
2.	Articles of clothing	2
3.	Tools	2
4.	Animals	2
5.	Areas of direction—directions	2
6.	Part of face	1
7.	Natural elements	1
8.	Furniture	2
9.	Food	0
10.	Expressions of artistic thoughts	2
11.	Both burn	1
12.	Rewards for actions	0
13.	I don't know.	0
	Total	17

Digit Span

F7 + B5   Total Score   12

Vocabulary

		Score
1–3.		6
4.	Time of the year when it gets cold, from October to early March	2
5.	To fix something	2
6.	First meal of the day	2
7.	Piece of material, used in sewing	2
8.	A piece of something	1
9.	To put together	2
10.	To hide	2
11.	Very big or very large	2
12.	To hurry up	2
13.	Group of words to express complete thought	2
14.	To put in a certain order	2
15.	To start	2
16.	To think about	2
17.	Sort of a tent	0
18.	To assign	2
19.	Has to do with home	2
20.	To use up	2
21.	To end	2
22.	To get in the way	2
23.	Sorry	1

24.	Peaceful	0
25.	Without a match—being unable to be matched	2
26.	Means you really don't want to do something	2
27.	Accident	1
28.	I don't know.	0
29.	Peaceful	2
30.	Building	2
31.	Concern	1
32.	Can be seen	2
33.	The outside of an object	2
34.	Person creating a scene	0
35.	Threatening	2
36.	Like a tantrum	2
37.	Don't know.	0
38.	Steal someone else's writings and claim it as your own	2
39.	To put on a point	1
40.	Don't know.	0

Total   63

Digit Symbol   Total Score   70

Picture Completion

		Score
1.		1
2.		1
3.		1
4.		1
5.		1
6.		1
7.		1
8.	One string.	0
9.		1
10.		0
11.	I don't know.	0
12.		1
13.		1
14.	Steam things—I don't know what they're called.	1
15.		1
16.		1
17.		0
18.		1
19.	I don't know.	0
20.	No snow on top of the wood.	1
21.	No ear.	0

Total   15

Block Design

	Time	Score
1.		4
2.		4
3.	4"	4
4.	7"	4
5.	7"	4

6.	70"	0
7.	60"	4
8. I don't think I can do it.	100"	4
9.	OT	0
10.	OT	0
	Total	28

Picture Arrangement

	Time	Order	Score
1.			4
2.			4
3.	5"	ABCD	4
4.	15"	ATOMIC	4
5.	33"	OPENS	4
6.	20"	JANET. All men are lechers	4
7.	27"	EFGHIJ	5
8.	30"	SALUME. He blushed because of fantasy. *(Q)* My imagination is dead.	0
		Total	29

Object Assembly

	Time	Score
M	15"	7
P	35"	12
H	100"	7
E	60"	8
	Total	34

Bender–Gestalt

[*after instructions*] On the same page?

2. [*Counts dots.*]

[*Pressed pencil very hard in copying designs.*]

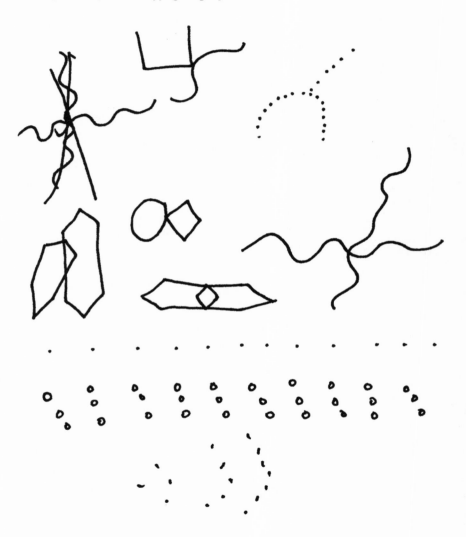

Figure Drawing

[*After instructions*] Woman? Man? [*referring to female drawing*] Pretty lousy. She's about 30, can't really tell—she's chunky. [*referring to male drawing, which she drew on same piece of paper*] Face looks womanish.

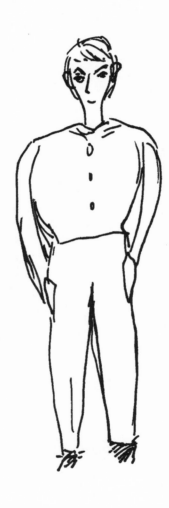

Rorschach

I.   10"

1. Two old women arguing with each other—not arguing—making faces.

   1. Frowning, have permanents.

2. Two young birds.

   2. Mouths open—up to neck.

→ 3. A man getting up after hiding in a bush.

4. Profile of Abraham Lincoln.

5. A fat woman raising her hands. She must have been a thalidomide baby, because they're stumpy hands.

II.

1. Two baby bears pushing snouts up to food.

   1. Short, fat, flattish head bigger than body.

2. An insect—red insect.

   2. Beetle type, shape of what is called ladybug

3. A man kneeling down—receiving football in football games.

III.

1. Hmm—two cannibals cooking something in a pot.

   1. Just cannibals. [Q] Men don't have hair— heads shaved—like cannibal men that I've seen.

2. Bottom half of a leg and a high heel shoe.

3. Outline of the U.S.—little distorted.

4. X ray of rib portion of a person.

IV.

1. A man with big feet lying down.

→ 2. A French poodle standing on hind legs.

2. Outline and texture of a French poodle.

3. Inside parts look like . . . what you see from the parkway, going up to the mews—dense, grassy, trees.

3. Dense, texture.

4. A man with a chin.

5. And a lizard on a branch, getting ready to jump at something.

V.

1. A bat.

1. It's flying.

2. A woman wearing a cape and arms spread.

2. Funny hat on—I've always wanted to own one.

3. A man with a pointed beard— wearing glasses.

VI.

1. A cat's face—looking from the back—back of cat's head.

↓ 2. Two people—men with beards sitting back to back with hands out [*demonstrates*].

3. Two little ducks— heads sticking out of nest.

4. Middle looks like a bedpost.

4. I've been looking at furniture.

5. Outline of the state of Florida.

VII.

1. Two young girls making faces at each other.

→ 2. A pig's face.

3. An elephant moving its trunk.

4. Land with water in middle—connected by canal in bottom.

VIII.

1. Different flavors of ice cream.

   1. Hazy, fuzzy, bright, color, texture, shape.

2. Some kind of mountain animal climbing on a rock.

3. A circus performer—standing on top of a ladder getting ready to jump.

IX.

1. Ice cream that's getting mushy.

   1. All over.

2. An ape with hand outstretched.

3. Elf—with hat that comes to a point—one of Santa Claus's helpers.

X.

1. A lot of sea fish, sea animals, having a meeting—guarding the King are two squid—it's a Queen, by the way. [Q] Of the Underworld.

   1. Because walking towards middle, to the Queen figure.

2. A cricket on its back.

3. Two deformed yellow chickens.

4. Two little girls with red paint on their faces.

5. A wishbone—chicken.

6. Continent of Australia.

   6. Round, down at tip.

TAT

1. The violin was given to the little boy as a present. His father was a great violinist, or someone in the family was very good—they want the boy to start studying it. . . . He wants to be good, but he's afraid or something and resents it. [*Q*] That they want him to play. He's ambivalent at the same time. . . . Can I tell you about my brother?

3 BM. What is the object over here? Fat girl who's been rejected. Not rejected, unhappy over something, end of the world and she's crying. [*Q*] Boy she liked didn't like her . . . anything that makes people unhappy. [*Q*] Stay there another hour and then get up.

10. This man is dancing with his girlfriend or wife, most probably girlfriend, and the music is beautiful—they're in love, eyes closed. That's that.

4. A woman is trying to pull a man back . . . man is sort of mad and trying to pull away [*looks at picture on wall*], but he isn't really paying attention to her . . . that's about it. [*Q*] Looks like he's mad at somebody and trying to pull away . . . an argument, she's trying to explain, but he's pulling away. [*Q*] He eventually pulls away, and she doesn't have a chance to explain herself.

2. Looks like schoolgirl coming home from school—and the mother's standing there talking to father . . . and the father's getting ready to plow the farm. That's it.

18 GF. Looks like a woman is holding a man . . . looks like he's sick or something. She looks at him . . . like she's scared he's going to die. That's all. [*Sick?*] Might have fallen on stairs. [*Q*] I guess he eventually dies. [*Related?*] Husband and wife.

5. [*studies card*] A mother goes to kid's room to check on kid. She finds the kid asleep . . . so she just leaves. She was just checking to make sure he was all right. That's it.

7 GF. A girl is sitting on the couch with her doll while her mother reads her a story. But the girl doesn't really want to hear the story, so she ignores it. [*Q*] Just boring.

16. There once were two friends. One cared about the other friend a lot, and one pretended to care. But one day the friend that cared a lot finally figured out that everyone around her were all actors who have a performance to make. So she decided to build a wall that will never be broken around herself. [*Q*] She becomes lonely.

Psychological Test Portrait

Q: 21–0 Female

Q, a 21-year-old female, came seeking psychotherapy because she was not satisfied with her school performance and suffered gastrointestinal problems.

She is a junior in college and is maintaining a B+ average. She is bothered often by abdominal discomfort with no known medical etiology.

Q lives at home with her widowed mother and younger brother. She felt herself to be favored by her father and still mourns his death from two years ago.

The therapist requested psychological testing to clarify the diagnostic picture. *Q* worked hard throughout the testing and looked forward to the results.

Cognitive Functioning

WAIS: Q scores a Very Superior Full Scale IQ of 134, with a Very Superior Verbal Score of 136 and a Superior Performance Score of 128. There is little inter- or intratest scatter among subtests, with the notable exception of Comprehension. Her lowered score in Comprehension will be discussed under *Dynamics* and *Defenses*. Otherwise her cognitive functioning in language, memory, abstractive ability, general knowledge, and perceptual-motor integration are all excellent.

B–G: Q's Bender is done in a well-organized fashion, with accurate reproduction of the designs.

FD: Both of Q's figure drawings are well proportioned, clearly sexually differentiated, and of appropriate size. In striking contrast to the male drawing (her first drawing), the female's hands are hidden, and the legs are not completed. This suggests poor planning on her part.

Rorschach: Q provides an adequate number of responses, using all aspects of the blot areas and varied determinants. Her language, however, is often confused and not at the level expressed in the WAIS.

TAT: Although Q's stories are adequately rendered, she often loses the picture as her thoughts become confused and/or tangential.

Summary Statement of Cognitive Functioning: Given a structured intelligence test, Q is able to demonstrate her very superior cognitive abilities. When faced with projective material, however, her level of functioning regresses, and she expresses confusion in her thinking and language.

Dynamic Picture

WAIS: Q's WAIS is free of dynamic intrusions, with the notable exception of Comprehension. Here we hypothesize that the questions (4, 5, 6, 10, 11, 12, and 14) trigger a threat to her ego integrity. This taps into her narcissism, which precludes an accurate interpretation of the questions (see answer to 5 as a striking example).

B–G: Q's Bender does not reveal any dynamic considerations.

FD: Q's choice to draw a male first may reflect a sexual identification conflict of earlier adolescence. The inward-turned hands of the male and the hidden hands on the female speak to a lack of interest in reaching out to others. Insecurity is suggested by the lack of feet on the female.

Rorschach: The content of Q's responses to the Rorschach reveal several basic areas of conflict. She feels herself vulnerable and fragile on the most primitive level of body integrity (I, 3; II, 3; III, 2, 3; IV, 2, 3; VII, 1, 2; VIII, 4; IX, 1, 2; X, 4, 6). These feelings are juxtaposed with aggressive impulses, sometimes sadistic in intent (I, 1; II, 3, 4; III, 5; IV, 1; X, 5). She wishes to be dependent (i.e., to regress: I, 2; II, 3; III, 3; IV, 3; VII, 1, 2; VIII, 3; IX, 1, 3), which is in conflict with her need for independence (i.e., achievement; see excessive concern with precision notably in I, 3; V, 2; VIII, 1; IX, 2). There is a suggestion, as in the order in which she drew her figures in the FD, of a sexual identification conflict (see confused description of female in I, 3; feminized male in III, 1). These conflict areas produce a great deal of inner tension and anxiety (*m*'s in II, 4, 5; VIII, 4; IX, 3; X, 5).

Q does not feel herself to be acceptable in relating to others (*c* in II, 1; IV, 3; V, 2; VI, 1 and 2; VIII, 1, 2, and 4; X, 1). Her only responses using C (II, 4; VIII, 2; IX, 1; X, 1 and 2) do not reflect a mature capacity for interpersonal relationships, in spite of a desire to relate.

TAT: The essential dynamic in Q's stories is a narcissistic self-involvement. This is seen in her inability to describe meaningful interactions between the characters she develops. She implies a kind of relationship between people but maintains it on a most superficial level. In fact, she often dispenses with presumably important people by having them die (6 GF, 10, 12 M) or even be killed (3 BM and 6 GF).

Similarly to the conflict raised in the Rorschach over dependence, Q can express the greatest degree of relatedness when she describes the nurturing of children (5 and 7 GF). She seems to experience comfort when she is alone (3 BM, 9 GF, and 14) or identified as a child (5 and 7 GF).

The sexual identity conflict seen in the FD and Rorschach is reflected here in a perception of males as more important (2, 4, 5, 6 GF, 7 GF, and 13 MF).

Feelings of body vulnerability and concern over body integrity are present in her stories (6 GF, 18 GF, and 13 MF), but to a lesser extent than in the Rorschach.

Summary Statement of Dynamic Picture: Driven by narcissistic preoccupations, Q is unable to achieve satisfying interpersonal relationships. In spite of a wish to relate to others, her unresolved aggressivity intrudes into her ability to relate. This seems to stem from feelings of body vulnerability accompanied by the profound sense of a lack of body integrity, which leaves her tense and anxious. With this basic problem, she cannot reconcile dependency longings with her need to achieve independence. She still struggles with the earlier adolescent's sexual identity conflict.

Defenses

WAIS: *Q*'s intellectual defenses are excellent and make it possible for her to perform on an intellectual level that gives the outward appearance of seeing the world as others do. She can become obsessive and overly intellectualized (see response to Information, 29 at beginning of Comprehension; Comprehension, 7; Similarities, 7 and 8; Vocabulary, 4, 6, and 8) at times when she seemingly wishes to impress with her knowledge.

Comprehension, which tests an awareness of societal interaction, elicits the only examples of failures in her intellectual prowess. When faced with the threat of danger, her defenses fail and she seeks an impulsive solution (Comprehension, 5), responding only to her own needs. This personal concern is also seen in her personalizing responses (Comprehension, 4 and 11) and concreteness (Comprehension, 10 and 14), where she loses the point of the question.

The effort to achieve an integration of the parts of the Profile and the Hand (Object Assembly)—in which she achieved the unusual scores of 13 and 11, respectively—speaks to the extent to which *Q* can utilize her excellent intellectual ability when faced with the experienced threat to her body integrity.

B–G: There are no indications of any defensive maneuvers in *Q*'s reproduction of the Bender figures.

FD: *Q*'s need to maintain distance from others is emphasized in the lack of hands and feet on the female and the inward-turning hands on the male.

Rorschach: The intellectual control *Q* has manifests itself with her high number of responses, her proper use of locations, and no *F*–'s on the blots. This supports what we saw in the WAIS as her ability to perceive the world as others do.

At an age when introspection is prevalent, *Q* notably has only one *K* response. In addition, her *C* responses are limited and when produced have an arbitrary quality (X, 1 and 2) reflecting, again, her intellectualizing efforts.

In her responses, *Q*'s excessive intellectualizing and obsessive detailing produce extraneous material (I, 1, 2, 3; II, 3; III, 1, 3; IV, 2, 3; V, 2; VIII, 1), concreteness (I, 2; VI, 2), and even a positional response (I, 4). Her perfectionistic demands lead her into obsessiveness (most notably seen in II, 2 and 3). Also, the imprecision of the blots causes her to project criticism onto the blots themselves (I, 3; VII, 2; VIII, 1).

TAT: *Q*'s TAT stories are notable for the predominant use of avoidance of interpersonal interrelatedness. In cards where there are more than one person depicted she describes individual actions, isolating the characters from each other (2, 6 GF, 10, 13 MF, 12 M). Avoidance is also achieved by intellectualization and distancing. The need for intellectual control is handled by leaving (2, 3 BM, 9 GF, 7 GF), distancing through social righteousness (4, 9 GF), presenting a demographic picture (10), evoking magic (13 MF), being alone with nature (3 BM, 9 GF, 14), and at times sounding grandiose and pretentious (9 GF, 13 MF, and 8 GF).

Projection is used infrequently but is notable in two instances (4 and 9 GF), and the obsessiveness seen in the Rorschach is to all intents and purposes absent (see remark at beginning of Card 1).

Summary Statement of Defenses: Q's primary defense is intellectualization. In impersonal, structured situations this works extremely well for her. In the projective tests, in addition to intellectualization, she relies on avoidance to cope with her affective response to the material. These defenses are rigidly maintained, thereby resulting in distortions in her language and confusion in her thinking.

Affective Expression

WAIS: Q's intellectal competence on the WAIS precludes affective expression, with the notable exception of Comprehension. Her response to question 5 implies a fearful reaction, but otherwise she expresses no affect to the confusion she exhibits to the other items.

B–G: There is no evidence of affective responsiveness on Q's part in the Bender.

FD: Q's remarks reflect an anxiety about her competence in drawing. Her excessive self-criticism reflects an unhappiness about the way she is doing the task. The drawings themselves reflect an impersonal pleasantness.

Rorschach: Q seemed comfortable in describing her percepts in the Rorschach test. There is only evidence of her inner tension and anxiety in her *m*'s. There is the suggestion of longing for contact with others in her *c*'s.

TAT: Q blames the TAT cards for eliciting feelings of sadness or unhappiness (1, 6 GF, 3 GF, 18 GF). Otherwise her stories are bland, intellectualized, and devoid of affect.

Summary Statement of Affective Expression: Q, for the most part, responds to the tests with bland affect. On the rare occasions when she mentions a feeling, it is a sad or unhappy one. Only on the Rorschach is there evidence of inner tension and anxiety.

Summary

Q is an exceptionally intelligent young woman who is able to utilize her intellectual defenses to see the world as others do. This conveys the impression that she is based in the same reality as others. When faced with material that elicits affect, however, it becomes clear that Q is a narcissistically self-involved woman who is affectively detached from interactions with others. She feels herself to be vulnerable and fragile on the most primitive level of body integrity, which is juxtaposed with aggressive impulses that are sometimes sadistic in intent. In order to protect herself she utilizes defenses of obsessiveness, avoidance, distancing, and at times, projection. The projection is seen in magical thinking, righteousness, and grandiosity that gives a paranoid flavor to her thinking. With little expression of affect in the projectives, it is possible to hypothesize that Q excessively relies on fantasy. This fantasy life provides affective gratification unavilable to her through interpersonal interactions.

These difficulties produce confused and tangential thinking, which results in peculiar language usage at times. The combination of her distorted thinking, bland affect, and inability to relate to others presents the picture of a borderline.

Diagnosis

DSM-III-R

Axis I: 300.70 Undifferentiated Somatoform Disorder

Axis II: 301.83 Borderline Personality Disorder with Paranoid Traits

Axis III: None

Axis IV: 2-Mild

Axis V: 60-Moderate

Q's seeking therapy, along with her excellent intellect, should enable her to benefit from psychotherapy. The primary goal for the therapy will be in enabling Q to establish a meaningful affective relationship with the therapist. Q may become discouraged that she does not see improvement in her school performance; however, this will not occur until she is able to experience satisfaction in her relationships to others, rather than from her fantasy life.